MEGALITHIC ˙

STONEHENGE, GOBEKLI TEPE, GGANTIJA TEMPLES & BAALBEK

4 BOOKS IN 1

BOOK 1
MYSTERIES OF THE MEGALITHS: UNRAVELING THE SECRETS OF STONEHENGE
BOOK 2
TIMELESS GUARDIANS: EXPLORING THE ENIGMATIC GOBEKLI TEPE
BOOK 3
THE FORGOTTEN GIANTS: JOURNEY TO THE GGANTIJA TEMPLES OF MALTA
BOOK 4
LEGENDS OF THE ANCIENT STONES: UNVEILING THE POWER OF BAALBEK'S
MEGALITHIC TEMPLE

BY A.J. KINGSTON

Published by A. J. Kingston
Library of Congress Cataloging-in-Publication Data
ISBN 978-1-83938-393-9
Cover design by Rizzo

Disclaimer

The contents of this book are based on extensive research and the best available historical sources. However, the author and publisher make no claims, promises, or guarantees about the accuracy, completeness, or adequacy of the information contained herein. The information in this book is provided on an "as is" basis, and the author and publisher disclaim any and all liability for any errors, omissions, or inaccuracies in the information or for any actions taken in reliance on such information.

The opinions and views expressed in this book are those of the author and do not necessarily reflect the official policy or position of any organization or individual mentioned in this book. Any reference to specific people, places, or events is intended only to provide historical context and is not intended to defame or malign any group, individual, or entity. The information in this book is intended for educational and entertainment purposes only. It is not intended to be a substitute for professional advice or judgment. Readers are encouraged to conduct their own research and to seek professional advice where appropriate.

Every effort has been made to obtain necessary permissions and acknowledgments for all images and other copyrighted material used in this book. Any errors or omissions in this regard are unintentional, and the author and publisher will correct them in future editions.

Join Our Productivity Group and Access your Bonus

If you're passionate about history books and want to connect with others who share your love of the subject, joining our Facebook group (search for "History Books by A.J.Kingston") can be a great way to do so. By joining a group dedicated to history books, you'll have the opportunity to connect with like-minded individuals, share your thoughts and ideas, and even discover new books that you might not have come across otherwise. You can also access your FREE BONUS once you joined our Facebook group called "History Books by A.J.Kingston".

One of the biggest advantages of joining our Facebook group is the sense of community it provides. You'll be able to interact with other history book enthusiasts, ask questions, and share your own knowledge and expertise. This can be especially valuable if you're a student or someone who is just starting to explore the world of history books.

If you love audiobooks, then joining our YouTube channel that offers free audiobooks on a weekly basis can be a great way to stay entertained and engaged. By subscribing to our channel, you'll have access to a range of audiobooks across different genres, all for free. Not only this is a great opportunity to enjoy some new audiobooks, but it's also a chance to discover new authors and titles that you might not have come across otherwise.

Lastly, don't forget to follow us on Facebook and YouTube by searching for A.J. Kingston.

Table of Contents – Book 1 - Mysteries Of The Megaliths: Unraveling The Secrets Of Stonehenge

Table of Contents – Book 2 - Timeless Guardians: Exploring The Enigmatic Gobekli Tepe

Table of Contents – Book 3 - The Forgotten Giants: Journey To The Ggantija Temples Of Malta

Table of Contents – Book 4 - Legends Of The Ancient Stones: Unveiling The Power Of Baalbek's Megalithic Temple

Introduction

Welcome to the captivating world of megalithic temples, where ancient mysteries and remarkable achievements of human civilization await. In this extraordinary book bundle, "Megalithic Temples," we embark on a transformative journey through the enigmatic realms of Stonehenge, Gobekli Tepe, Ggantija Temples, and Baalbek. Across four volumes, we delve into the secrets, symbolism, and profound significance of these awe-inspiring structures, shedding light on the wonders of our ancient past.

In "Mysteries of the Megaliths: Unraveling the Secrets of Stonehenge," we step into the presence of an iconic wonder that has stood for millennia. Through meticulous research and archaeological insights, this volume explores the enigmas of Stonehenge, delving into its celestial alignments, intricate construction, and the spiritual beliefs that may have guided its creators. Join us on a quest to understand the purpose and mysteries that continue to captivate the imagination.

"Timeless Guardians: Exploring the Enigmatic Gobekli Tepe" invites us to witness the dawn of civilization. In this volume, we embark on a journey to an ancient site that has rewritten the narrative of human history. Gobekli Tepe unveils its secrets through its magnificent architecture, intricate carvings, and the tantalizing clues it offers about early religious and societal practices. Together, we delve into the rich tapestry of this archaeological wonder, unlocking the mysteries of our distant past.

"The Forgotten Giants: Journey to the Ggantija Temples of Malta" takes us to the idyllic Mediterranean island of Malta, where we discover the remnants of an ancient civilization. The Ggantija Temples, with their colossal stone structures, transport us to a time long forgotten. In this volume, we unravel the mysteries surrounding their construction, explore the rituals and beliefs of their creators, and contemplate the cultural legacy left behind by this enigmatic society.

Lastly, "Legends of the Ancient Stones: Unveiling the Power of Baalbek's Megalithic Temple" immerses us in the captivating realm of Baalbek, an ancient site steeped in myth and wonder. Through meticulous research and vivid storytelling, we unravel the significance of its monumental stones, marvel at the engineering feats that created them, and explore the enduring legends that have woven themselves into the tapestry of this sacred place.

Together, these four volumes present a comprehensive exploration of megalithic temples, inviting you on a mesmerizing journey through time and space. With each turn of the page, you will be transported to ancient landscapes, walk in the footsteps of ancient civilizations, and witness the profound impact of human ingenuity and spirituality.

Whether you are a history enthusiast, an archaeology aficionado, or simply a curious explorer of the past, "Megalithic Temples" offers a treasure trove of knowledge and wonder. So, embark on this extraordinary adventure with us and immerse yourself in the mysteries, legends, and profound significance of Stonehenge, Gobekli Tepe, Ggantija Temples, and Baalbek—the magnificent megalithic temples that continue to inspire awe and ignite the imagination.

BOOK 1

MYSTERIES OF THE MEGALITHS UNRAVELING THE SECRETS OF STONEHENGE

BY A.J. KINGSTON

Chapter 1: The Enigmatic Origins

In the annals of antiquity, amidst the fading echoes of distant ages, lie concealed the enigmatic legends and myths that have captivated the minds of scholars, poets, and dreamers alike. These tales, handed down through the veil of time, whisper of gods, heroes, and extraordinary feats, transporting us to a realm where reality and fantasy intermingle. To unravel the mysteries that shroud these ancient narratives is to embark upon an intellectual journey that traverses the boundaries of the known world and delves into the depths of human imagination.

To approach these myths, one must adopt the spirit of an intrepid explorer, ready to navigate the treacherous terrains of conflicting accounts, cultural variations, and allegorical interpretations. With each step, the veils of antiquity are gradually lifted, revealing glimpses of the truths that lie at the heart of these captivating tales. It is through meticulous examination, scrupulous comparison, and discerning analysis that the fragments of reality concealed within the mythological tapestry begin to coalesce into a coherent narrative.

Among the most enduring legends is that of the heroic demigod Hercules, whose mighty deeds and trials have enthralled generations. From the sacred groves of ancient Greece to the temples of Rome, Hercules' exploits have been recounted in countless variations. Yet, amidst the manifold accounts, one can discern certain common threads that persist, transcending cultural boundaries and evoking a shared human fascination with the extraordinary.

Unraveling the true essence of Hercules necessitates an exploration of the historical context from which he emerged. By peering through the fog of time, one discerns that the mythic figure finds its roots in the deep well of the human psyche, embodying the eternal struggle between virtue and vice, strength and weakness. Hercules becomes a symbol of the indomitable human spirit, battling against insurmountable odds and transcending mortal limitations.

But Hercules is not alone in his mythical splendor. In the labyrinthine recesses of ancient lore, one encounters a multitude of divine beings, such as the cunning and ever-shifting Hermes, the radiant and wise Athena, and the enigmatic and unpredictable Apollo. Each god embodies facets of the human experience, offering glimpses into the intricate tapestry of ancient beliefs and the profound truths that shaped human understanding.

The unraveling of these ancient legends is not a task for the faint-hearted, nor for those who seek facile answers. It demands an unyielding dedication to scholarship, an insatiable thirst for knowledge, and a willingness to embrace the multifaceted nature of human storytelling. As one peels back the layers of myth, a nuanced understanding emerges, revealing the complex interplay between historical events, cultural symbolism, and the innate human desire to make sense of the world.

In the pursuit of truth, one must not discount the inherent beauty and power of these ancient legends. They are the creative products of imaginative minds, the repositories of cultural wisdom, and the sparks that ignite the fires of imagination. To unravel their mysteries is to breathe life into forgotten worlds, to stand on the precipice between fact and fable, and to glimpse the eternal truths that transcend the boundaries of time.

Thus, as we venture forth into the realm of ancient legends and myths, let us embrace the challenges that lie ahead. With scholarly rigor and an appreciation for the poetic grandeur of the tales, we embark upon a journey that promises enlightenment, inspiration, and a deeper connection to the timeless threads that bind humanity across the ages. In the pursuit of truth, we unravel the veils of myth, bringing to light the enduring wonders of the ancient world.

Tracing the historical roots of the megalithic temples is an endeavor that takes us deep into the annals of time, to epochs when civilizations were just beginning to take shape. These awe-inspiring structures, composed of colossal stones and intricate architectural designs, bear witness to the ingenuity, skill, and sacred beliefs of our ancient ancestors. Standing in solemn splendor, they are a testament to the human capacity to conceive and construct monumental edifices that have withstood the test of time.

To embark upon the journey of tracing the historical roots of these megalithic temples is to delve into the recesses of prehistoric societies, where the seeds of civilization were sown. As we peel back the layers of time, we are confronted with a tapestry of ancient cultures that span continents and millennia, from the towering monoliths of Stonehenge in the misty plains of England, to the enigmatic Gobekli Tepe in the Anatolian highlands, and the grand Ggantija temples of Malta. Each site carries with it a unique story, interwoven with the traditions, beliefs, and aspirations of the people who erected them.

Stonehenge, shrouded in the mists of Salisbury Plain, has captivated the imagination for centuries. Its massive stone circles, aligned with celestial bodies, evoke a sense of wonder and reverence. As we trace its historical roots, we find ourselves transported back to a time when ancient communities carefully selected, transported, and arranged these colossal stones with precision, creating a sacred space that served as a celestial observatory and ceremonial center. The significance of Stonehenge lies not only in its grandeur but also in the enigmatic purpose it served, invoking questions that continue to elude us.

Moving across continents to Gobekli Tepe, we encounter a site that challenges our understanding of human history. Dating back over 11,000 years, Gobekli Tepe predates the advent of agriculture and settled societies, forcing us to reassess our assumptions about the capabilities of early hunter-gatherer communities. Its intricately carved T-shaped pillars, arranged in circular enclosures, hint at a sophisticated social organization and a deep spiritual connection to the cosmos. The presence of monumental architecture in a time of apparent simplicity compels us to rethink the narrative of human progress.

In the sun-drenched landscapes of Malta, the Ggantija temples stand as testament to the skill and ambition of Neolithic builders. These towering structures, composed of massive limestone blocks, bear witness to the communal efforts and engineering prowess of a civilization that flourished over 5,000 years ago. As we explore the historical roots of the Ggantija temples, we uncover a glimpse into the lives, beliefs, and rituals of a society that venerated its ancestors and sought connection with the divine. The sacred landscape of Malta unfolds before our eyes, revealing a profound link between the physical realm and the spiritual realm.

Tracing the historical roots of these megalithic temples is a journey that transcends the boundaries of time and space. It invites us to contemplate the ingenuity, spirituality, and cultural richness of our ancient forebears. The stories etched in stone speak of our shared human heritage, reminding us of our connection to the past and our responsibility to preserve and honor these ancient marvels. As we gaze upon these megalithic temples, we are reminded that they are not mere relics of the past, but living testament to the enduring human quest for meaning, transcendence, and the eternal pursuit of knowledge.

Examining early archaeological discoveries is akin to unraveling a tapestry of human history. These remarkable findings, unearthed from the depths of time, provide a window into the lives, customs, and achievements of our ancient ancestors. As we delve into the annals of archaeological exploration, we are transported to a time when the science of uncovering the past was still in its infancy, yet brimming with the promise of unearthing secrets long buried.

One such pioneering discovery was that of the Egyptian pharaoh Tutankhamun's tomb in 1922 by Howard Carter. This remarkable find sent shockwaves through the archaeological community and captivated the world's imagination. The intact burial chamber, adorned with golden treasures and intricate funerary objects, provided an unprecedented glimpse into the opulence and religious beliefs of ancient Egypt. Carter's meticulous documentation and preservation techniques set new standards for archaeological excavation and shed light on the rich tapestry of Egyptian civilization.

Another significant milestone in the realm of early archaeology was the excavation of the ancient city of Pompeii, which lay buried beneath volcanic ash after the cataclysmic eruption of Mount Vesuvius in 79 AD. The meticulous work of archaeologists like Giuseppe Fiorelli in the 19th century unveiled a perfectly preserved snapshot of Roman life, frozen in time. The unearthed ruins, frescoes, and artifacts provided invaluable insights into daily life, urban planning, and social dynamics of a bygone era.

Further afield, in the fertile lands of Mesopotamia, the discovery of the royal tombs of Ur by Sir Leonard Woolley in the 1920s offered a treasure trove of artifacts and insights into the ancient Sumerian civilization. The opulent burials, replete with jewelry, weapons, and intricate artwork, provided a glimpse into the social hierarchy and religious beliefs of this early urban society. Woolley's meticulous excavations and groundbreaking techniques paved the way for the systematic study of ancient Mesopotamia.

In the realm of prehistoric archaeology, the discovery of the Lascaux cave paintings in southwestern France in 1940 proved to be a revelation. The vivid depictions of animals and human figures, dating back over 17,000 years, showcased the artistic skills and spiritual beliefs of Paleolithic hunters. These cave paintings opened a window into a world long lost, allowing us to marvel at the artistic talents and deep-seated connections between humans and the natural world in prehistoric times.

As we reflect on these early archaeological discoveries, we recognize the dedication, vision, and meticulous attention to detail displayed by these pioneering archaeologists. Their groundbreaking work laid the foundation for modern archaeological practices and ignited a passion for unearthing the mysteries of the past. These discoveries not only expanded our knowledge but also awakened a sense of wonder and fascination with our shared human heritage.

Today, as we continue to explore the far corners of the world and employ ever-advancing technologies, the legacy of these early discoveries serves as a reminder of the importance of preserving and studying our archaeological heritage. Each find contributes a piece to the vast puzzle of human history, painting a more comprehensive picture of our collective journey through time. It is through the examination of these early archaeological discoveries that we come to appreciate the profound depths of our past and the enduring significance of our archaeological heritage.

The origins of the megalithic temple builders have long been shrouded in mystery, leaving room for speculation and a multitude of theories. As we delve into the realm of speculation, we encounter a tapestry of hypotheses that seek to unravel the enigmatic origins of these ancient architects. While definitive answers remain elusive, these theories offer valuable insights and avenues for exploration, inviting us to ponder the extraordinary capabilities and motivations of our ancient ancestors.

One theory posits that the megalithic temple builders were part of an advanced seafaring civilization that traversed the ancient world. Proponents of this theory point to the widespread distribution of megalithic structures across different continents as evidence of a global maritime network. They propose that these seafarers possessed navigational skills, engineering knowledge, and a deep understanding of celestial alignments. By harnessing the power of the seas, they purportedly established trade routes, exchanged ideas, and disseminated their architectural prowess across distant lands.

Another hypothesis suggests that the megalithic temple builders were an indigenous group with a profound connection to the natural landscape. Advocates of this theory emphasize the intricate alignments of these structures with celestial bodies, geographical features, and local topography. They argue that these alignments reflect a deep spiritual reverence for the surrounding environment and a desire to establish harmonious relationships with the forces of nature. By harnessing and manipulating the energies of the earth and sky, these ancient builders sought to create sacred spaces that bridged the human and divine realms.

A third line of thought revolves around the idea of a lost civilization or an advanced ancient society that possessed technological knowledge far beyond what is commonly attributed to their time. This theory suggests that the megalithic temple builders possessed sophisticated engineering techniques, precision tools, and a comprehensive understanding of mathematical principles. The intricacy and precision of their constructions, proponents argue, surpass what could be achieved by the societies typically associated with that era. This hypothesis sparks intrigue and raises questions about the potential existence of forgotten civilizations that rose and fell in the mists of time.

Alternatively, some theories propose that the megalithic temple builders were the result of a gradual cultural evolution within specific regions. They suggest that the construction of megalithic structures arose as a response to societal needs, such as communal gathering spaces, ceremonial centers, or symbols of power and authority. Over time, advancements in architectural techniques and knowledge were passed down through generations, leading to the construction of ever more sophisticated and awe-inspiring temples.

As we explore these theories, it is important to acknowledge the limitations of our current knowledge and the fragmentary nature of the archaeological record. Each theory offers a unique perspective, shedding light on different aspects of the megalithic temple builders' origins. Yet, definitive evidence to support or disprove any single theory remains elusive.

In the absence of conclusive answers, it is perhaps the convergence of these theories that holds the greatest potential for uncovering the truth. By embracing multidisciplinary approaches, incorporating archaeological, anthropological, geological, and astronomical perspectives, we can weave together a more comprehensive narrative of the origins of the megalithic temple builders.

Ultimately, the search for the origins of these ancient architects is an ongoing endeavor, a tapestry woven through the collaboration of diverse disciplines and the unquenchable human curiosity. The theories put forth provide a starting point for further exploration and a testament to our relentless pursuit of understanding the extraordinary achievements of our ancient ancestors.

The construction of temples, particularly megalithic structures, was shaped by a complex interplay of genetic and cultural influences. Genetic factors refer to the hereditary traits and capabilities passed down through generations, while cultural factors encompass the beliefs, practices, and knowledge shared within a specific community or society. Examining the role of genetics and culture provides valuable insights into the motivations and abilities of the ancient builders who created these awe-inspiring architectural marvels.

From a genetic perspective, researchers have explored the possibility of genetic traits or predispositions that may have contributed to the construction of megalithic temples. Some argue that certain populations may have possessed inherent physical characteristics, such as exceptional strength or stature, that facilitated the movement of massive stones. These physical attributes, if present in specific populations, could have been advantageous in the construction process, allowing for the manipulation and transport of heavy building materials.

Furthermore, genetic factors can influence cognitive abilities, spatial perception, and engineering aptitude, which are crucial for designing and constructing complex architectural structures. While no specific "temple-building" gene has been identified, the genetic variations that impact cognitive and spatial abilities could have played a role in the development of architectural skills among certain populations. However, it is important to note that genetic factors alone are not sufficient to explain the monumental achievements of ancient builders. Cultural influences and accumulated knowledge were also critical components in temple construction.

Cultural influences encompass a wide range of factors, including religious beliefs, social organization, technological advancements, and accumulated knowledge. These cultural elements played a significant role in shaping the design, construction techniques, and purpose of temples. Religious beliefs and rituals, in particular, often served as the driving force behind the construction of these monumental structures. Temples were constructed as sacred spaces, intended to connect the physical and spiritual realms, and to honor deities or ancestors. Cultural beliefs surrounding the afterlife, divinity, and cosmic order influenced the design principles, orientations, and symbolism incorporated into the temple structures.

Technological advancements and accumulated knowledge also played a crucial role in temple construction. Ancient societies developed sophisticated techniques for quarrying, shaping, and transporting massive stones. These methods were refined over time, passed down through generations, and embedded in the cultural knowledge of specific communities. Techniques such as stone dressing, lever systems, and pulleys were utilized to overcome the challenges posed by the sheer size and weight of the stones, enabling the creation of megalithic structures.

The transmission of architectural knowledge within a society was a cultural process, involving apprenticeship, shared experiences, and communal learning. As successive generations built upon the accumulated knowledge and skills of their ancestors, temple construction techniques evolved, leading to the creation of increasingly complex and awe-inspiring structures.

In summary, the construction of temples, including megalithic structures, was influenced by both genetic and cultural factors. Genetic factors may have contributed to physical attributes and cognitive abilities that facilitated the construction process. Cultural influences, on the other hand, encompassed religious beliefs, social organization, technological advancements, and accumulated knowledge. Together, these factors shaped the motivations, skills, and techniques employed by ancient builders, resulting in the creation of magnificent temples that continue to inspire awe and curiosity to this day.

Chapter 2: Alignments and Astronomical Significance

Celestial alignments have long fascinated humanity, offering a window into the vast cosmos and inspiring awe and wonder. Ancient cultures across the globe recognized the profound connection between celestial bodies and earthly phenomena, incorporating celestial alignments into their architectural designs, religious practices, and cultural beliefs. Through careful observation and precise measurement, these civilizations sought to align their sacred structures with celestial events, creating a harmonious link between the terrestrial and celestial realms.

One of the most notable examples of celestial alignments can be found in the megalithic temples of ancient civilizations. These awe-inspiring structures, crafted with meticulous precision and remarkable engineering, were often aligned with celestial bodies such as the sun, moon, and stars. The alignment of these temples served multiple purposes, including religious significance, agricultural calendars, and spiritual beliefs.

In many cultures, the alignment of temples with the sun played a crucial role in marking the solstices and equinoxes, key events in the celestial calendar. The rising or setting of the sun in specific alignments with the temple's architecture served as a symbolic representation of the cycle of life, death, and rebirth. It also provided practical benefits, aiding in the determination of the agricultural seasons and ensuring the appropriate timing for planting, harvesting, and other vital activities.

The alignment of temples with the moon also held great significance. The lunar cycles, with their rhythmic waxing and waning, were believed to influence fertility, tides, and the ebb and flow of life. Temples aligned with lunar events allowed for the observation and reverence of the moon's phases, reinforcing the cultural and religious connection between humanity and the celestial realm.

Stellar alignments were another captivating aspect of ancient temple construction. Some megalithic structures were designed to align with specific stars or constellations, serving as celestial markers or navigational aids. These alignments not only demonstrated advanced astronomical knowledge but also played a role in religious and mythological narratives. The movements of stars and constellations were associated with divine beings, heroes, or mythical stories, further enriching the cultural and spiritual significance of the temples.

The precise nature of these celestial alignments showcases the ingenuity, mathematical understanding, and engineering skills of our ancient ancestors. These alignments required careful observation, accurate measurement, and sophisticated calculations. The ability to create structures that precisely aligned with celestial events speaks to the depth of knowledge, reverence for the cosmos, and the desire to establish a profound connection between the earthly and divine realms.

Beyond the practical and religious implications, celestial alignments provided a source of wonder and inspiration. They invited contemplation of humanity's place within the vast cosmos, encouraging a sense of humility and awe in the face of the grandeur of the universe. The alignment of temples with celestial events continues to captivate us today, reminding us of the enduring human fascination with the stars, and the universal quest to comprehend the mysteries of the cosmos.

In summary, celestial alignments represent a remarkable aspect of ancient cultures' relationship with the cosmos. They served as a bridge between the earthly and celestial realms, symbolizing the interconnectedness of all things. These alignments, meticulously incorporated into the architecture of temples and other sacred structures, allowed ancient civilizations to honor celestial events, maintain agricultural calendars, and express their spiritual beliefs. Through their pursuit of celestial alignment, our ancestors sought to understand and commune with the cosmic forces that shape our world, leaving behind a legacy that continues to awe and inspire us today.

Solstices, equinoxes, and astrological connections have played significant roles in human cultures throughout history. These celestial events mark key points in the Earth's orbit around the sun and have been observed and celebrated by diverse civilizations, influencing various aspects of human life, including religious beliefs, agricultural practices, and even the development of astrology.

Solstices occur twice a year, marking the longest and shortest days of the year. The summer solstice, typically around June 21st in the Northern Hemisphere, represents the peak of sunlight and the beginning of summer. In contrast, the winter solstice, around December 21st in the Northern Hemisphere, marks the shortest day and the beginning of winter. These solstices have held great significance for ancient cultures, symbolizing the cyclical nature of life, death, and rebirth. Many megalithic structures, such as Stonehenge, are aligned to capture the sun's rays during these solstices, highlighting their cultural and spiritual importance.

Equinoxes, occurring around March 21st (spring equinox) and September 21st (autumn equinox) in the Northern Hemisphere, mark the moments when day and night are of equal length. These events hold profound symbolism, representing balance and harmony in nature. Equinoxes have been associated with the transition of seasons, influencing agricultural practices and the planning of religious ceremonies. Temples and other structures were often built with alignments that allowed sunlight to penetrate specific areas during the equinoxes, further emphasizing their cultural and spiritual significance.

Astrological connections, particularly within the realm of astrology, focus on the relationship between celestial bodies and human affairs. Astrology is the belief that the positions and movements of celestial objects can influence human behavior, personality traits, and future events. Ancient civilizations, such as the Babylonians, Egyptians, and Greeks, developed intricate systems of astrology based on their observations of the stars, planets, and other celestial phenomena. These astrological connections were often associated with specific zodiac signs, each linked to different personality traits and astrological interpretations.

The solstices, equinoxes, and astrological connections share a common thread in their deep-rooted connection to celestial events. These phenomena have inspired diverse cultural beliefs, religious practices, and societal customs throughout history. They have shaped the way ancient civilizations perceived and interacted with the natural world, influencing everything from agricultural calendars and the timing of religious ceremonies to the development of complex astrological systems.

While modern science has provided explanations for the astronomical causes of solstices and equinoxes, their cultural and symbolic significance continues to resonate today. Festivals, celebrations, and spiritual practices still revolve around these celestial events, honoring the cycles of nature and acknowledging our place in the cosmos. Astrology, too, persists as a belief system, albeit with varying interpretations and degrees of acceptance.

In summary, solstices, equinoxes, and astrological connections represent profound links between the celestial and human realms. These celestial events have influenced cultural practices, religious beliefs, and our understanding of the natural world throughout history. They serve as reminders of our connection to the larger universe, prompting contemplation of the mysteries of the cosmos and the interplay between celestial rhythms and human existence.

Investigating astronomical observatories is a fascinating journey that unveils the intricate relationship between humanity and the cosmos. These remarkable structures, carefully designed to study and understand the celestial bodies, showcase the innate curiosity and scientific prowess of ancient civilizations. As we delve into the study of these observatories, we gain insights into the remarkable astronomical knowledge, advanced engineering, and cultural significance that underpinned their construction.

One of the most renowned ancient observatories is Stonehenge, located on the Salisbury Plain in England. This megalithic monument, composed of massive standing stones, has captivated scholars and visitors for centuries. While the precise purpose of Stonehenge continues to be debated, its alignment with the solstices and equinoxes suggests an intimate connection with the movements of the sun. The careful positioning of the stones allowed ancient observers to track the changing seasons, marking important agricultural and religious events.

Moving across continents, we encounter Chichen Itza in present-day Mexico. This Mayan observatory, known as El Caracol, stands as a testament to the astronomical knowledge of the ancient Maya. El Caracol's circular design with narrow windows aligns with key celestial events, such as the movement of Venus. The Maya's meticulous observations and understanding of celestial cycles enabled them to create precise calendars, navigate the seas, and make predictions about the cosmos.

In India, the Jantar Mantar complex in Jaipur offers further evidence of ancient astronomical pursuits. Built by the Rajput king Sawai Jai Singh II in the 18th century, this collection of architectural instruments served as an observatory and an astronomical laboratory. The instruments, constructed with exceptional precision and large-scale proportions, facilitated the measurement of celestial phenomena, including the positions of celestial bodies and the calculation of eclipses.

Delving into the ancient world, we encounter the Antikythera mechanism, a remarkable device discovered in a shipwreck off the coast of Greece. Dating back to the 2nd century BCE, this intricate mechanism displayed an astonishing level of mechanical sophistication. The Antikythera mechanism, often referred to as the world's oldest analog computer, was used to track celestial positions, predict eclipses, and perform complex calculations. Its discovery highlights the advanced astronomical knowledge and technological capabilities of ancient Greek civilization.

Each of these observatories, and many others scattered across the globe, serves as a testament to humanity's ceaseless fascination with the cosmos. They demonstrate the profound connection between ancient cultures and the celestial bodies that influenced their lives, religious beliefs, and agricultural practices. These observatories were not only scientific instruments but also cultural and spiritual symbols, embodying a society's reverence for the heavens and its quest to understand the universe.

Investigating astronomical observatories allows us to appreciate the remarkable achievements of our ancestors. The meticulous observations, precise measurements, and architectural ingenuity embedded within these structures provide glimpses into the ancient scientific mindset and their quest to comprehend the cosmos. Through the lens of these observatories, we gain a deeper understanding of the interconnectedness between humanity and the vast celestial realm, bridging the gaps between past and present, science and culture, and inspiring future generations to explore the mysteries of the universe.

Mapping the skies through astronomical alignments in megalithic temples is a captivating journey that reveals the profound connection between ancient civilizations and the celestial realm. These architectural marvels, crafted with precision and purpose, served as celestial observatories, aligning with significant celestial events and embodying the cultural and spiritual beliefs of their creators. Exploring the astronomical alignments in megalithic temples allows us to peer into the minds of our ancient ancestors, marvel at their astronomical knowledge, and understand the profound significance they attributed to the celestial bodies.

One of the most renowned examples of astronomical alignments can be found in Stonehenge, standing sentinel on the Salisbury Plain in England. The carefully placed stones, arranged in concentric circles and horseshoe shapes, align with the movements of the sun during the solstices and equinoxes. As the sun rises or sets in specific positions, rays of light filter through the stone formations, marking significant moments in the solar calendar. These alignments suggest that Stonehenge was not merely a gathering place or burial site but also a sophisticated celestial observatory, enabling precise astronomical observations and calculations.

In Malta, the megalithic temples of Mnajdra and Ħaġar Qim exhibit remarkable alignments with celestial events. These temples, dating back over 5,000 years, are intricately positioned to capture the rising sun during the equinoxes and solstices. As the sun's rays pierce through specific apertures and passageways, they illuminate designated areas within the temples, indicating the precise timing of celestial events and highlighting the importance of these moments in the cultural and religious practices of the ancient Maltese society.

Moving across continents to the New World, the Mayan city of Chichen Itza in Mexico boasts the impressive El Castillo pyramid. During the equinoxes, the setting sun casts shadows on the pyramid's staircases, creating the illusion of a serpent slithering down the steps. This remarkable alignment symbolizes the changing seasons and serves as a visual representation of the Mayan agricultural and cosmological beliefs. The precision required to create this alignment speaks to the advanced astronomical knowledge and architectural skills of the Mayan civilization.

In Egypt, the temples of Abu Simbel offer another testament to the celestial alignments in megalithic structures. The Great Temple of Ramses II, constructed over 3,000 years ago, features an awe-inspiring phenomenon twice a year. On February 22nd and October 22nd, the rising sun aligns with the temple's entrance, illuminating the inner sanctuary and illuminating the statues of the pharaoh and gods within. This alignment likely served a religious and symbolic purpose, reinforcing the divine connection between the pharaoh and the celestial realm.

These examples represent a mere fraction of the many megalithic temples worldwide that exhibit astronomical alignments. The intricate knowledge of celestial events displayed by these ancient civilizations is a testament to their keen observations, mathematical understanding, and reverence for the cosmos. By aligning their temples with the movements of the sun, moon, and stars, these cultures sought to establish a profound connection between the earthly and celestial realms, infusing their daily lives, religious rituals, and cultural practices with cosmic significance.

Mapping the skies through astronomical alignments in megalithic temples enables us to unravel the intricate tapestry of human fascination with the cosmos. It demonstrates the universal yearning to comprehend and connect with the celestial bodies that have inspired wonder, curiosity, and spiritual contemplation throughout the ages. These alignments serve as lasting testaments to the intellectual prowess, spiritual beliefs, and enduring legacy of our ancient ancestors, reminding us of the enduring human quest to understand our place in the vastness of the universe.

The spiritual and symbolic meaning of celestial alignments has been the subject of speculation and interpretation by various cultures throughout history. These alignments, where the positions of celestial bodies coincide with specific locations or structures on Earth, have often been attributed profound significance, connecting the celestial and terrestrial realms and carrying deep spiritual and symbolic meaning. Several theories have emerged to explain the spiritual and symbolic implications of celestial alignments in different cultural contexts.

One theory proposes that celestial alignments were believed to signify the presence of deities or divine beings. The precise alignment of temples, monuments, or other sacred sites with celestial bodies was seen as a manifestation of the gods' influence or communication with the human realm. The alignment of a structure with the rising or setting sun, for example, could be interpreted as a direct interaction between the divine and human spheres, signifying blessings, guidance, or a sacred connection.

Another theory suggests that celestial alignments were perceived as representations of cosmic order and harmony. The precise positioning of structures in alignment with celestial events reflected a belief in the interconnectedness of all things, symbolizing the unity and balance between the earthly and celestial realms. These alignments were seen as expressions of cosmic laws or principles governing the natural world and human existence, imparting a sense of order and purpose to life.

Celestial alignments also often held agricultural and seasonal significance. The observation and marking of solstices, equinoxes, and other celestial events helped societies track the changing seasons and determine the optimal timing for agricultural activities. These alignments were intertwined with fertility rites, harvest celebrations, and agrarian rituals, reflecting the deep spiritual connection between the celestial cycles and the sustenance of life.

Symbolically, celestial alignments represented transitions and transformations. The alignment of a structure with the sun during solstices or equinoxes, for example, could symbolize the passage from darkness to light, or the shift from one season to another. These alignments were associated with themes of renewal, rebirth, and the cyclical nature of existence. They provided an opportunity for reflection, introspection, and spiritual growth, inviting individuals to align themselves with the cosmic rhythms and embrace personal transformation.

In some cultures, celestial alignments were linked to mythological narratives and folklore. The movements and alignments of celestial bodies were connected with stories of gods, heroes, and legendary events. These alignments were seen as a physical representation or enactment of mythological tales, allowing individuals to participate in and witness the cosmic dramas embedded in their cultural narratives.

While these theories provide insight into the possible spiritual and symbolic meanings attributed to celestial alignments, it is important to remember that interpretations varied across cultures and epochs. Celestial alignments carried different significance depending on the specific religious, mythological, and cultural contexts in which they were situated. Furthermore, our understanding of these ancient beliefs and interpretations may be limited by the fragmentary nature of historical records and the passage of time.

Nevertheless, the spiritual and symbolic meanings assigned to celestial alignments by various cultures illuminate the universal human fascination with the cosmos and the desire to find meaning in the celestial realm. These alignments bridged the gap between the earthly and celestial planes, offering glimpses into the mysteries of the universe and inviting contemplation of our place within the cosmic order. They served as reminders of the interconnectedness of all things, the cycles of life and nature, and the enduring quest for spiritual understanding.

Chapter 3: Construction Techniques and Engineering Marvels

Mastering megalithic masonry, the art of crafting and erecting massive stone structures, required a combination of innovative techniques and specialized tools. The ancient builders who undertook these monumental tasks displayed remarkable engineering skills, creativity, and perseverance. Although precise methods varied across different cultures and time periods, several common techniques and tools emerged as key elements in the mastery of megalithic masonry.

One of the fundamental techniques employed by megalithic builders was the process of quarrying. Selecting suitable stone from natural outcrops or quarries required careful consideration. The chosen stone had to possess durability, strength, and workability. Quarrying techniques involved the use of wedges, wooden or stone levers, and hammers to split the stone from its original location. Cleverly placed wedges and the application of force allowed the stone to be separated along natural lines of weakness, creating workable blocks for further processing.

Once the stones were quarried, shaping and dressing became crucial. Ancient masons employed a range of tools to shape the stones to precise dimensions and create the desired aesthetic effects. For rough shaping, stone hammers and chisels were used to chip away excess material. As the work progressed, finer tools such as bronze or iron chisels, drills, and scrapers were employed to achieve smoother surfaces and more intricate details.

The transportation of megalithic stones posed a significant challenge. Ancient builders employed various ingenious methods to move these massive blocks over long distances. One technique involved the use of wooden sledges or rollers, along with ropes and levers, to facilitate sliding or rolling the stones across specially constructed tracks or earthen ramps. Water was also employed to create temporary pathways for the stones to glide upon, reducing friction and easing transportation.

Lifting and placing the stones into their designated positions required sophisticated techniques and the coordination of many workers. Ramps, scaffolding, and earthwork embankments were commonly used to elevate the stones to their desired heights. The application of leverage, pulleys, and counterweights enabled the controlled lifting and precise positioning of the stones.

In addition to the physical techniques, ancient masons utilized various measurement and leveling tools to ensure accuracy and alignment.

String lines, plumb bobs, and spirit levels were employed to assess verticality and straightness. Sight lines and astronomical observations aided in achieving precise alignments with celestial events or desired orientations.

The mastery of megalithic masonry also required a deep understanding of the properties of different stone types, including their resistance to weathering, load-bearing capacities, and interlocking qualities. Skilled masons knew how to exploit these properties to ensure the stability and longevity of the structures they erected.

The tools used by ancient masons were predominantly made of stone, bronze, or iron, reflecting the technological capabilities available during specific time periods. Stone hammers, chisels, and mallets were common, while bronze and iron chisels, drills, and saws provided greater efficiency and precision.

The techniques and tools employed by ancient builders for megalithic masonry were a testament to their ingenuity and expertise. These craftsmen mastered the art of working with massive stones, transforming raw materials into awe-inspiring structures that have withstood the test of time. Their innovative methods and careful planning allowed for the creation of architectural marvels that continue to captivate and inspire us today.

The transportation of enormous stones for megalithic construction is a remarkable feat that has puzzled researchers and sparked various theories and hypotheses. The movement of these massive stones over long distances required innovative methods, ingenuity, and considerable manpower. While definitive answers regarding transportation techniques may remain elusive, several theories and methods have been proposed to shed light on this intriguing aspect of megalithic construction.

One prevalent theory suggests that ancient builders used simple yet effective techniques involving sledges, rollers, and manpower to transport the enormous stones. Wooden sledges, often lubricated with animal fat or water, were placed underneath the stones to reduce friction and facilitate sliding. Teams of workers pulled or pushed the sledges, while others cleared the path and potentially applied temporary ramps or inclined planes to navigate uneven terrain. This theory proposes that by repeating these incremental movements, the stones were gradually transported to their intended locations.

Another theory posits the use of round logs or cylindrical rollers, possibly made from tree trunks or other materials, to create a rolling platform for the stones. By placing the stones on top of these rollers and using ropes or levers for guidance and control, ancient builders could roll the stones along carefully constructed tracks or earthen ramps. This method would have required continuous repositioning of the rollers at the front, allowing the stone to roll over them and be moved forward.

Water-based transportation methods have also been proposed for areas with accessible waterways. These theories suggest that megalithic stones were transported via rafts or boats, taking advantage of buoyancy and water currents. The stones would have been loaded onto the rafts or boats and floated to their destinations, reducing friction and simplifying the movement process. Additionally, temporary canals or channels might have been constructed to create smoother pathways for the stones to navigate overland, utilizing the power of water to aid in their transportation.

In certain cases, theories propose the implementation of an "earth ramp" technique. This method involves the construction of earthen ramps, gradually built up alongside the structure being erected. The stones could then be transported up the ramp using sledges, rollers, or other means. As the construction progressed, the ramp would be extended, allowing for the continued ascent of the stones to higher levels. Once the construction was complete, the ramp would be removed or incorporated into the final structure.

It is important to note that the specific transportation methods likely varied depending on factors such as the available technology, local geography, and cultural practices of the ancient builders. Different theories may be more applicable to specific regions or time periods, and it is possible that a combination of techniques was employed to overcome various challenges.

While these theories offer plausible explanations for transporting enormous stones, the precise methods employed by ancient builders remain speculative to some extent. The absence of detailed historical records and the passage of time have made it challenging to definitively determine how these impressive engineering feats were accomplished. However, ongoing research, experimental archaeology, and the study of historical accounts and cultural practices continue to provide valuable insights into the transportation methods used by our ancient ancestors.

In summary, the transportation of enormous stones for megalithic construction remains a subject of intrigue and speculation. Theories propose the use of sledges, rollers, water-based transportation, and earth ramps, among other techniques. While these theories provide plausible explanations, further research and discoveries are needed to gain a more comprehensive understanding of the remarkable methods employed by ancient builders. The transportation of these massive stones stands as a testament to the ingenuity, resourcefulness, and determination of our ancestors, who overcame significant challenges to create enduring architectural wonders.

Architectural marvels throughout history have showcased a remarkable level of precision in both design and construction. From ancient megalithic structures to modern skyscrapers, these awe-inspiring buildings stand as testaments to human ingenuity, technological advancements, and a pursuit of perfection. Achieving precision in architectural design and construction requires meticulous planning, innovative techniques, and attention to detail at every stage of the process.

In the realm of ancient architecture, megalithic structures such as Stonehenge, the Pyramids of Egypt, and the temples of ancient Greece and Rome continue to amaze us with their precision and durability. These monumental structures, often created without the aid of advanced machinery, exhibit exceptional accuracy in their alignments, proportions, and intricate detailing. The stones used in their construction were precisely cut, shaped, and fitted together to create harmonious and visually stunning edifices.

The precision in design starts with careful planning and calculation. Ancient architects employed mathematical principles, geometry, and ratios to ensure the proper proportions and harmony of their structures. The Golden Ratio, for example, was often used to create aesthetically pleasing and balanced compositions. These meticulous calculations and proportions contributed to the visual appeal and perceived harmony of the buildings.

In terms of construction techniques, ancient architects and builders displayed remarkable craftsmanship and engineering skills. Stone-cutting tools such as chisels, saws, and drills were used to shape the stones with precision. Mortar, when employed, was mixed to exact proportions, allowing for sturdy and enduring structures. Advanced techniques, such as arches, vaults, and domes, enabled the creation of large, open spaces and distributed the weight of the structures effectively.

Moving into the modern era, technological advancements have allowed for even greater precision in architectural design and construction. Computer-aided design (CAD) and Building Information Modeling (BIM) software have revolutionized the way architects plan and visualize their designs. These tools enable precise 3D modeling, accurate calculations, and detailed simulations, resulting in more efficient construction processes and improved accuracy.

In construction, advanced machinery, such as tower cranes and robotic systems, facilitates the precise assembly of building components. Laser-guided leveling systems ensure the accuracy of floors and surfaces, while high-precision cutting tools and equipment enable the fabrication of intricate details with exceptional accuracy. These technological advancements have revolutionized the construction industry, allowing for the realization of complex and precise architectural visions.

Achieving precision in architectural design and construction is not solely about mathematical calculations and advanced technology. It also requires meticulous craftsmanship, attention to detail, and a deep understanding of materials and their properties. Skilled craftsmen, such as masons, carpenters, and metalworkers, play a crucial role in translating the architect's vision into reality, ensuring that every element is meticulously executed.

Precision in architectural design and construction not only produces visually striking buildings but also ensures structural integrity, durability, and functionality. It enhances the user experience, creating spaces that are not only aesthetically pleasing but also practical and comfortable.

In summary, architectural marvels across the ages demonstrate the extraordinary level of precision achieved in both design and construction. From ancient megalithic structures to modern skyscrapers, these buildings reflect the human pursuit of perfection, technological advancements, and the marriage of creativity and craftsmanship. Achieving precision in architecture requires meticulous planning, innovative techniques, attention to detail, and a harmonious blend of art and science. These remarkable structures inspire awe, captivate our imagination, and stand as enduring testaments to the power of human ingenuity and the beauty of precision in architecture.

Megalithic temples, with their massive stone constructions, stand as awe-inspiring engineering feats that continue to captivate researchers and visitors alike. The analysis and discoveries surrounding these ancient structures provide valuable insights into the advanced engineering techniques employed by our ancestors and the remarkable achievements they accomplished.

One key aspect of megalithic temples is their impressive stone-cutting and shaping techniques. Ancient builders utilized various methods to extract, shape, and transport enormous stones with precision. The discovery of tool marks, such as chisel marks and abrasions, on the surfaces of megalithic stones has revealed the use of stone hammers, chisels, and other cutting tools. The meticulous shaping and fitting of these stones, often without the aid of mortar, demonstrate the skill and craftsmanship of ancient masons.

The transportation and positioning of these massive stones are also remarkable engineering achievements. Researchers have proposed different theories and experimental reconstructions to understand how these stones were moved over long distances and lifted into position. The use of sledges, rollers, ramps, and ingenious techniques involving leverage and counterweights have been hypothesized and tested to replicate the transportation methods employed by ancient builders. These investigations have shed light on the level of planning, organization, and collaborative efforts required to achieve such monumental tasks.

The structural stability and durability of megalithic temples have also fascinated researchers. The precise interlocking of stones, careful weight distribution, and incorporation of load-bearing elements, such as corbels and lintels, have contributed to the longevity of these structures. The use of post-and-lintel construction, where vertical stones (posts) support horizontal stones (lintels), provided structural integrity and allowed for the creation of large interior spaces. The discovery of stone wedges and other devices used to secure the stones together further demonstrates the attention given to structural stability.

Furthermore, the acoustic properties of megalithic temples have been a subject of investigation. Researchers have observed that certain structures exhibit enhanced acoustic qualities, with specific spots within the temples resonating or amplifying sound. The deliberate design of these spaces suggests that acoustics played a role in the rituals and ceremonies conducted within the temples, creating immersive and reverberating experiences for the participants.

Archaeological excavations and surveys around megalithic temples have uncovered additional engineering features and insights. The discovery of drainage systems, water management techniques, and ventilation systems indicate the careful consideration given to practical aspects of the temples' construction. These features ensured the longevity of the structures by preventing water damage and maintaining a comfortable environment within the sacred spaces.

Advancements in modern technology, such as ground-penetrating radar and laser scanning, have allowed for non-invasive investigations of megalithic temples. These techniques have revealed hidden chambers, complex architectural features, and potential patterns in the construction methods employed. The integration of these modern tools with traditional archaeological methods has provided a comprehensive understanding of the temples' engineering and architectural characteristics.

In summary, the analysis and discoveries surrounding megalithic temples have deepened our appreciation for the remarkable engineering feats achieved by ancient civilizations. The stone-cutting techniques, transportation methods, structural stability, acoustic properties, and practical considerations demonstrate the ingenuity, skill, and knowledge of our ancestors. These temples stand as enduring testaments to human creativity, craftsmanship, and the pursuit of spiritual and cultural expression. The ongoing research and exploration of these magnificent structures continue to uncover new insights and enhance our understanding of ancient engineering practices.

In the annals of historical inquiry, few subjects have engendered as much controversy and scholarly debate as the unconventional construction theories surrounding ancient monuments. These enigmatic structures, with their intricate designs and colossal proportions, have confounded researchers for centuries, giving rise to a plethora of unconventional theories that challenge conventional wisdom. In this discourse, we shall delve into the realm of unconventional construction theories and explore the controversies that have stirred the minds of historians, architects, and archaeologists alike.

One of the most contentious topics in the realm of unconventional construction theories revolves around the construction methods employed in ancient megalithic structures. These awe-inspiring monuments, constructed with massive stones, defy the imagination and have elicited various speculative hypotheses. While conventional wisdom attributes their construction to the meticulous efforts of skilled craftsmen utilizing primitive tools, proponents of unconventional theories posit alternative explanations.

Some theorists propose that these colossal stones were not quarried and transported by human hands alone. Instead, they suggest the involvement of extraterrestrial or supernatural forces in the construction process. According to this line of thinking, ancient civilizations received assistance or guidance from beings of superior intelligence or technology. Such theories, often dismissed as products of wild imagination, challenge the conventional understanding of human capabilities at the time, leaving room for imaginative speculation.

Another controversial aspect of unconventional construction theories pertains to the astronomical alignments observed in many ancient structures. The meticulous positioning of these monuments in alignment with celestial events, such as solstices or equinoxes, has sparked debates regarding the purpose and significance of such alignments. While mainstream explanations suggest a connection to religious or calendrical practices, proponents of unconventional theories propose that these alignments reflect a profound understanding of celestial mechanics and the manipulation of cosmic energies.

One widely debated theory revolves around the idea of ancient knowledge lost to time. Proponents argue that ancient civilizations possessed advanced technologies, scientific knowledge, or architectural techniques that have been lost or suppressed over the millennia. According to this view, these forgotten advancements allowed for the construction of monuments that defy conventional explanations. While some dismiss these theories as mere speculation, others argue that the historical record may not fully capture the extent of ancient achievements.

Controversial theories also extend to specific monuments, such as the Great Pyramids of Egypt or the intricate stonework of Machu Picchu. Theories questioning the conventional understanding of the construction methods used in these iconic structures abound. Some suggest the involvement of advanced machinery or levitation techniques, while others propose that these structures were pre-existing and later modified by ancient civilizations. These unconventional ideas challenge the accepted narratives surrounding these monuments and invite further exploration and investigation.

Unconventional theories, by their very nature, often run counter to established academic consensus and face significant scrutiny from the scholarly community. Critics argue that proponents of such theories rely on speculative evidence, cherry-picked data, or subjective interpretations. They caution against straying too far from the established historical record and urge rigorous scrutiny of alternative ideas to ensure a grounded approach to the study of ancient construction.

Nevertheless, the allure of unconventional construction theories persists, capturing the imagination and stimulating further inquiry. They serve as a reminder that historical understanding is an evolving process, subject to reinterpretation and revision as new evidence emerges. While some theories may be dismissed as pseudoscientific or fantastical, others may contribute to new discoveries, fostering a deeper understanding of ancient civilizations and their architectural achievements.

Ultimately, it is the spirit of intellectual inquiry and the pursuit of knowledge that drive the exploration of unconventional construction theories. Even in the face of controversy, these theories inspire new avenues of research, challenge preconceived notions, and encourage critical thinking. As historians, archaeologists, and architects continue to delve into the mysteries of the past, it is this spirit of curiosity and open-mindedness that will shed light on the unconventional and shape the future of our understanding of ancient construction.

Chapter 4: Theories on Purpose and Function

The religious and spiritual significance of megalithic temples is a subject that has fascinated scholars and researchers for generations. These monumental structures, with their grandeur and intricate designs, were not merely architectural marvels but also sacred spaces where ancient communities conducted rituals and ceremonies of deep spiritual importance. Exploring the religious and spiritual significance of megalithic temples allows us to gain insights into the beliefs, practices, and cultural expressions of the civilizations that built and utilized these sacred sites.

Rituals and ceremonies held within megalithic temples were central to the religious and spiritual lives of ancient societies. These rituals served as a means of communing with the divine, honoring ancestors, seeking blessings, expressing gratitude, and fostering social cohesion within the community. They formed a fundamental part of the religious fabric and were often tied to the cycles of nature, the agricultural calendar, or celestial events.

The alignment of megalithic temples with celestial phenomena, such as the rising or setting sun during solstices or equinoxes, played a crucial role in religious rituals. The precise positioning of these temples allowed for the observation and celebration of celestial events, which were believed to hold deep spiritual significance. These astronomical alignments marked important moments in the annual calendar, serving as triggers for religious observances, feasts, and communal gatherings.

The architecture and layout of megalithic temples often reflected the cosmological beliefs and mythologies of the societies that built them. The spatial arrangement of chambers, corridors, altars, and sacred niches within the temples held symbolic meaning and were used for specific ritual purposes. Sacred objects, statues, and artifacts were placed strategically within the temples to invoke the presence of deities, ancestors, or spirits and to facilitate communication with the spiritual realm.

The act of pilgrimage to megalithic temples was another important aspect of religious practice. People traveled from distant regions to visit these sacred sites, often engaging in arduous journeys as an expression of their devotion and faith. Pilgrimage served as a transformative experience, allowing individuals to connect with the divine, seek spiritual guidance, and participate in communal worship.

Music, dance, and chanting were integral components of religious rituals and ceremonies held within megalithic temples. These expressive forms of worship helped create an immersive and transcendent experience, fostering a collective sense of spirituality and facilitating a deep connection with the divine. The rhythmic movements, harmonious melodies, and repetitive chants were believed to induce altered states of consciousness and facilitate communication with the spiritual realm.

The rituals and ceremonies conducted within megalithic temples often involved offerings and sacrifices. These acts of devotion included the presentation of food, drink, incense, or precious objects as offerings to deities or ancestral spirits. Animal sacrifices were also common in some cultures, symbolizing the exchange of life force and demonstrating commitment and reverence.

The religious and spiritual significance of megalithic temples extended beyond individual rituals and ceremonies. These sacred sites served as cultural and social centers, fostering a sense of community and shared identity. They provided spaces for important social events, such as weddings, funerals, or initiation ceremonies, further strengthening the bonds within the community and reinforcing the collective religious and spiritual beliefs.

It is important to note that the specific religious beliefs and practices associated with megalithic temples varied across cultures and time periods. The interpretation of these ancient rituals and ceremonies relies on a combination of archaeological evidence, historical accounts, comparative studies, and an understanding of the cultural context in which these structures were built.

In summary, the religious and spiritual significance of megalithic temples reveals the deep reverence and connection ancient societies had with the divine and the spiritual realm. These sacred sites were not mere architectural achievements but embodied the cultural, religious, and communal values of the civilizations that built and utilized them. The rituals, ceremonies, and practices conducted within these temples provided a means for individuals and communities to express their spirituality, seek divine guidance, and find solace in the mysteries of the universe. Studying the religious and spiritual significance of megalithic temples enhances our understanding of the profound and enduring human quest for transcendence, meaning, and connection with the divine.

Temples have long served as sacred spaces that hold profound cultural significance. These architectural marvels, constructed with meticulous craftsmanship and imbued with symbolic meaning, provide a physical embodiment of the cultural practices and beliefs of the societies that built them. Exploring the cultural practices associated with temples allows us to gain a deeper understanding of the rituals, traditions, and social dynamics of ancient civilizations.

Temples were central to religious practices and played a crucial role in the spiritual lives of ancient communities. They served as sanctuaries where people could connect with the divine, seek blessings, offer prayers, and engage in acts of worship. Temples were often dedicated to specific gods, goddesses, or deities associated with various aspects of life, such as fertility, agriculture, wisdom, or war. These divine beings were revered as protectors, guides, and sources of spiritual power.

The rituals and ceremonies conducted within temples were important cultural events that fostered a sense of community and shared identity. These practices varied across cultures but commonly included offerings, prayers, hymns, processions, and symbolic acts performed by priests, priestesses, or designated individuals. The rituals were often performed at specific times of the year, such as harvest festivals or celestial events, and were closely tied to the cycles of nature or important milestones in the community.

Temples also served as repositories of knowledge, housing sacred texts, religious scriptures, and historical records. Priests and religious scholars acted as custodians of this knowledge, interpreting and preserving the cultural and religious heritage of the society. Temples were centers of learning, where individuals could receive education, engage in philosophical discussions, and seek guidance on matters of morality, ethics, and spirituality.

The architecture and design of temples reflected the cultural aesthetics and beliefs of the civilization. Elaborate carvings, intricate sculptures, and colorful murals adorned the walls, depicting mythological stories, legendary figures, or historical events. These artistic representations served to convey religious narratives, cultural ideals, and moral teachings. Symbolism played a significant role in temple design, with specific architectural elements representing cosmic forces, the hierarchy of the divine realm, or the journey of the soul.

Temples were not solely places of religious worship but also hubs of social and communal activities. They functioned as gathering places for festivals, celebrations, and social events. These occasions provided opportunities for community members to interact, strengthen social bonds, and partake in collective festivities. Temples often hosted cultural performances, music, dance, and theater, enriching the cultural fabric of the society and fostering a sense of shared heritage.

Additionally, temples served as centers for charitable activities and community welfare. They functioned as economic engines, employing artisans, priests, and temple staff. Donations and offerings made by devotees supported the maintenance and upkeep of the temple, as well as charitable endeavors such as feeding the poor, providing medical aid, or supporting education. Temples played a role in the socioeconomic development of the communities, acting as redistributive institutions that promoted social cohesion and helped address the needs of the less fortunate.

The cultural practices associated with temples evolved over time, reflecting the dynamic nature of societies and the influence of external factors. Changes in political power, contact with neighboring civilizations, and shifts in religious ideologies often impacted temple practices and architectural styles. Temples were also influenced by the social structures and values of the society, mirroring the hierarchical systems or gender roles prevalent at the time.

In summary, temples served as sacred spaces that encompassed the religious, cultural, and social aspects of ancient civilizations. They were centers of worship, repositories of knowledge, and focal points of communal activities. Temples embodied the cultural practices, beliefs, and aspirations of the societies that constructed and utilized them. Exploring the cultural practices associated with temples allows us to delve into the rich tapestry of ancient civilizations, offering insights into their religious devotion, artistic expression, community cohesion, and quest for meaning and transcendence.

Temples have long served as centers of community gathering and social functions, playing a pivotal role in the social fabric of ancient civilizations. These sacred spaces provided a venue for people to come together, engage in shared activities, and foster a sense of unity and collective identity. Exploring the community gathering and social functions associated with temples allows us to understand the important role these structures played in the social dynamics and cohesion of ancient societies.

One of the primary functions of temples as community gathering spaces was to facilitate religious ceremonies and rituals. These events brought people together to participate in acts of worship, prayer, and offerings to the divine. Temples served as focal points for religious festivals, where the community would congregate to celebrate important occasions, such as harvest festivals, solstices, or the birthdays of revered deities. These religious gatherings fostered a sense of communal spirituality, allowing individuals to connect with the divine and reinforce their shared religious beliefs and practices.

Temples also functioned as venues for cultural and artistic expressions. They provided a platform for performances of music, dance, theater, and other forms of artistic expression. Cultural festivals, musical recitals, and dramatic performances were held within temple premises, enriching the cultural landscape of the community. These events not only entertained but also served to pass down cultural traditions, preserve historical narratives, and instill a sense of cultural identity and pride among the attendees.

Beyond religious and artistic functions, temples served as spaces for educational and intellectual pursuits. They acted as centers of learning, where priests, scholars, and wise individuals imparted knowledge on various subjects, including philosophy, ethics, and religious teachings. Temples provided a forum for intellectual debates, discussions, and the exchange of ideas. They were repositories of sacred texts, historical records, and cultural wisdom, making them educational institutions that nurtured the intellectual growth and enlightenment of the community.

Temples played a significant role in fostering social cohesion and strengthening community bonds. They provided opportunities for social interactions, facilitating the formation of friendships, alliances, and communal ties. People from different social strata and backgrounds would come together within the temple precincts, fostering a sense of equality and camaraderie. Temples also acted as meeting places for community gatherings, where important decisions, discussions, and communal matters were deliberated upon.

Social functions held within temple premises extended beyond religious and cultural events. Temples often hosted communal feasts, banquets, and celebratory meals, where the community shared food and engaged in conviviality. These occasions served as a means of socializing, reinforcing kinship ties, and fostering a sense of solidarity and unity. The act of sharing a meal within the temple environment created a sense of communal belonging and promoted social harmony.

Temples also played a role in charitable activities and community welfare. They served as platforms for acts of benevolence, with devotees making donations and offerings to support the less fortunate members of the community. Temples often distributed food, provided healthcare services, or supported educational initiatives, thereby promoting social justice, compassion, and the well-being of the community at large.

In summary, temples functioned as vital spaces for community gathering and social functions in ancient civilizations. These sacred structures provided settings for religious ceremonies, cultural events, intellectual pursuits, and social interactions. Temples fostered a sense of communal spirituality, facilitated the transmission of cultural heritage, and played a role in shaping the social dynamics and cohesion of the community. Exploring the community gathering and social functions associated with temples offers insights into the significance of these structures beyond their religious roles, highlighting their broader impact on the social, cultural, and intellectual aspects of ancient societies.

Megalithic temples, with their imposing structures and central locations, often served as cultural centers and administrative hubs in ancient civilizations. These architectural marvels played a crucial role in the social, cultural, and administrative aspects of the communities that built and utilized them. Exploring the functions of megalithic temples as cultural centers and administrative hubs allows us to understand the significance of these structures beyond their religious and architectural aspects.

One important function of megalithic temples as cultural centers was to preserve and transmit cultural heritage. These temples served as repositories of knowledge, housing sacred texts, historical records, and cultural artifacts. Priests and religious scholars acted as custodians of this knowledge, ensuring its preservation and passing it down to future generations. Temples played a role in educating the community, teaching religious beliefs, moral codes, and cultural traditions. They were centers of learning, where individuals could receive education in various disciplines, including theology, philosophy, literature, and the arts.

The architecture and design of megalithic temples also reflected the cultural aesthetics and beliefs of the civilization. Intricate carvings, sculptures, and paintings adorned the temple walls, depicting mythological stories, historical events, and cultural symbolism. These artistic representations served to convey cultural narratives, express religious ideologies, and preserve the cultural identity of the community. Temples became living museums of art and culture, showcasing the artistic achievements and cultural expressions of the civilization.

Megalithic temples often served as venues for cultural events, festivals, and performances. These gatherings brought together community members, allowing them to celebrate important occasions, share in cultural festivities, and engage in collective expressions of joy and reverence. Theatrical performances, musical recitals, dance ceremonies, and poetry readings were held within the temple precincts, fostering artistic talent and contributing to the cultural vibrancy of the community. The central location and grandeur of megalithic temples made them natural focal points for administrative activities. Temples often housed administrative offices, where local authorities and religious leaders made decisions, resolved disputes, and administered justice. These structures served as administrative hubs, facilitating governance, and acting as meeting places for community leaders and representatives. Temples played a role in the organization of communal affairs, coordination of public works, and management of resources.

Furthermore, megalithic temples served as gathering places for community assemblies and discussions. These assemblies provided an opportunity for the community to come together, voice concerns, deliberate on important matters, and make decisions that affected the collective well-being. Temples acted as platforms for community engagement and participatory democracy, allowing individuals to actively shape the social, cultural, and administrative landscape of their society.

Temples also played a role in economic activities, functioning as centers of trade and commerce. The influx of people into the temple precincts during festivals and ceremonies created opportunities for economic exchange. Artisans, merchants, and traders set up stalls, offering goods and services to the temple visitors. Temples became vibrant marketplaces, where goods were bought, sold, and bartered, contributing to the economic vitality of the community.

In summary, megalithic temples served as cultural centers and administrative hubs in ancient civilizations. These structures preserved cultural heritage, facilitated education, and acted as repositories of knowledge. They provided venues for cultural events, festivals, and performances, fostering artistic expression and cultural vibrancy. Temples served as gathering places for community assemblies and discussions, playing a role in governance, decision-making, and community engagement. Their central location and economic activities made them hubs of trade and commerce. Exploring the functions of megalithic temples as cultural centers and administrative hubs offers insights into the multi-faceted roles these structures played in the social, cultural, and administrative dynamics of ancient societies.

Megalithic temples, with their intriguing architectural features and enigmatic history, continue to be the subject of modern interpretations and debates regarding their purpose and function. As scholars and researchers delve deeper into the study of these ancient structures, varying theories and hypotheses have emerged, shedding new light on their significance and challenging long-held beliefs. The modern interpretations and debates surrounding the purpose and function of megalithic temples reflect the evolving nature of archaeological and historical research.

One prominent area of debate revolves around the religious and spiritual significance of megalithic temples. Traditional views propose that these structures served primarily as places of worship and religious rituals, dedicated to specific deities or ancestral spirits. However, modern interpretations have expanded the understanding of their religious function, suggesting that they also played a role in cosmological beliefs, celestial observations, and the performance of sacred rites. These interpretations consider the alignment of megalithic temples with celestial events, such as solstices or equinoxes, as evidence of their connection to astronomical observations and the pursuit of a deeper understanding of the cosmos.

Another ongoing debate concerns the social and communal functions of megalithic temples. While religious activities likely formed the core purpose of these structures, some scholars argue that they also served as community gathering places, administrative centers, or symbols of collective identity. These interpretations propose that megalithic temples functioned as focal points for communal events, such as festivals, ceremonies, or assemblies, where social interactions, cultural expressions, and governance activities took place. They suggest that the grandeur and central location of these temples were deliberate choices to enhance their role as social and political hubs.

The architectural and engineering aspects of megalithic temples have also spurred discussions on their purpose and function. Some scholars emphasize the sophisticated construction techniques and precise stonework of these structures, suggesting that their primary function was to showcase the advanced architectural skills and engineering prowess of the ancient civilizations. Others propose that the monumental scale and impressive designs were intended to evoke a sense of awe and reverence, emphasizing the sacredness of the space and elevating the religious experience for worshippers.

Additionally, debates persist regarding the economic and practical functions of megalithic temples. While it is widely accepted that these structures required significant resources and labor to construct, the exact nature of their economic impact is subject to interpretation. Some argue that the construction and maintenance of megalithic temples contributed to local economies by providing employment opportunities, stimulating trade, or attracting pilgrims and visitors who would contribute to the local economy. Others contend that the resources invested in temple construction may have been driven more by religious or symbolic motivations rather than purely economic considerations.

Moreover, alternative theories propose that megalithic temples had multifunctional purposes, serving a combination of religious, social, economic, and symbolic roles. These interpretations emphasize the complexity and diversity of these ancient structures, suggesting that their purpose and function may have evolved over time or varied across different cultures and regions.

The ongoing debates and varying interpretations surrounding the purpose and function of megalithic temples highlight the challenges inherent in understanding the motivations and beliefs of ancient civilizations. As new archaeological discoveries are made, technological advancements enable more precise measurements and analyses, and interdisciplinary approaches are employed, our understanding of these enigmatic structures continues to evolve. Through open dialogue, rigorous research, and the integration of diverse perspectives, scholars strive to unravel the mysteries surrounding megalithic temples, offering ever-deeper insights into their purpose, function, and the societies that created them.

Chapter 5: The Sacred Landscape

One of the fascinating aspects of megalithic temples is their integration with the natural environment, where the architects and builders incorporated natural features into the design of these sacred structures. This intentional alignment with nature reflects the deep reverence and connection ancient civilizations had with the natural world. By incorporating natural features into temple design, they sought to create a harmonious relationship between the human-made and the surrounding natural landscape.

One common practice observed in megalithic temples is the selection of sacred sites with natural elements that hold symbolic or spiritual significance. Temples were often situated near rivers, lakes, or springs, emphasizing the importance of water as a life-giving force and a symbol of purification and renewal. These natural water sources were integrated into temple complexes, sometimes with ceremonial baths or pools used for ritualistic purposes.

The choice of specific geological formations or natural landmarks was also significant in the design and placement of megalithic temples. Mountains, hills, or cliffs were often incorporated into the temple complex, either as a backdrop or as integral parts of the architectural layout. These natural features were seen as sacred manifestations of the divine or as conduits for spiritual energy. Temples built on elevated locations or nestled within the embrace of hills symbolized a connection between the earthly realm and the celestial realm.

In some instances, the natural landscape itself was shaped or modified to enhance the sacredness of the temple. Terracing, leveling, or reshaping of the land created a platform for the temple, blending the man-made and natural elements seamlessly. These modifications not only served functional purposes but also conveyed a symbolic message of the human desire to create a sacred space in harmony with the surrounding environment.

The orientation and layout of megalithic temples often took into account celestial alignments and natural phenomena. The rising or setting of the sun, moon, or stars during specific astronomical events, such as solstices or equinoxes, played a role in the design and positioning of temples. Alignments with celestial bodies were believed to connect the earthly realm with the celestial realm, emphasizing the interplay between human existence and cosmic forces. These alignments were often incorporated into the architectural elements, such as doorways, windows, or openings, allowing light to penetrate and illuminate specific areas of the temple during significant astronomical events.

The materials used in the construction of megalithic temples were often sourced from the local natural environment, further emphasizing the connection to the land. Stone, in particular, was a prevalent choice, as it symbolized endurance, stability, and the eternal nature of the divine. The stones used in temple construction were carefully selected and shaped, blending with the natural geology of the area and creating a seamless integration between the human-made and the natural surroundings.

By aligning with nature and incorporating natural features into temple design, ancient civilizations sought to create a spiritual sanctuary that harmonized with the world around them. The deliberate integration of natural elements into temple complexes emphasized the interdependence between humans and the environment, fostering a sense of reverence, gratitude, and humility. It also served as a reminder of the interconnectedness of all living beings and the divine forces that permeate the natural world.

The incorporation of natural features into megalithic temples not only enhanced the aesthetic beauty of these structures but also deepened the spiritual experience for worshippers. The alignment with nature fostered a sense of sacredness, tranquility, and connectedness, allowing individuals to connect with the divine and experience a profound sense of unity with the natural world. Through their intentional integration of natural elements, megalithic temples exemplify the timeless wisdom of ancient civilizations in recognizing and honoring the sanctity of the natural environment.

Sacred geography played a significant role in the design and symbolism of megalithic temples, as ancient civilizations sought to create a profound connection between the physical environment and their religious and spiritual beliefs. The surrounding landscapes, topographical features, and geographical locations were incorporated into the design and symbolism of these sacred structures, imbuing them with deeper meaning and significance.

The choice of a specific location for a megalithic temple was not arbitrary but often based on the perceived spiritual qualities of the surrounding landscape. Temples were constructed in areas believed to possess inherent sacredness, such as mountains, caves, forests, or riverbanks. These natural environments were seen as gateways to the divine or as realms where the spiritual and earthly realms intersected. The presence of these sacred landscapes added a layer of spiritual significance to the temples, enhancing their perceived connection with the divine.

The orientation and alignment of megalithic temples with natural features were integral to their symbolism. Temples were often positioned in alignment with significant landmarks, such as mountains, rivers, or specific celestial bodies. These alignments were believed to establish a connection between the temple and the natural world, as well as to the cosmic forces or deities associated with those features. The alignment with mountains, for example, symbolized the ascent to higher realms or the dwelling place of gods, while alignment with rivers represented purification, fertility, and the flow of life.

The natural elements and topographical features surrounding megalithic temples also held symbolic significance. Mountains represented stability, transcendence, and the abode of deities. Forests were associated with fertility, regeneration, and the mystical realm. Caves symbolized the womb of the Earth, serving as gateways to the underworld or as places of initiation and transformation. These natural features were not only integrated into the temple design but also became part of the sacred narrative and symbolism associated with the temple.

Water bodies, such as rivers, lakes, or springs, played a prominent role in the symbolism of megalithic temples. Water was viewed as a purifying and life-giving force, symbolizing renewal, fertility, and spiritual cleansing. Many temples were strategically positioned near water sources, and sometimes ceremonial pools or baths were constructed within the temple complexes for ritualistic purposes. The presence of water in and around the temples heightened their spiritual significance and emphasized the connection between the human and divine realms.

The surrounding landscapes and geographical locations also influenced the cultural narratives and mythologies associated with megalithic temples. The natural features and landmarks became part of the sacred narratives, legends, and origin myths of the communities that built and worshipped at these temples. They formed the backdrop for the stories of gods, heroes, and ancestral beings, enriching the cultural heritage and collective memory of the society.

Symbolism in megalithic temples extended beyond the natural landscape to include architectural elements and sacred geometry. The arrangement of stones, the positioning of doorways and entrances, and the layout of chambers and corridors held symbolic meanings. Sacred numbers, geometric proportions, and spatial alignments were believed to enhance the energetic flow, harmonize the spiritual forces, and create a sacred space conducive to worship and communion with the divine.

In summary, the symbolism of megalithic temples was intricately intertwined with the surrounding landscapes and geographical features. The choice of location, orientation, and alignment with natural elements reflected a profound understanding of the sacredness of the environment and the interplay between the physical and spiritual realms. The incorporation of natural symbolism in megalithic temples enriched the religious experience, deepened the connection between humans and the natural world, and reinforced the cultural narratives and spiritual beliefs of ancient civilizations. These sacred landscapes and their symbolic significance continue to captivate our imagination and inspire awe, offering glimpses into the ancient wisdom and reverence for the interconnectedness of the Earth and the divine.

The concept of earth energies and ley lines has gained interest in the investigation of spiritual connections associated with megalithic temples. Earth energies refer to subtle energy currents or forces believed to flow through the Earth's crust, while ley lines are thought to be energetic pathways that connect sacred sites and landmarks. Exploring these phenomena provides a framework to understand the spiritual significance attributed to megalithic temples and their connection to the broader landscape.

According to proponents of earth energies, megalithic temples were strategically positioned to harness and interact with these subtle energy currents. It is believed that certain locations possess higher concentrations of these energies, which can be felt and utilized for spiritual purposes. Temples were constructed in alignment with these energetic currents, tapping into their transformative and healing qualities. This connection between the temples and earth energies was believed to enhance the spiritual experience of worshippers and amplify the divine presence within the sacred space.

Ley lines, on the other hand, are thought to be energetic pathways that connect sacred sites, including megalithic temples, across vast distances. These alignments are often attributed to ancient civilizations' understanding of the energetic properties of the Earth and their desire to establish connections between important spiritual or power centers. Ley lines are believed to create a network of energetic flow, enabling the transfer of spiritual energy, wisdom, and cosmic forces between these sacred sites. Exploring the ley line connections between megalithic temples offers insights into the intentional design and placement of these structures, emphasizing their role in a broader spiritual network.

Investigations into earth energies and ley lines often involve dowsing, a practice that uses tools such as rods or pendulums to detect and map these subtle energy patterns. Dowsers claim to identify the flow of earth energies and ley lines, contributing to our understanding of the energetic landscape and the relationship between megalithic temples and the natural environment.

While the concepts of earth energies and ley lines are intriguing, they remain subjects of debate and skepticism within the scientific community. Critics argue that the perception of these subtle energies may be subjective, influenced by cultural beliefs and personal experiences. The patterns identified as ley lines may be coincidental alignments rather than intentional energetic pathways. Skeptics also point to the lack of empirical evidence to support these claims, challenging their validity as scientific phenomena.

Nonetheless, the exploration of earth energies and ley lines contributes to a holistic understanding of the spiritual connections associated with megalithic temples. It highlights the deep reverence ancient civilizations had for the natural environment and their desire to establish harmonious relationships with the Earth and the cosmos. Even if viewed metaphorically or symbolically, the notion of earth energies and ley lines offers a framework to interpret the intentional placement and alignment of megalithic temples, emphasizing their role as conduits between the human and divine realms.

In summary, investigations into earth energies and ley lines provide a lens through which to explore the spiritual connections associated with megalithic temples. While these concepts are subject to debate and skepticism, they contribute to our understanding of the intentional placement, alignment, and symbolic significance of these sacred structures within the broader natural landscape. The exploration of earth energies and ley lines adds depth to our comprehension of the spiritual beliefs and practices of ancient civilizations, inviting us to contemplate the profound interplay between the physical and metaphysical aspects of our world.

Sacred geometry played a significant role in the architecture of megalithic temples, reflecting the belief that certain geometric proportions and patterns held sacred and divine significance. The incorporation of sacred geometry into temple design was seen as a way to create harmony, balance, and spiritual resonance within the sacred space. Exploring the use of sacred geometry in megalithic temple architecture provides insights into the symbolic language and mathematical precision employed by ancient civilizations.

One of the fundamental geometric principles observed in megalithic temples is the use of basic shapes, such as circles, squares, and triangles.

These shapes were believed to embody specific qualities and represent various aspects of the divine. Circles symbolized unity, wholeness, and the eternal nature of the divine. Squares represented stability, balance, and the earthly realm. Triangles were associated with spirituality, ascension, and the connection between the earthly and celestial realms. The intentional use of these shapes in temple architecture aimed to invoke a sense of sacredness and align the space with divine energies.

Proportional relationships and ratios were another crucial aspect of sacred geometry in megalithic temple design. The Golden Ratio, also known as the Divine Proportion, was believed to embody beauty and perfection. This ratio, approximately 1.618, was considered aesthetically pleasing and was thought to resonate with the inherent harmony of the cosmos. The application of the Golden Ratio in temple architecture ensured balanced and visually appealing proportions, evoking a sense of awe and transcendence in worshippers.

Additionally, the Fibonacci sequence, a mathematical series in which each number is the sum of the two preceding ones (0, 1, 1, 2, 3, 5, 8, 13, 21, and so on), was often found in the dimensions and arrangements of temple structures. This sequence, believed to reflect the inherent order and growth found in nature, was used to create aesthetically pleasing and harmonious proportions. The Fibonacci spiral, derived from this sequence, was sometimes incorporated into temple designs, symbolizing the spiraling evolution and interconnectedness of all things.

Symmetry, another key element of sacred geometry, was highly valued in megalithic temple architecture. Symmetrical designs, whether axial or radial, were seen as manifestations of divine order and perfection. The use of symmetrical elements in temple facades, floor plans, or interior spaces created a sense of balance, rhythm, and visual harmony. Symmetry was not only present in the overall architectural layout but also extended to intricate decorative motifs and carvings, reinforcing the sacredness of the space.

The integration of geometric patterns and symbols further enhanced the sacred geometry of megalithic temples. Intricate geometric motifs, such as interlocking circles, hexagons, or spirals, adorned the temple walls, floors, and decorative elements. These patterns were believed to represent cosmic forces, spiritual energies, or the interplay between the earthly and divine realms. They served as visual reminders of the sacredness of the space and offered contemplative focal points for worshippers.

The precision and attention to sacred geometry in megalithic temple architecture were not merely aesthetic considerations but were thought to have profound spiritual and metaphysical implications. The intentional use of geometric principles aimed to create an environment that resonated with higher energies, facilitating a deeper connection with the divine. The harmonious proportions, symbolic patterns, and mathematical precision of megalithic temples served as vehicles for spiritual transformation, fostering a sense of awe, reverence, and transcendence.

In summary, sacred geometry played a vital role in the architecture of megalithic temples, incorporating geometric shapes, proportions, and patterns believed to hold sacred and divine significance. The intentional use of sacred geometry aimed to create harmonious and spiritually resonant spaces. The exploration of sacred geometry in megalithic temple architecture offers insights into the symbolic language, mathematical precision, and metaphysical concepts employed by ancient civilizations, revealing their deep understanding of the interplay between mathematics, aesthetics, and the spiritual realms.

In the annals of human history, few phenomena evoke a sense of wonder and intrigue as much as the megalithic temples scattered across the ancient landscape. These monumental structures, crafted by the hands of our ancestors, stand as enduring testaments to their ingenuity and reverence for the natural world. The relationship between megalithic temples and the natural environment is a captivating subject, offering profound insights into the ways in which ancient civilizations interacted with and perceived the world around them.

To comprehend the profound connection between megalithic temples and the natural environment, one must first examine the locations chosen for their construction. It is no mere coincidence that these temples were often sited in areas of outstanding natural beauty or geological significance. Majestic mountains, tranquil valleys, or the serene embrace of forests frequently played host to these hallowed structures. The selection of such locales was a testament to the ancient civilizations' recognition of the spiritual energy that coursed through the land, an energy they sought to harness and channel within the sacred confines of their temples.

Consider the awe-inspiring presence of Stonehenge, its enigmatic stone circle standing in resolute defiance of time. Situated upon Salisbury Plain, this megalithic marvel is surrounded by a vast expanse of rolling grasslands, gently undulating like a sea frozen in stone. One cannot help but be captivated by the sight of these colossal stones, hewn from the earth and placed with such precise intent. Their arrangement aligns with the solstices, evoking a profound connection to the celestial realm. This harmonious union of earth and sky speaks to the intricate relationship between megalithic temples and the natural environment.

Equally compelling is the megalithic complex of Gobekli Tepe, nestled amidst the ancient landscape of southeastern Turkey. Here, amidst the rugged terrain, stands a series of monumental stone pillars adorned with intricate carvings. The site's elevated position provides a commanding view of the surrounding plains, granting a sense of dominion over the land. The very act of raising these monolithic structures speaks to the ancient civilization's desire to transcend the earthly realm, reaching towards the heavens. Gobekli Tepe serves as a poignant reminder that our ancestors understood the inherent power that resided in the natural environment and sought to capture it within their sacred spaces.

The relationship between megalithic temples and the natural environment extended beyond mere geographical placement. It found expression in the architectural design, where the natural world's features were often incorporated into the very fabric of the temples. Architectural elements mirrored the contours of the land, seamlessly blending the human-made with the earth's own form. The curvature of temple walls mirrored the undulations of nearby hills, while doorways and entrances echoed the graceful arches of stone bridges spanning rivers. Such harmonious integration was a testament to the ancient civilizations' recognition of the natural environment as both a source of inspiration and a divine blueprint for their architectural endeavors.

One cannot discount the role that the natural world played in shaping the spiritual beliefs and practices associated with megalithic temples. The ancient civilizations perceived the world around them as imbued with sacredness, each element possessing its own spiritual essence. The sun, moon, stars, mountains, rivers, and trees were seen as living entities, interconnected and deserving of reverence. In the sanctuaries of megalithic temples, these elements found expression through intricate carvings, murals, and symbols adorning the walls. The celestial bodies and natural phenomena were celebrated and venerated, allowing worshippers to forge a profound connection with the cosmos.

The profound connection between megalithic temples and the natural environment also manifested in the rituals and ceremonies conducted within their sacred precincts. Ancient civilizations understood that their spiritual practices needed to be intimately intertwined with the natural rhythms of the world. They marked the solstices and equinoxes, celebrating the changing seasons and the eternal cycle of life, death, and rebirth. The very act of congregating within these temples was an acknowledgment of their dependence on the land, the rivers, and the skies for sustenance, inspiration, and divine communion.

In summary, the relationship between megalithic temples and the natural environment is a testament to the ancient civilizations' profound understanding of the world's interconnectedness. These magnificent structures were not mere testaments to human ingenuity but rather a profound expression of the human desire to forge a harmonious union with the natural world. Whether through the careful selection of awe-inspiring locations, the integration of natural elements into architectural design, or the incorporation of the natural world's symbolism into religious rituals, megalithic temples stand as testament to the ancient civilizations' deep reverence for the environment. In their pursuit of spiritual transcendence, they recognized that the natural world held the key to unlocking the mysteries of existence. Even today, as we marvel at these megalithic marvels, we are reminded of the enduring relationship between humanity and the natural environment that continues to shape our collective consciousness.

Chapter 6: Stonehenge through the Ages

The enigmatic stone circle known as Stonehenge has long captured the imagination of scholars and enthusiasts alike. Its origins, construction, and purpose have been the subject of countless investigations and theories. Tracing the development of Stonehenge through its early phases offers valuable insights into the evolution of this ancient monument and the motivations of its builders.

The earliest phase of Stonehenge, referred to as the "Henge Phase," dates back to around 3100 BCE. During this period, a circular bank and ditch were constructed, creating a roughly circular enclosure measuring approximately 110 meters in diameter. The bank, made of chalk and earth, was piled up from the material excavated during the creation of the ditch, which was about 7 meters wide and 1.5 meters deep. The sheer effort and organization required to construct such an earthwork in the Neolithic period is a testament to the ancient people's determination and engineering capabilities.

Within the enclosed area of the henge, a series of large timber posts, known as "Aubrey Holes" after their discoverer John Aubrey, were positioned. These holes, numbering 56 in total, held the timber posts that stood proud within the henge. Although the precise purpose of these posts remains a matter of speculation, they are believed to have served as markers or possibly supported a timber circle or other structures.

The second phase of Stonehenge, known as the "Stone Settings Phase," began around 2600 BCE. During this period, the construction focus shifted from timber to stone. Large sarsen stones, weighing up to 50 tons, were brought from Marlborough Downs, about 20 miles to the north. These massive stones were carefully shaped and arranged in an outer circle, with lintels resting on top to create a continuous ring.

The inner part of the stone circle was composed of smaller, bluestones, some of which were sourced from the Preseli Hills in Wales, over 150 miles away. The transportation of these bluestones across such a significant distance is a testament to the organization and ingenuity of the ancient builders. The arrangement of the bluestones within the circle was precise, with some forming an inner horseshoe and others positioned radially within the circle.

The third and final phase of Stonehenge's development occurred around 2400 BCE, known as the "Final Stone Circle Phase." During this period, the iconic stone trilithons were erected. These trilithons consist of two upright stones with a lintel stone placed on top, forming a distinctive portal-like structure. The largest trilithons, positioned in the horseshoe arrangement within the stone circle, stand at the center of the monument, dominating the landscape.

The purpose and significance of Stonehenge's early phases remain shrouded in mystery. The henge enclosure, with its timber posts, likely served ceremonial or ritualistic functions, acting as a gathering place for the ancient community. The stone circles, with their precise alignments to celestial events, suggest an association with astronomical observations and a deeper understanding of the cosmos. The symbolism of the stones, their arrangement, and their relationship to the surrounding landscape all point to the monument's spiritual and cultural significance.

The construction of Stonehenge and its evolution through its early phases was a testament to the ancient people's ability to organize and undertake monumental projects. The transportation of massive stones over great distances, the precision in shaping and arranging them, and the astronomical alignments demonstrate the depth of knowledge and expertise possessed by the builders.

Tracing the development of Stonehenge through its early phases allows us to glimpse into the ancient world and the motivations behind this remarkable monument. While many questions remain unanswered, the ongoing exploration and study of Stonehenge offer hope that we may uncover further insights into its purpose, the beliefs of its builders, and the cultural and spiritual significance it held for the ancient people who created it. Stonehenge's early phases stand as enduring testaments to human ingenuity, captivating our imagination and inviting us to unravel the mysteries of our distant past.

Stonehenge, the iconic stone circle that has stood for millennia on the Salisbury Plain, has undergone changes and additions throughout its long history. These alterations reflect the evolving beliefs, cultural practices, and religious rituals of the civilizations that interacted with this enigmatic monument. Tracing the evolution of Stonehenge over time offers insights into the complex and dynamic nature of its significance and purpose.

One of the notable changes to Stonehenge occurred during the early Bronze Age, around 2000 BCE. This period saw the addition of a unique feature known as the "Avenue." The Avenue consists of parallel banks and ditches that extend for nearly 2 miles, leading from the River Avon to Stonehenge. This deliberate construction created a ceremonial pathway, emphasizing the ritualistic approach to the monument and further emphasizing the sacred nature of the site.

Another significant alteration took place during the late Bronze Age, around 1500 BCE. The Bluestones, originally positioned within the inner circle, were rearranged and reconfigured. Some were removed, while others were repositioned to create the horseshoe arrangement that is a defining characteristic of Stonehenge. The exact reasons for this rearrangement remain a subject of debate, with theories ranging from shifts in religious beliefs to changes in cultural practices.

During the Iron Age, between 800 BCE and 43 CE, Stonehenge continued to evolve. The Heel Stone, a massive upright stone located just outside the main circle, was erected during this period. Its positioning holds astronomical significance, aligning with the summer solstice sunrise when viewed from the center of the stone circle. This addition further enhanced the celestial connections and heightened the ritualistic and astronomical aspects of Stonehenge.

Over the centuries, Stonehenge also experienced alterations due to human activities and natural processes. Excavations and archaeological investigations have revealed evidence of burials and cremations within and around the monument, indicating the site's continued significance as a sacred burial ground. Additionally, erosion and weathering have affected the stones and the surrounding landscape, prompting conservation efforts to preserve this ancient wonder for future generations.

The multifaceted nature of Stonehenge's evolution suggests that its purpose and significance were dynamic, responding to the changing beliefs and practices of the civilizations that interacted with it. From its early phases as a timber henge to the incorporation of massive sarsen stones, the alterations to Stonehenge demonstrate a profound commitment to preserving and adapting this sacred site.

The ongoing exploration and study of Stonehenge continue to shed light on its evolution and offer tantalizing glimpses into the beliefs and rituals of the past. Archaeological discoveries, technological advancements, and interdisciplinary research have expanded our understanding of this ancient monument, revealing intricate details about its construction techniques, astronomical alignments, and cultural context.

Tracing the changes and additions to Stonehenge over time underscores its enduring significance and the cultural legacy it represents. As successive civilizations left their mark upon this sacred landscape, they contributed to its mystique and perpetuated the sense of awe and wonder that Stonehenge inspires to this day. The monument stands as a testament to the resilience of human creativity, spirituality, and the enduring power of ancient wonders to captivate and provoke our imagination.

In summary, Stonehenge's evolution over time reflects the ever-changing beliefs, rituals, and cultural practices of the civilizations that engaged with this remarkable monument. The additions, rearrangements, and adaptations demonstrate the dynamic nature of Stonehenge's significance and purpose. Through the centuries, Stonehenge has stood as a timeless symbol of human ingenuity, serving as a bridge between the past and the present, and reminding us of the enduring allure and enigmatic nature of our ancient heritage.

The illustrious history of Stonehenge is not devoid of periods of abandonment and neglect, during which this majestic monument fell into a state of disrepair. These periods of decline serve as a poignant reminder of the ebb and flow of human reverence and interest in ancient structures, as well as the challenges posed by time and changing societal priorities.

One of the earliest instances of abandonment occurred during the Roman occupation of Britain in the first few centuries CE. With the decline of the indigenous Celtic societies and the spread of Roman influence, Stonehenge gradually lost its cultural and religious significance. The pagan practices associated with the monument were superseded by Christianity, and Stonehenge ceased to serve as a central hub of religious activity. As a result, the stones and surrounding landscape were left largely untouched and forgotten, standing as silent witnesses to a bygone era.

Throughout the medieval period, Stonehenge remained a mysterious and enigmatic structure, inspiring awe and wonder among those who encountered it. However, the monument's significance and purpose were largely lost to the annals of history. It became subject to folklore, myth, and legend, with imaginative tales spun to explain its origins and purpose. The gradual deterioration of the stones due to weathering and occasional acts of vandalism further contributed to the monument's neglected state.

By the 17th and 18th centuries, Stonehenge began to attract the attention of antiquarians and scholars who sought to unravel its mysteries. In 1680, the first recorded archaeological excavation was conducted by John Aubrey, sparking renewed interest in the monument. Despite these early efforts, Stonehenge remained in a state of disrepair and suffered from neglect.

The situation worsened during the 19th century when Stonehenge faced a new threat: commercial exploitation. The land surrounding the monument was privately owned and subjected to agricultural use. Encroaching fences, livestock grazing, and even attempts to blast the stones for building materials posed significant risks to the preservation of Stonehenge. Concerned individuals and organizations, recognizing the monument's historical and cultural importance, began advocating for its protection.

In the early 20th century, the British government acquired the land surrounding Stonehenge and implemented measures to safeguard the monument. The Ancient Monuments Consolidation and Amendment Act of 1913 offered legal protection, and subsequent restoration efforts were undertaken to stabilize the stones and mitigate the effects of erosion. The establishment of the Stonehenge Landscape in 1986 further enhanced the preservation and management of the site, ensuring its long-term protection.

Today, Stonehenge is under the care of English Heritage, and considerable efforts have been made to preserve and interpret the monument for future generations. Ongoing research, conservation projects, and visitor management strategies aim to strike a delicate balance between preserving the monument's integrity and providing educational and enjoyable experiences for visitors.

The story of abandonment and neglect in Stonehenge's history serves as a cautionary tale, reminding us of the need for active stewardship and the recognition of our responsibility to protect and preserve our ancient heritage. The decline of Stonehenge underscores the vulnerability of ancient sites to the passage of time, changing social and religious practices, and human actions. It is a reminder that our understanding and appreciation of such cultural treasures are not static but require ongoing commitment and engagement.

In summary, Stonehenge experienced periods of abandonment and neglect throughout its storied history. From the decline during the Roman occupation to the medieval era of mystery and folklore, and the threats posed by commercial exploitation in more recent times, the monument faced significant challenges. However, efforts by concerned individuals, organizations, and the British government have enabled its preservation and restoration. The story of decline and subsequent revival highlights the importance of active stewardship and the need to recognize and protect our ancient heritage for future generations to appreciate and cherish.

The story of Stonehenge is not merely one of abandonment and decline but also of rediscovery and restoration efforts that have breathed new life into this ancient monument. Over the centuries, Stonehenge has captured the imagination of scholars, antiquarians, and the general public, sparking a desire to unravel its mysteries and ensure its preservation for future generations. The rediscovery and subsequent restoration of Stonehenge are testaments to the enduring fascination and dedication of individuals and organizations in reviving its historical and cultural significance.

The first steps towards rediscovering Stonehenge can be traced back to the 17th century when the monument attracted the attention of pioneering antiquarians and scholars. Figures such as John Aubrey, William Stukeley, and Sir Richard Colt Hoare conducted early investigations and excavations, attempting to unravel the purpose and origins of the enigmatic stone circle. Their efforts shed light on Stonehenge's historical context and inspired further interest and exploration.

In the 19th century, the advent of more systematic archaeological methods and the rise of professional archaeology brought renewed attention to Stonehenge. Notable figures such as Sir Flinders Petrie and Lieutenant Colonel William Hawley conducted detailed surveys, excavations, and documentation of the monument, laying the foundations for a scientific understanding of its construction and chronology. Their meticulous work provided valuable insights into Stonehenge's complex history and fueled public interest in the site.

By the 20th century, growing concerns about the preservation of Stonehenge led to significant restoration and conservation efforts. The site's acquisition by the British government in 1918 marked a turning point in its care and protection. Restoration projects aimed to stabilize and preserve the stones, address erosion issues, and mitigate the impact of weathering and human activities.

In the 1950s, a major restoration campaign led by archaeologist Richard Atkinson focused on repositioning fallen stones and stabilizing the monument. This ambitious endeavor aimed to restore Stonehenge to a state that closely resembled its presumed original form, based on archaeological evidence and historical records. The project involved meticulous planning, engineering expertise, and careful consideration of the monument's historical and cultural significance.

In recent years, restoration efforts have continued with a more nuanced approach that prioritizes preservation, interpretation, and public access.

Advances in scientific techniques and technologies have enabled detailed analysis of the stones, their geological sources, and the methods of their construction. Non-invasive surveys, such as ground-penetrating radar and laser scanning, have provided valuable data for research and conservation purposes.

Alongside restoration, the development of visitor facilities and interpretation centers has aimed to enhance the visitor experience while respecting the monument's integrity. Educational programs, exhibitions, and guided tours offer visitors the opportunity to engage with Stonehenge's history, archaeology, and cultural significance. Visitor management strategies, including timed tickets and controlled access, ensure the preservation of the site and a more immersive experience for visitors.

The rediscovery and restoration efforts surrounding Stonehenge exemplify the collaborative endeavors of archaeologists, conservationists, government agencies, and the public. The revival of this ancient monument has rekindled public interest, fostering a deeper appreciation of its historical and cultural importance. It serves as a testament to our collective responsibility to preserve and celebrate our shared heritage.

In summary, the rediscovery and restoration of Stonehenge have breathed new life into this ancient monument, rekindling our understanding and appreciation of its historical and cultural significance. From the early investigations of antiquarians to the modern-day scientific analysis and visitor management, dedicated individuals and organizations have played a pivotal role in reviving and safeguarding Stonehenge. Through their efforts, the monument stands not only as a remarkable archaeological site but also as a symbol of our enduring fascination with the mysteries of the past. The ongoing restoration and interpretation of Stonehenge ensure that future generations will have the opportunity to explore and appreciate its ancient wonders.

The recognition of Stonehenge as a World Heritage Site by UNESCO in 1986 marked a significant milestone in the ongoing efforts to preserve and protect this ancient monument. As a World Heritage Site, Stonehenge is internationally recognized for its outstanding universal value and its contribution to human civilization. The designation has played a crucial role in raising awareness, promoting conservation, and fostering appreciation for this remarkable cultural treasure.

Stonehenge's inclusion on the World Heritage List is a testament to its global significance and the recognition of its exceptional archaeological and cultural value. The inscription acknowledges the monument's remarkable construction, its alignment with celestial phenomena, and its enduring enigma, which continues to captivate and intrigue scholars and visitors alike. Stonehenge stands as a symbol of human ingenuity, spiritual exploration, and the rich tapestry of human history.

The World Heritage status has provided Stonehenge with a platform for increased protection, conservation, and research. It has encouraged international collaboration among experts, fostering the exchange of knowledge and best practices in archaeological preservation and management. The designation has also facilitated access to funding and resources for ongoing conservation projects, ensuring the long-term stability and sustainability of the site.

Preservation efforts at Stonehenge have been guided by the principles of the World Heritage Convention, which emphasizes the protection of cultural and natural heritage for future generations. Conservation measures have focused on maintaining the integrity of the monument, safeguarding its physical structures, and mitigating the impact of natural forces and human activities. These efforts include regular monitoring, stabilization of the stones, erosion control, and the management of visitor access to minimize potential damage.

In addition to preservation, the World Heritage status has also led to enhanced interpretation and public engagement. Stonehenge's significance as a World Heritage Site is communicated through educational programs, visitor centers, exhibitions, and guided tours. These initiatives offer visitors the opportunity to deepen their understanding of Stonehenge's historical context, cultural importance, and the ongoing research conducted at the site.

The designation as a World Heritage Site has also stimulated tourism and economic development in the surrounding region. Stonehenge attracts visitors from all corners of the globe, contributing to the local economy and providing opportunities for sustainable tourism initiatives. The revenue generated from tourism is reinvested in the preservation and management of the site, ensuring its long-term viability.

While the World Heritage status has brought numerous benefits to Stonehenge, it has also presented challenges. Managing the delicate balance between visitor access and site preservation remains an ongoing endeavor. Striking the right balance between providing an enriching visitor experience and safeguarding the monument's integrity requires careful planning, monitoring, and adaptation of visitor management strategies.

In summary, Stonehenge's recognition as a World Heritage Site has been instrumental in the preservation, research, and promotion of this iconic monument. The designation has elevated Stonehenge to a position of global significance, ensuring its protection and fostering international collaboration in heritage conservation. As a World Heritage Site, Stonehenge serves as a timeless reminder of the ingenuity, spirituality, and cultural diversity of our human heritage. Its designation continues to inspire appreciation, curiosity, and a sense of wonder, preserving this ancient wonder for generations to come.

Chapter 7: Rituals and Ceremonies

Stonehenge, with its imposing stone circle and enigmatic presence, has long been associated with sacred rituals and ceremonies. The site's alignment with celestial events and its awe-inspiring architecture have led scholars and enthusiasts to speculate about the nature and purpose of the ancient practices that took place within its hallowed confines. While the precise details of these rituals remain shrouded in the mists of time, archaeological evidence and comparative studies provide valuable insights into the possible nature of the sacred rites performed at Stonehenge.

The astronomical alignments of Stonehenge are among its most striking features, suggesting a strong connection to celestial events and the passage of time. The axis of the monument is aligned with the rising and setting of the sun at the solstices, particularly the summer solstice when the sun rises over the Heel Stone, creating a dramatic spectacle. This alignment highlights the importance of the solstices in the ancient calendar and suggests that Stonehenge served as a focal point for observing and celebrating these significant astronomical moments.

The celestial associations of Stonehenge extend beyond the solstices. The stones and architectural features of the monument also align with other celestial phenomena, such as lunar positions and specific stars. This suggests that celestial observation and the tracking of astronomical events played a central role in the rituals and ceremonies performed at Stonehenge. The celestial alignments likely guided the timing of important religious festivals and marked the transitions of the seasons.

Stonehenge's layout and architecture also offer clues about the nature of the rituals that took place within its sacred precincts. The monument's circular shape, the arrangement of the stones, and the presence of distinct features such as the central altar stone suggest a structured space for religious practices. The horseshoe-shaped arrangement of stones, known as the "horseshoe setting," may have been a focal point for specific rituals or processions, while the central altar stone may have been a site for offerings or ceremonial activities.

Archaeological excavations and discoveries around Stonehenge have yielded important evidence of past rituals and activities. The presence of human remains, including cremated remains and burial sites, indicates the performance of funerary rites and the reverence for ancestors. Artefacts found in the vicinity, such as pottery fragments, animal bones, and personal items, provide insights into the material culture associated with the rituals conducted at the site.

The rituals and ceremonies at Stonehenge likely encompassed a range of activities, including communal gatherings, processions, music, dance, feasting, and possibly even healing practices. The monument's scale and capacity to accommodate large numbers of people suggest that it served as a focal point for community celebrations and religious observances. Stonehenge may have been a site for social cohesion, the reinforcement of shared beliefs, and the strengthening of community bonds.

The exact beliefs and mythology associated with the rituals at Stonehenge are largely speculative, as the ancient people who constructed and utilized the monument left no written records. However, comparative studies with other ancient societies and ethnographic research provide valuable insights into possible interpretations. Stonehenge's astronomical alignments, for example, have parallels with the cosmological beliefs of other ancient cultures, where the heavens were often seen as a bridge between the earthly and divine realms.

The significance of Stonehenge as a sacred site likely extended beyond the rituals performed within its boundaries. The monument's imposing presence and its strategic location within the landscape would have imbued it with symbolic and spiritual meaning, making it a powerful and revered place within the ancient worldview.

In summary, Stonehenge's association with sacred rituals and ceremonies is deeply rooted in its celestial alignments, architectural design, and archaeological evidence. The monument's alignment with astronomical events suggests a profound connection between the ancient people who built Stonehenge and the celestial realm. The rituals performed at Stonehenge likely involved communal gatherings, observance of celestial phenomena, and the reinforcement of social and spiritual bonds. While the specifics of these rituals may remain elusive, the enduring legacy of Stonehenge as a sacred site invites us to contemplate the profound spiritual and cultural practices of our ancient ancestors.

The solstices, marking the longest and shortest days of the year, have held immense cultural and spiritual significance throughout human history. Stonehenge, with its precise alignments to the rising and setting sun during these celestial events, stands as a testament to the importance of solstice celebrations in the ancient world. The alignment of Stonehenge with the solstices provides insights into the beliefs, practices, and reverence for the cycles of nature that shaped the lives of our ancient ancestors.

At Stonehenge, the alignment of the Heel Stone with the rising sun during the summer solstice is one of the most renowned features of the monument. This phenomenon creates a dramatic spectacle as the sun appears to rise directly over the Heel Stone, casting its first rays into the heart of the stone circle. The precision of this alignment suggests a deep understanding of the movements of the celestial bodies and the changing seasons.

The summer solstice, with its longest day and shortest night, holds profound symbolic significance. It marks the zenith of the sun's power and the abundant growth and vitality of the natural world. For agricultural societies dependent on the cycles of planting and harvesting, the summer solstice represented a pivotal moment of transition and celebration. It was a time to express gratitude for the bountiful gifts of the earth and to invoke blessings for a fruitful season ahead.

Stonehenge's alignment with the winter solstice is equally significant. Although less visually dramatic than the summer solstice alignment, the winter solstice marks the longest night and the gradual return of light. It represents the turning point of the year, when the sun begins its ascent from its lowest point in the sky. The winter solstice held a profound meaning for ancient cultures, symbolizing the triumph of light over darkness, the rebirth of the sun, and the renewal of life.

The solstice celebrations at Stonehenge would have involved rituals, ceremonies, and communal gatherings. The alignment of the monument with the solstices served as a focal point for these observances, providing a tangible connection between the earthly realm and the celestial forces that governed the natural world. It is likely that the rituals performed at Stonehenge during the solstices involved prayers, offerings, dances, chants, and other symbolic acts to honor and invoke the powers of the sun.

The solstice celebrations also fostered a sense of community and unity. Ancient societies would have gathered at Stonehenge, coming together from distant places to mark this significant moment in the annual cycle. The rituals and festivities would have reinforced social bonds, strengthened communal identity, and affirmed the interconnectedness of humans with the larger web of life.

The alignment of Stonehenge with the solstices demonstrates the profound connection between our ancient ancestors and the cycles of nature. It reflects their deep reverence for the sun as a life-giving force, a symbol of divinity, and a source of spiritual and cosmic energy. The solstice celebrations at Stonehenge provided a profound sense of meaning, purpose, and connection to the ancient people who participated in these sacred rituals.

Today, the solstice celebrations at Stonehenge continue to draw people from around the world, perpetuating the tradition of honoring these celestial events. The gathering of diverse individuals to witness the solstice alignments at Stonehenge highlights the enduring fascination and universal human longing for connection with the cycles of nature and the transcendent forces that shape our existence.

In summary, the alignment of Stonehenge with the solstices serves as a testament to the profound significance of these celestial events in the ancient world. The solstice celebrations at Stonehenge provided a sacred space for communal gatherings, rituals, and the expression of gratitude and reverence for the cycles of nature. The alignments symbolized the eternal dance between light and darkness, life and death, and the perpetual renewal of the cosmos. Today, Stonehenge stands as a timeless reminder of our ancient ancestors' deep connection to the rhythms of the natural world and their profound sense of awe and wonder.

The equinoxes, marking the points in the year when day and night are of equal length, have long held significance in human culture. At Stonehenge, the alignment of the monument with the vernal and autumnal equinoxes reveals a deep connection to the changing seasons and the cyclical nature of life. These alignments provide insights into the ancient observances and rituals that accompanied the equinoxes, reflecting humanity's profound relationship with the natural world.

The vernal equinox, also known as the spring equinox, occurs around March 20th in the northern hemisphere. It heralds the arrival of spring, a season associated with new life, growth, and rejuvenation. At Stonehenge, the monument's alignment with the vernal equinox suggests a reverence for this moment of balance between light and darkness, as well as a celebration of the return of warmth and the awakening of nature.

The alignment of Stonehenge with the autumnal equinox, which takes place around September 22nd, highlights the transition from summer to autumn. This equinox signals the approaching harvest season, when the fruits of the earth are gathered and preparations are made for the colder months ahead. Stonehenge's alignment with the autumnal equinox indicates an acknowledgment of the changing seasons and the importance of harvest, abundance, and gratitude.

The equinox observances at Stonehenge would have likely involved ceremonies, rituals, and communal gatherings. The alignments of the monument with the equinoxes served as focal points for these activities, providing a connection between the earthly realm and the cosmic forces governing the seasons. It is believed that rituals performed during the equinoxes involved offerings, prayers, dances, and symbolic acts to honor the natural cycles and invoke blessings for the coming season.

The equinoxes also symbolize balance and harmony, as they mark the moments when day and night are in perfect equilibrium. The alignment of Stonehenge with the equinoxes may have represented a striving for equilibrium within the human experience, a recognition of the interconnectedness of all things, and a desire to align with the rhythms of nature.

Stonehenge's alignment with the equinoxes reflects the deep reverence and understanding our ancient ancestors had for the cycles of the natural world. It is a testament to their observation of the heavens, their connection to the land, and their belief in the interplay between the celestial and earthly realms. The equinox observances at Stonehenge provided a sense of continuity, purpose, and connectedness to the ancient people who participated in these sacred rituals.

Today, the equinoxes continue to be recognized and celebrated at Stonehenge, drawing visitors from around the world who seek to experience the alignment with these celestial events. The gatherings at Stonehenge during the equinoxes serve as a reminder of our enduring fascination with the cycles of nature, our longing for balance and harmony, and our deep connection to the Earth and the cosmos.

In summary, the alignment of Stonehenge with the equinoxes reveals the profound significance of these celestial events in the ancient world. The observances and rituals conducted at Stonehenge during the equinoxes were expressions of gratitude, celebration, and reverence for the changing seasons and the natural cycles of life. The alignments symbolize the delicate balance and interconnectedness of all things, offering a profound reminder of our place in the grand tapestry of the universe. Stonehenge stands as a timeless testament to our ancient ancestors' wisdom, their connection to the rhythms of nature, and their eternal quest for harmony and meaning.

Stonehenge, with its mysterious stone circle and ancient history, has been a site of burial and commemorative ceremonies for thousands of years. The presence of human remains and funerary practices in and around the monument provides valuable insights into the beliefs, rituals, and reverence for ancestors that shaped the lives of our ancient predecessors.

Excavations and archaeological discoveries have revealed evidence of burials at Stonehenge dating back to its earliest phases of construction. Human remains, including cremated bones and grave goods, have been found in and around the monument, indicating that it served as a sacred burial ground. These burials are testament to the deep connection between Stonehenge and the cycle of life, death, and the afterlife.

The exact nature of the burial practices at Stonehenge remains a subject of ongoing research and interpretation. The presence of cremated remains suggests a belief in the transformation of the deceased from the earthly realm to the spiritual realm. The act of cremation may have been seen as a means of facilitating this transition, while the burial of the ashes within or near the monument could have represented a symbolic link between the deceased and the sacred site.

The burials at Stonehenge were not mere interments; they were accompanied by rituals, ceremonies, and commemorative practices. The placement of grave goods, such as pottery vessels, tools, and personal items, alongside the remains suggests a belief in an afterlife and the provision of items necessary for the deceased's journey or continued existence. These offerings may have been intended to honor and appease the spirits of the departed and to maintain a connection between the living and the dead.

The significance of burial at Stonehenge is further emphasized by its association with commemorative ceremonies. The gathering of individuals at the monument for ceremonies and rituals provided an opportunity for the community to come together to honor and remember their ancestors. These gatherings may have included speeches, music, dance, and feasting, creating a space for collective remembrance and the reaffirmation of communal bonds.

The presence of burials and commemorative ceremonies at Stonehenge speaks to the enduring belief in the importance of ancestral connections and the role of the deceased in the lives of the living. It reflects a reverence for the past, a recognition of the ongoing presence of ancestors in daily life, and a desire to maintain a spiritual and cultural link between past and present.

The burials and commemorative ceremonies at Stonehenge also highlight the monument's multifaceted role as a sacred space. It served not only as an astronomical observatory and a center for religious rituals but also as a place of reverence for ancestors and a site for communal remembrance. The integration of burial practices within the monument further imbued Stonehenge with spiritual significance and underscored its role as a nexus between the human realm and the realm of the divine. In summary, the burials and commemorative ceremonies at Stonehenge provide a glimpse into the ancient beliefs and rituals associated with death, ancestor veneration, and the cycle of life. The presence of human remains within the monument reflects the enduring connection between Stonehenge and the commemoration of the deceased. The burial practices and associated ceremonies at Stonehenge served to honor ancestors, maintain communal bonds, and affirm the spiritual and cultural identity of the ancient people who gathered at this sacred site. Stonehenge stands as a testament to the enduring significance of burial and commemoration in human societies, reminding us of the deep roots of our reverence for the departed and the timeless connection between the living and the dead.

In modern times, Stonehenge has become a site of fascination, inspiration, and spiritual exploration. While the original purpose and precise nature of the ancient rituals performed at Stonehenge remain shrouded in mystery, the monument's enigmatic aura has led to various interpretations and reimagined rituals by contemporary individuals and groups.

One of the notable modern interpretations of Stonehenge is its association with neo-pagan and New Age spiritual practices. Many individuals drawn to these belief systems view Stonehenge as a sacred site that resonates with their spiritual or mystical inclinations. They may engage in rituals, meditations, or ceremonies at Stonehenge that draw upon ancient symbolism, earth-centered spirituality, or personal connection with the natural world. These reimagined rituals often seek to tap into the perceived energy and spiritual power of the site, fostering a sense of connection with the ancient past and the mysteries of the universe.

The summer and winter solstices, in particular, have gained prominence in modern celebrations at Stonehenge. Thousands of people gather at the monument during these astronomical events to witness the sunrise or sunset alignments and to partake in contemporary interpretations of solstice rituals. These gatherings often include music, dance, drumming, and communal celebrations, fostering a sense of unity, renewal, and connection with nature.

In addition to spiritual interpretations, Stonehenge has also inspired artistic expressions and cultural events. The monument has served as a backdrop for performances, concerts, art installations, and theatrical productions. These creative endeavors often explore themes of ancient history, spirituality, and the enduring allure of Stonehenge as a cultural icon. They offer a platform for artists, musicians, and performers to interpret and reimagine the monument's significance through their craft, contributing to its ongoing cultural resonance.

Stonehenge's association with solstice and equinox alignments has also attracted scientific research and astronomical investigations. Astronomers and archaeoastronomers study the alignments and explore their astronomical significance, shedding light on the ancient people's understanding of celestial phenomena. Through advanced technologies and calculations, they seek to uncover the precise astronomical knowledge embedded within Stonehenge's design and to deepen our understanding of its relationship with the cosmos.

The reimagined rituals and interpretations of Stonehenge reflect the enduring fascination and desire for connection with our ancient past. They serve as reminders of our innate curiosity, our longing to comprehend the mysteries of the universe, and our yearning for a spiritual connection with the natural world. Whether through spiritual practices, artistic expressions, or scientific exploration, these modern interpretations contribute to the ongoing narrative surrounding Stonehenge and its significance in contemporary culture.

It is important to note that access to Stonehenge is managed and regulated by English Heritage, the organization responsible for the site's preservation and visitor management. Special arrangements are made for solstice and equinox events, allowing controlled access to the monument during these periods to ensure the preservation of the site and the safety of visitors.

In summary, Stonehenge's enigmatic presence continues to captivate and inspire modern interpretations and reimagined rituals. From spiritual practices and artistic expressions to scientific investigations, contemporary individuals and groups engage with the monument in diverse ways, seeking personal connections, cultural expressions, and deeper insights into our ancient past. Stonehenge stands as a timeless symbol that transcends time, inviting us to explore our place in the cosmic order and to forge connections with the mysteries of the universe.

Chapter 8: Mythology and Folklore Surrounding Stonehenge

Stonehenge, with its ancient stones and mysterious aura, has been the subject of numerous legends, myths, and stories throughout the ages. These tales have woven a rich tapestry of folklore and imagination around the monument, adding to its allure and capturing the imagination of generations. While these stories may vary in details and interpretations, they reflect the enduring fascination and the desire to uncover the secrets hidden within Stonehenge's ancient stones.

One popular legend surrounding Stonehenge is the story of Merlin, the great wizard of Arthurian lore. According to the myth, Merlin transported the massive stones of Stonehenge from Ireland to Salisbury Plain using his magical powers. This tale attributes the construction of Stonehenge to supernatural forces and connects it to the legendary figure of Merlin, further enshrouding the monument in mysticism and wonder.

Another captivating story is that Stonehenge was built by giants or mythical creatures. According to this folklore, the stones were either placed by giants as a testament to their immense strength or were formed by the tears of a giantess who mourned the loss of her lover. These tales of giants and mythical beings infuse Stonehenge with an air of enchantment and imbue the monument with a sense of otherworldly origin.

The story of Stonehenge as a healing site is also prevalent in folklore. It is said that the stones possess healing powers, and people would come from far and wide seeking remedies for their ailments. The belief in the stones' healing properties reflects the ancient connection between sacred sites and the restoration of health, fostering a sense of hope and wonder in the power of the natural world.

Stonehenge is also associated with various folk customs and traditions. For example, it is said that if a couple holds hands while walking around the stones, their love will endure forever. Other tales speak of Stonehenge as a site of mystical energy, a portal to other dimensions, or a place where time itself is altered. These stories add layers of intrigue and magic to Stonehenge's mystique, perpetuating the notion that the monument holds secrets waiting to be unlocked.

In addition to local folklore, Stonehenge has inspired countless literary works, poems, and artistic creations. Writers and artists have drawn upon the monument's enigmatic nature to explore themes of spirituality, timelessness, and human connection. Stonehenge has become a symbol of the enduring mysteries of the past, a muse for artistic expression, and a source of inspiration for the human imagination.

While these legends, myths, and stories may not provide factual explanations for the construction and purpose of Stonehenge, they play a vital role in shaping our cultural understanding and fascination with the monument. They embody the human desire to seek meaning, to connect with the ancient past, and to find wonder in the enigmatic remnants of bygone civilizations.

In summary, the legends, myths, and stories surrounding Stonehenge add depth and enchantment to its historical significance. These tales, whether passed down through generations or born from the creative minds of writers and artists, contribute to the enduring allure of the monument. Stonehenge's ability to inspire such tales speaks to its timeless appeal and the profound impact it has had on human imagination throughout history. It stands as a testament to the enduring power of storytelling and the captivating nature of ancient mysteries.

The legendary figure of King Arthur and his connection to Stonehenge have long been subjects of fascination and speculation. According to Arthurian lore, Stonehenge plays a prominent role in the tales of King Arthur and his Knights of the Round Table. While these connections are rooted in mythology rather than historical fact, they have contributed to the enduring association between Stonehenge and the Arthurian legends.

One of the most famous Arthurian connections to Stonehenge is the tale of the giant wizard Merlin and the construction of the monument. According to the legend, Merlin had the ability to move the stones with his magical powers. He supposedly brought the stones from Ireland and erected them at Salisbury Plain to create Stonehenge as a memorial to fallen knights. This story imbues Stonehenge with a sense of mythical origin and emphasizes the monument's significance as a symbol of Arthurian legend.

In Arthurian tales, Stonehenge is often portrayed as the site of significant events in King Arthur's story. It is said to be the place where Arthur was crowned and where he held court with his Knights of the Round Table. Some legends even depict Stonehenge as the location of Arthur's final battle, where he fought against his nemesis, Mordred. The association of Stonehenge with these pivotal moments in Arthurian lore adds to the monument's allure and elevates its mythical status.

The connection between Stonehenge and King Arthur reflects the cultural and literary fascination with both the monument and the legendary figure. The Arthurian legends emerged during the medieval period and have captured the imaginations of countless writers, poets, and artists throughout history. Stonehenge's inclusion in these tales adds a touch of mysticism and ancient grandeur to the Arthurian narrative, further solidifying its place in the realm of myth and legend.

While the Arthurian connections to Stonehenge may be steeped in fantasy, they illustrate the enduring power of storytelling and the interplay between myth and history. The tales of King Arthur and Stonehenge have become intertwined, contributing to the cultural tapestry that surrounds both. They inspire the imagination and ignite the sense of wonder and possibility that lies within the realms of myth and legend.

In summary, the Arthurian connections to Stonehenge have firmly entrenched the monument within the tapestry of Arthurian legends. While these connections may be the product of medieval storytelling and imagination, they have added to the allure and mystique of Stonehenge. The association of the monument with King Arthur and his legendary exploits reflects our human fascination with grand tales of heroism, destiny, and the interplay between the earthly and the mythical realms. Stonehenge stands as a testament to the enduring power of mythology and its ability to capture the human imagination across time and generations.

Stonehenge, with its ancient stones and enigmatic presence, has been linked to Druidic lore and spirituality. The Druids, a learned and revered class of ancient Celtic priests, held a deep reverence for nature and are believed to have performed rituals and ceremonies at sacred sites, including Stonehenge. While the precise nature of the Druidic practices and their connection to Stonehenge remains a subject of debate and speculation, the association has contributed to the perception of Stonehenge as a sacred Druid site.

Druidic lore is rooted in oral tradition and mystical beliefs, making it challenging to discern the exact rituals and practices carried out by the Druids at Stonehenge. However, some theories propose that the Druids may have utilized Stonehenge as an outdoor temple, a place to commune with the spirits of nature, and to engage in spiritual and ceremonial activities.

The alignment of Stonehenge with celestial events, such as the solstices and equinoxes, has led to the belief that the monument held special significance for the Druids. These astronomical alignments would have provided the Druids with a means to mark the changing seasons and perform rituals tied to the cycles of nature. Stonehenge's orientation towards the rising sun during the summer solstice, in particular, has been interpreted as a focal point for Druidic ceremonies celebrating the power of the sun and the abundance of the natural world.

The reverence for nature and the spiritual connection to the land that characterized Druidic beliefs align with the aura of sanctity attributed to Stonehenge. The monument's location in the midst of a natural landscape, surrounded by open fields and rolling hills, adds to its mystical allure and evokes a sense of harmony with the environment. It is within this context that the association between Stonehenge and the Druids arises, as both embody a deep appreciation for the natural world and a desire to connect with its spiritual essence.

The association between Stonehenge and Druidic lore has been perpetuated through various sources, including medieval texts, folklore, and later literary and artistic interpretations. These sources often romanticize the Druids and their connection to Stonehenge, portraying them as wise, mystical figures who communed with the spirits of the land and held deep knowledge of the natural world. While these depictions may contain elements of fiction, they contribute to the enduring perception of Stonehenge as a sacred site intertwined with Druidic practices.

It is important to note that our understanding of the Druids and their practices is limited, primarily derived from ancient texts written by outsiders and fragmented archaeological evidence. The Druids themselves did not leave behind written records, and their oral traditions were largely lost over time. As a result, the true nature and extent of their connection to Stonehenge and other ancient sites remain veiled in mystery.

In summary, the association of Stonehenge with Druidic lore adds to the monument's mystical and spiritual aura. While the precise nature of the Druidic rituals at Stonehenge may remain elusive, the belief in a connection between the monument and the Druids reflects our human longing for a deeper connection with the natural world and the spiritual realms. Stonehenge stands as a symbol of the timeless quest to comprehend the mysteries of the past and our place within the greater cosmic order.

Stonehenge, with its imposing stone circle and ancient history, has been the subject of supernatural beliefs and attributed with mystical powers. Throughout the ages, people have ascribed magical and otherworldly qualities to the monument, fostering a sense of awe and wonder. While these beliefs may vary in details and interpretations, they reflect the human fascination with the mysterious and the desire to attribute extraordinary powers to extraordinary places.

One prevalent supernatural belief surrounding Stonehenge is its association with ley lines, invisible energy pathways that are said to crisscross the Earth. It is believed that Stonehenge sits at the convergence of multiple ley lines, amplifying its spiritual energy and connection to the cosmos. According to this belief, these ley lines serve as conduits for mystical forces, and being in the presence of Stonehenge can enhance one's spiritual experiences or enable access to higher realms of consciousness.

Another supernatural belief associated with Stonehenge is its alleged ability to heal ailments or possess transformative energies. Some individuals claim that by standing or meditating within the stone circle, one can experience physical or emotional healing, or undergo spiritual transformations. These beliefs stem from the perception that the stones themselves emit unique energies or resonate with the natural forces of the Earth, allowing for personal growth and well-being.

Stonehenge's alignment with celestial events, such as the solstices and equinoxes, has further contributed to its mystical reputation. The precise alignment of the stones with astronomical events is believed to grant the monument special powers or imbue it with cosmic significance. Some people visit Stonehenge during these celestial occurrences, seeking to harness the heightened spiritual energies or to partake in rituals that are believed to be more potent during these times.

The supernatural beliefs surrounding Stonehenge also encompass notions of time manipulation, interdimensional portals, and contact with otherworldly beings. Some individuals claim to have experienced time anomalies or encountered strange phenomena while in proximity to the monument. Others believe that Stonehenge serves as a gateway between realms or dimensions, allowing for communication or interaction with spiritual entities or beings from other worlds.

It is important to recognize that these supernatural beliefs are rooted in personal experiences, spiritual practices, and individual interpretations. While they may lack empirical evidence or scientific validation, they contribute to the enduring fascination and allure of Stonehenge as a place of mystery, spirituality, and the extraordinary.

In summary, the supernatural beliefs and mystical powers attributed to Stonehenge highlight the human propensity to seek the extraordinary and the transcendental. They reflect our innate curiosity, our desire to connect with something greater than ourselves, and our yearning to explore the boundaries of the natural and the supernatural realms.

Stonehenge stands as a testament to the enduring power of the human imagination, inspiring awe and wonder in those who encounter its ancient stones and contributing to the rich tapestry of beliefs and experiences that surround this remarkable monument.

Stonehenge, with its ancient and enigmatic allure, has had a profound influence on literature, art, and popular culture throughout history. The monument's mystique, grandeur, and enduring mysteries have inspired countless creative minds, fostering a rich tapestry of literary works, artistic expressions, and cultural references.

In literature, Stonehenge has been featured in various forms, ranging from historical novels to fantasy epics. Writers have drawn upon the monument's captivating presence to weave stories of ancient civilizations, mythical realms, and time-traveling adventures. Its enigmatic nature and the associations with legends and folklore have provided fertile ground for authors to explore themes of mystery, destiny, and the human quest for understanding. From Thomas Hardy's "Tess of the d'Urbervilles" to Bernard Cornwell's "Stonehenge" and countless other works, Stonehenge continues to captivate and inspire literary imaginations.

Artists across different mediums have also been drawn to Stonehenge as a subject of creative expression. Painters, photographers, and sculptors have sought to capture the monument's grandeur, the play of light and shadow upon its stones, and the sense of mystery that envelops it. Stonehenge's striking silhouette against the backdrop of the English countryside has become an iconic image, appearing in countless artworks and becoming a symbol of ancient wonder. From the Romantic paintings of John Constable to contemporary photographic masterpieces, artists have translated the monument's presence into visual representations that evoke a sense of awe and contemplation.

Stonehenge's pervasive influence extends into popular culture, where it has become a recognizable and iconic symbol. The monument has been featured in films, television series, and video games, often serving as a backdrop for stories that encompass themes of time travel, fantasy, and ancient mysteries. Stonehenge's appearance in popular culture has helped to maintain its relevance and ensure its continued recognition among audiences of all ages.

Music has also been profoundly influenced by Stonehenge. From classical compositions to rock ballads, musicians have been inspired by the monument's mysticism and historical significance. Songs such as "Stonehenge" by Spinal Tap, "Stonehenge" by Ylvis, and "Druid's Chant" by Lisa Thiel reflect the fascination and reverence for the monument, creating a sonic connection between the ancient stones and the world of music.

Furthermore, Stonehenge's cultural significance has led to its recognition as a UNESCO World Heritage Site, underscoring its enduring value and the global recognition of its historical and artistic importance. The monument's status as a symbol of human ingenuity, ancient history, and timeless mysteries ensures its place in the collective imagination and ensures its continued influence on literature, art, and popular culture.

In summary, Stonehenge's impact on literature, art, and popular culture is far-reaching and profound. From the pages of novels to the strokes of a painter's brush, from the screens of movies to the melodies of songs, the monument continues to captivate and inspire generations of creative minds. Stonehenge's enigmatic presence, its connection to ancient history and legends, and its symbolic resonance make it an enduring muse that transcends time and continues to shape the cultural landscape of our world.

Chapter 9: Archaeological Discoveries and Insights

The early excavations at Stonehenge, carried out by pioneering archaeologists, played a crucial role in unraveling the mysteries of the monument and establishing its significance as a world-renowned archaeological site. These dedicated individuals, driven by curiosity and a desire to uncover the secrets of the past, embarked on groundbreaking excavations that laid the foundation for our understanding of Stonehenge today.

One of the key figures in the early exploration of Stonehenge was Colonel William Hawley. In the early 20th century, Hawley conducted extensive excavations at the site, meticulously documenting and mapping the positions of the stones and uncovering crucial evidence about its construction and history. His detailed surveys and comprehensive records formed the basis for subsequent research and provided valuable insights into the monument's layout and development over time.

Another notable archaeologist associated with Stonehenge is Professor Richard Atkinson. In the 1950s and 1960s, Atkinson led a series of excavations that shed light on the monument's chronology and the sequence of its construction phases. His work revealed the presence of burial mounds and the positioning of stones that had fallen or been removed. Atkinson's meticulous excavation methods and his commitment to understanding the monument's complex history paved the way for future studies and interpretations.

The efforts of archaeologists like Stuart Piggott, Richard J.C. Atkinson, and many others have further advanced our understanding of Stonehenge. Piggott's work in the 1930s focused on examining the surrounding landscape and its connection to the monument, highlighting the intricate relationship between Stonehenge and its broader context. His research into the monument's astronomical alignments and his exploration of the site's religious and cultural significance contributed to a more nuanced understanding of Stonehenge's purpose.

Excavations at Stonehenge have not only yielded important discoveries but also influenced the development of archaeological techniques and methodologies. Archaeologists utilized innovative methods such as carbon dating, stratigraphic analysis, and geophysical surveys to gain insights into the monument's construction phases, its use over time, and its relation to surrounding features. These advancements in archaeological practice have not only enhanced our understanding of

Stonehenge but have also influenced archaeological investigations worldwide.

It is important to acknowledge that the early excavations at Stonehenge were conducted in an era when archaeological practices and conservation ethics were still developing. Some of the methods employed, such as reconstruction efforts and rearrangement of stones, may be viewed differently in the context of modern archaeological principles. However, the pioneering work of these early archaeologists set the stage for subsequent research, and their dedication to uncovering the mysteries of Stonehenge laid the groundwork for the rigorous and systematic approach to studying ancient sites that we employ today.

In summary, the early excavations at Stonehenge by pioneering archaeologists were pivotal in unraveling the mysteries surrounding the monument. Through their dedicated efforts, meticulous surveys, and groundbreaking research, they shed light on its construction, chronology, and cultural significance. Their work not only deepened our understanding of Stonehenge but also influenced archaeological methodologies and shaped the study of ancient sites worldwide. The pioneering archaeologists' contributions continue to inspire and guide contemporary researchers as they strive to uncover the secrets of Stonehenge and to illuminate the lives and beliefs of those who built and used this remarkable monument.

The process of unearthing Stonehenge's secrets has been marked by a series of groundbreaking discoveries that have transformed our understanding of the monument and its place in ancient history. These significant findings, made by archaeologists and researchers over the years, have shed light on various aspects of Stonehenge, ranging from its construction methods to its cultural and ceremonial significance.

One of the most pivotal discoveries at Stonehenge was made during the 20th century when the Aubrey Holes were excavated. In the 1920s, archaeologist William Hawley uncovered these circular pits surrounding the central stone structure. The meticulous excavation and analysis of the Aubrey Holes revealed that they likely held timber posts, creating a palisade that encircled the monument. This finding challenged earlier theories and deepened our understanding of Stonehenge's architectural evolution and layout.

Another significant breakthrough came with the discovery of the bluestones' origin. In the 1920s and 1930s, geologist Herbert Thomas studied the geological composition of the bluestones and traced their source to the Preseli Hills in southwest Wales, over 200 miles away. This finding was a revelation, as it indicated that the builders of Stonehenge had transported massive stones across such a considerable distance, providing insights into the monument's construction methods and the immense efforts undertaken by its builders.

In recent years, non-invasive techniques such as ground-penetrating radar and 3D laser scanning have played a crucial role in uncovering hidden features and subsurface structures at Stonehenge. In 2011, a groundbreaking survey known as the Stonehenge Hidden Landscapes Project employed cutting-edge technology to reveal an array of previously unknown features surrounding the monument, including buried stone circles, pathways, and barrows. This discovery has reshaped our understanding of Stonehenge's landscape and suggests a more extensive complex of ceremonial and funerary structures.

Furthermore, the excavations of the nearby site known as Durrington Walls, which took place in the late 20th and early 21st centuries, have provided valuable insights into the purpose and function of Stonehenge. The discovery of a vast Neolithic village at Durrington Walls, complete with dwellings and evidence of feasting, has led to the theory that it served as a gathering place for the builders and users of Stonehenge. This finding has deepened our understanding of the monument's social and cultural context, highlighting its role as a focal point for communal activities.

One of the most recent and significant discoveries at Stonehenge relates to the cremated human remains found at the site. In 2008, during a re-excavation of Aubrey Hole 7, archaeologists uncovered fragments of cremated human bone. Radiocarbon dating of these remains indicated that they dated back to the period of Stonehenge's construction. This finding has opened up new avenues of research into the people who were buried at Stonehenge, their social status, and the rituals associated with the monument.

These groundbreaking discoveries, along with numerous others, have revolutionized our understanding of Stonehenge. They have challenged long-held assumptions, provided insights into the monument's construction techniques, and deepened our understanding of its cultural and ceremonial significance. The combination of meticulous excavation, technological advancements, and interdisciplinary research has allowed us to peel back the layers of time and gain a more nuanced picture of Stonehenge's enigmatic past.

In summary, the groundbreaking discoveries made at Stonehenge have transformed our knowledge of the monument and its place in ancient history. From the identification of the bluestones' origin to the revelation of hidden structures through advanced surveying techniques, each finding has added a piece to the puzzle and advanced our understanding of this iconic site. The ongoing research and exploration at Stonehenge continue to captivate the archaeological community and offer the promise of uncovering even more secrets from its ancient past.

Excavations at Stonehenge have played a crucial role in unraveling the purpose and significance of this iconic monument. Over the years, archaeological research and discoveries have provided valuable insights into the functions, rituals, and cultural context of Stonehenge, allowing us to better understand its place in ancient society.

One of the earliest and most fundamental questions surrounding Stonehenge has been its purpose as a ceremonial or religious site. Excavations have revealed numerous artifacts and features that indicate its use for ritualistic activities. For instance, the discovery of human cremated remains and burial mounds in and around Stonehenge suggests that it served as a sacred burial ground. The alignment of the monument with celestial events, such as the solstices and equinoxes, has further supported the theory that it was used for astronomical observations and rituals tied to the cycles of nature.

Excavations have also shed light on the construction techniques employed at Stonehenge, providing clues about the purpose behind its distinctive layout. The discovery of the bluestones' origin in Wales and evidence of the transportation and repositioning of these massive stones highlight the monumental efforts invested in the construction of Stonehenge. The precise positioning of the stones and the intricate design of the monument suggest that it was carefully engineered to create specific alignments and visual effects. These deliberate choices indicate that Stonehenge had a ceremonial or symbolic purpose, potentially associated with the cycles of the sun and the seasons.

Further excavations at Stonehenge's surrounding landscape have revealed the presence of other structures and features that suggest its use as a complex ceremonial site. The discovery of the nearby site of Durrington Walls, a large Neolithic village, suggests that Stonehenge was part of a broader landscape of ritual activities and gatherings. The findings of feasting remains, animal remains, and evidence of communal activities at Durrington Walls provide insights into the social and cultural practices associated with Stonehenge.

Excavations have also uncovered evidence of past alterations and modifications to Stonehenge. The presence of fallen stones, repositioned stones, and the existence of various construction phases indicate that

Stonehenge was a site of ongoing importance and underwent changes over time. This suggests that the monument's purpose may have evolved or adapted to the needs and beliefs of different societies and generations.

While many aspects of Stonehenge's purpose remain open to interpretation, the accumulated evidence from excavations points to its significance as a place of ritual, ceremony, and communal gatherings. The monument's alignment with astronomical events, the presence of burials, the engineering prowess demonstrated in its construction, and its integration into a broader ceremonial landscape all contribute to our understanding of its multifaceted role in ancient society.

In summary, excavations at Stonehenge have provided invaluable insights into its purpose and function as a ceremonial and ritual site. The discoveries made through archaeological investigations have deepened our understanding of the monument's cultural context, construction techniques, and societal significance. While some questions still remain unanswered, the ongoing research and excavations at Stonehenge continue to offer new perspectives and fuel our curiosity about this remarkable monument and its role in the ancient past.

The examination of burials and human remains at Stonehenge has provided valuable insights into the lives, beliefs, and social practices of the people associated with the monument. The presence of human remains within and around Stonehenge indicates that it held significant funerary and commemorative roles in ancient times. Through careful analysis of these burials, archaeologists have been able to piece together important details about the individuals buried at the site and the rituals surrounding their interments.

Excavations at Stonehenge have uncovered a range of burial types, including both primary and secondary burials. Primary burials refer to individuals who were interred directly within the monument, while secondary burials involve the reburial of remains that were originally deposited elsewhere. The diversity of burial practices suggests that Stonehenge was not only a place of burial but also a site where ancestral connections were maintained and commemorated.

The examination of the human remains themselves has yielded valuable information about the individuals buried at Stonehenge. Anthropological analysis, such as age estimation, sex determination, and examination of dental health, has allowed researchers to gain insights into the demographics and lifestyles of the people associated with the monument. Isotopic analysis of teeth and bones has provided clues about diet, mobility, and geographical origins, revealing the diversity of the population and their connections to different regions.

Furthermore, the analysis of grave goods, objects buried alongside individuals, has shed light on the social and cultural practices of the time. Grave goods range from personal items such as beads, pottery, and tools to more elaborate offerings like weapons or jewelry. The presence of these objects suggests beliefs in an afterlife or the desire to provide comfort and provisions for the deceased in their journey beyond.

One of the notable discoveries at Stonehenge was the finding of cremated human remains. These cremations have been found within and outside the monument, indicating a variety of funerary practices. Radiocarbon dating and other analytical techniques have helped establish the chronology of these cremations and provided insights into the temporal sequence of burials at Stonehenge.

The examination of burials and human remains at Stonehenge has also raised questions and sparked debates among researchers. The purpose of certain burial practices, the social status of individuals buried within the monument, and the relationship between different burial sites in the surrounding landscape are topics of ongoing investigation and interpretation. The careful study of these remains continues to contribute to our understanding of the beliefs, social structures, and funerary customs of the ancient people connected to Stonehenge.

It is essential to approach the study of human remains at Stonehenge with respect and sensitivity, recognizing the dignity and cultural significance of the individuals who were laid to rest there. The ethical considerations surrounding the handling and analysis of human remains continue to evolve, and researchers adhere to professional guidelines and protocols to ensure that the study of these remains is conducted responsibly and with appropriate sensitivity.

In summary, the examination of burials and human remains at Stonehenge has deepened our understanding of the people who were associated with the monument. Through anthropological analysis, isotopic studies, and the investigation of grave goods, researchers have gained insights into the demographics, social practices, and beliefs of the individuals buried at Stonehenge. This knowledge contributes to our broader understanding of the cultural, spiritual, and funerary significance of the monument, shedding light on the lives and legacies of the ancient people who inhabited this remarkable site.

Advanced technologies have played a pivotal role in the archaeology of Stonehenge, providing researchers with powerful tools to explore, analyze, and preserve the monument and its surrounding landscape.

These innovative technologies have revolutionized our understanding of Stonehenge and have allowed us to uncover new insights into its construction, purpose, and cultural significance.

One of the most significant technological advancements in Stonehenge archaeology is remote sensing. Ground-penetrating radar (GPR) and magnetometry surveys have been employed to map and visualize the subsurface features and structures that are not visible to the naked eye. By sending electromagnetic waves into the ground and measuring their reflections, GPR can detect buried archaeological features, such as pits, ditches, and postholes. Magnetometry measures variations in the Earth's magnetic field, enabling the identification of buried structures and patterns. These non-invasive techniques have helped uncover previously unknown features and better understand the layout and organization of the landscape around Stonehenge.

Another technological breakthrough in Stonehenge archaeology is 3D laser scanning or LiDAR (Light Detection and Ranging). This technique captures high-resolution three-dimensional images of the monument and its surroundings, allowing for detailed analysis and virtual reconstructions. LiDAR surveys have revealed subtle details and variations in the landscape, assisting in the identification of hidden features and improving our understanding of the monument's context and relationship with its environment.

Advancements in geospatial technologies, such as Geographic Information Systems (GIS), have also enhanced our understanding of Stonehenge. GIS enables the integration and analysis of various types of spatial data, including topographic, archaeological, and environmental information. By digitally mapping and overlaying these datasets, researchers can explore relationships, patterns, and correlations, helping to formulate hypotheses and make informed interpretations about Stonehenge's construction, use, and cultural significance.

The application of isotopic analysis has been instrumental in understanding the origins, movements, and diet of the people associated with Stonehenge. Strontium, oxygen, and carbon isotopes found in human and animal remains provide clues about migration patterns, mobility, and dietary practices. Isotopic analysis has revealed that some individuals buried at Stonehenge may have come from distant regions, suggesting the monument's importance as a gathering place and ceremonial center for communities across the British Isles.

Furthermore, virtual reality (VR) and augmented reality (AR) technologies have offered new ways to engage with Stonehenge and its history. Virtual reconstructions and immersive experiences allow visitors and researchers to explore the monument and its surrounding landscape in a more interactive and informative manner. Through VR and AR, one can experience Stonehenge as it might have appeared in different time periods, gaining a deeper appreciation of its architectural complexity and cultural significance.

The application of advanced technologies in Stonehenge archaeology has not only facilitated new discoveries but also contributed to the preservation and conservation of the monument. Non-invasive techniques, such as GPR and LiDAR, minimize physical interventions, reducing the risk of damage to the site. Digital documentation, 3D models, and databases ensure the long-term preservation and accessibility of archaeological data, allowing for ongoing research and analysis while preserving the integrity of the physical site.

In summary, advanced technologies have transformed Stonehenge archaeology, providing researchers with powerful tools to explore and understand the monument in unprecedented ways. Remote sensing, 3D laser scanning, geospatial analysis, isotopic analysis, and virtual reality have revolutionized our ability to study Stonehenge, revealing hidden features, uncovering new insights, and facilitating public engagement. The application of these technologies continues to push the boundaries of our knowledge and enrich our understanding of this ancient and enigmatic monument.

Chapter 10: Stonehenge in the Modern World

Stonehenge has long captivated the imaginations of people worldwide, attracting visitors from all corners of the globe who seek to experience the grandeur and mystery of this iconic monument. As one of the most renowned archaeological sites in the world, Stonehenge offers a range of tourism and visitor experiences that aim to educate, inspire, and provide a deeper connection to its ancient past.

Upon arrival at Stonehenge, visitors are greeted by a visitor center that serves as a gateway to the monument. The visitor center offers a wealth of information, interactive exhibits, and displays that introduce the history, significance, and ongoing research surrounding Stonehenge. It serves as an educational hub, providing visitors with a contextual understanding of the monument before they embark on their journey to the site itself.

To enhance the visitor experience, guided tours led by knowledgeable experts are available. These tours offer in-depth explanations about the monument's construction, purpose, and cultural significance, providing historical and archaeological insights that bring Stonehenge to life. Expert guides share fascinating stories, theories, and interpretations, allowing visitors to delve into the mysteries and legends surrounding the monument.

To ensure the preservation of Stonehenge, access to the inner circle is restricted, and visitors are guided around the perimeter of the monument on a designated pathway. This management approach protects the stones and helps maintain the site's integrity while still providing visitors with an up-close experience. Viewing platforms and walkways allow visitors to appreciate the monument from different angles and vantage points, offering breathtaking views and opportunities for contemplation.

Interactive exhibits and displays within the visitor center and surrounding landscape allow visitors to engage with the history, archaeology, and cultural context of Stonehenge. Replicas, models, and interactive installations provide hands-on experiences, enabling visitors to understand the monument's construction methods, celestial alignments, and the daily lives of the people who built and used it. These exhibits foster a deeper appreciation for the remarkable engineering, astronomical knowledge, and cultural significance of Stonehenge.

Additionally, virtual reality and augmented reality experiences offer immersive and interactive encounters with Stonehenge. Through digital technologies, visitors can explore virtual reconstructions, journey back in time, and visualize the monument's past appearances and cultural contexts. These experiences bring a sense of immediacy and connection to the ancient world, providing a glimpse into the lives and beliefs of those who once inhabited the landscape.

To further enrich the visitor experience, Stonehenge hosts special events and activities throughout the year. These events range from solstice and equinox celebrations, where visitors can witness the alignment of the sun with the stones, to living history demonstrations that showcase ancient crafts, music, and traditions. These events offer a unique opportunity to engage with Stonehenge in a dynamic and interactive way, fostering a deeper connection to the monument's cultural heritage.

In recent years, efforts have been made to enhance the overall visitor experience at Stonehenge by improving amenities, facilities, and accessibility. Amenities such as cafes, gift shops, and picnic areas cater to the needs of visitors, ensuring a comfortable and enjoyable visit. Accessibility measures, including wheelchair ramps and audio guides, aim to make the site accessible to all, allowing everyone to appreciate and engage with Stonehenge's wonders.

In summary, the tourism and visitor experiences at Stonehenge provide an opportunity for people from around the world to encounter the awe-inspiring monument and connect with its ancient past. Through informative exhibits, guided tours, interactive displays, and immersive technologies, visitors can gain a deeper understanding of the monument's construction, purpose, and cultural significance. By fostering a sense of wonder, education, and preservation, Stonehenge continues to inspire and captivate visitors, ensuring that its legacy endures for future generations.

Stonehenge, as a site of global significance, has been subject to various contemporary controversies surrounding its management and access. These debates revolve around striking a balance between preserving the monument's integrity, facilitating visitor access, and ensuring sustainable management practices.

One of the ongoing controversies relates to the management of the site. Balancing conservation efforts with the demands of tourism and public access is a complex task. The management of Stonehenge involves maintaining the monument's physical condition, preserving its surroundings, and safeguarding its cultural significance. This includes considerations such as controlling visitor numbers, protecting the site from erosion, and managing the impact of foot traffic on the delicate archaeological remains. Finding the right balance between access and preservation is a continual challenge, with different perspectives and interests at play.

Access to the inner circle of Stonehenge has been a subject of debate. To protect the monument and its fragile surroundings, access to the stones themselves is restricted. While this approach ensures the preservation of the site, it has sparked debates about the degree of access granted to visitors. Some argue for more permissive access, allowing people to experience the monument up close and create a deeper personal connection. Others advocate for maintaining the current restrictions to prevent potential damage and to preserve the sense of awe and mystery associated with Stonehenge.

The issue of visitor management has also raised concerns. As one of the UK's most popular tourist attractions, Stonehenge attracts a large number of visitors each year, leading to challenges in managing crowds, traffic, and infrastructure. The need to provide adequate parking, facilities, and transportation while minimizing the impact on the surrounding landscape has prompted discussions about sustainable tourism practices and the development of appropriate visitor management strategies.

The involvement of various stakeholders in the management and decision-making processes has been another contentious topic. Balancing the perspectives of archaeologists, conservationists, local communities, tourism bodies, and government agencies can be complex. Different stakeholders often have differing priorities and interests, leading to debates about how best to incorporate multiple voices into the management and decision-making processes while ensuring the long-term preservation and sustainable use of the site.

Repatriation of cultural artifacts and human remains has emerged as a significant issue in recent years. Some Indigenous groups and communities have called for the return of ancestral remains and sacred objects that were taken from their original contexts and are now held in museums and institutions. This issue raises questions about the ethical and respectful treatment of cultural heritage and the need to consider the perspectives and rights of Indigenous communities in relation to Stonehenge and its associated artifacts.

The continued exploration and excavation of Stonehenge's surrounding landscape have also sparked discussions about the potential for new discoveries and their impact on the site. The use of advanced technologies, such as ground-penetrating radar and LiDAR, has revealed the presence of hidden features and structures in the vicinity of Stonehenge. The potential for further excavation and research has raised questions about the appropriate balance between exploration and preservation, with concerns about the potential disturbance of the site's delicate archaeology.

In summary, contemporary controversies surrounding the management and access to Stonehenge reflect the complex challenges of balancing preservation, visitor access, and sustainable management. Striking the right balance between protecting the site's integrity, facilitating visitor experiences, and incorporating the perspectives of various stakeholders requires ongoing dialogue, careful planning, and informed decision-making. Ultimately, these discussions and debates contribute to the ongoing stewardship and preservation of Stonehenge for future generations.

Stonehenge stands as a powerful symbol of British heritage, embodying the rich history, cultural identity, and enduring legacy of the United Kingdom. As one of the most recognizable and iconic landmarks in the world, Stonehenge represents a connection to the ancient past and serves as a source of national pride.

Stonehenge's significance as a symbol of British heritage lies in its age and enigmatic nature. Dating back thousands of years, the monument stands as a testament to the ingenuity and craftsmanship of our ancestors. It represents the enduring human desire to create and build monumental structures that transcend time. Stonehenge serves as a tangible link to the past, reminding us of the long-standing human presence on the British Isles and the accomplishments of our early civilizations.

The monument's distinct architectural design, with its imposing stone circles and lintels, evokes a sense of mystery and awe. The precision and intentionality of its construction demonstrate the remarkable engineering skills of ancient societies, raising questions about their cultural beliefs, technological abilities, and astronomical knowledge. Stonehenge's unique and enigmatic nature fuels the imagination, inspiring countless interpretations, myths, and legends that have woven themselves into the fabric of British folklore.

Stonehenge's association with the cycles of the sun and the changing seasons further enhances its symbolic significance. The alignment of the stones with the solstices and equinoxes reflects the close connection ancient societies had with the natural world and their deep understanding of celestial phenomena. Stonehenge's role as a celestial observatory and its ability to mark significant astronomical events serve as a reminder of the deep-rooted human connection to the rhythms of nature.

The enduring cultural and historical importance of Stonehenge is further reinforced by its recognition as a UNESCO World Heritage site. This prestigious designation acknowledges the universal value of the monument and its significance to humanity as a whole. Stonehenge's inclusion on this esteemed list highlights its importance not only to the British people but also to the global community, solidifying its position as an internationally recognized symbol of cultural heritage.

Stonehenge's iconic status is also reflected in its representation in British art, literature, and popular culture. The monument has been depicted in countless paintings, photographs, and illustrations, immortalizing its image in the collective consciousness. It has served as a backdrop for films, documentaries, and television shows, further cementing its status as a symbol of British identity and heritage.

As a popular tourist destination, Stonehenge attracts millions of visitors each year, both from within the UK and around the world. Its magnetic allure and cultural significance make it a must-see landmark for those seeking to immerse themselves in British history and heritage. The monument's ability to captivate and inspire visitors underscores its enduring importance as a symbol of national pride and identity.

In summary, Stonehenge stands as an iconic symbol of British heritage, representing the deep historical and cultural roots of the United Kingdom. Its age, mysterious nature, architectural prowess, and celestial alignments have made it an enduring source of fascination and national pride. Stonehenge's status as a UNESCO World Heritage site, its depiction in art and popular culture, and its significance as a tourist attraction all contribute to its symbolic importance as a cherished piece of British heritage, reflecting the timeless connection between the past, present, and future.

Stonehenge's enigmatic allure and historical significance have made it a captivating subject in popular culture, inspiring numerous films, books, and songs that explore its mysteries, legends, and cultural impact. From epic adventures to thought-provoking narratives, Stonehenge's presence in popular culture reflects its enduring fascination and its ability to captivate the imagination of artists and audiences alike.

In the realm of film, Stonehenge has served as a backdrop for numerous productions, adding an air of mystery and ancient wonder to the cinematic experience. Films like "National Lampoon's European Vacation" (1985) and "This Is Spinal Tap" (1984) humorously satirize the monument, while others like "King Arthur" (2004) and "The Omen" (1976) incorporate Stonehenge into their narrative as a site of mythical significance. The visual grandeur and mystique of Stonehenge make it an ideal setting for films that explore themes of ancient civilizations, magic, and the clash between the past and the present.

In literature, Stonehenge has inspired countless authors to weave its mysteries into their stories. Novels such as Bernard Cornwell's "Stonehenge" (1999) and Jean M. Auel's "The Clan of the Cave Bear" (1980) incorporate Stonehenge as a central element, exploring the monument's origins, cultural significance, and its impact on the lives of fictional characters. These works often blend historical fiction, fantasy, and archaeological research to create immersive narratives that transport readers to the ancient world and delve into the enigma of Stonehenge.

Music, too, has been profoundly influenced by Stonehenge's enigmatic presence. The rock band Spinal Tap famously immortalized the monument in their song "Stonehenge" (1984), humorously exaggerating its significance and calling attention to its mystique. The British rock band Black Sabbath also referenced Stonehenge in their song "Stonehenge" (1981), capturing its aura of mystery and ancient power. These songs, among others, highlight Stonehenge's symbolic resonance in the realm of music, evoking a sense of wonder and awe associated with the monument.

Beyond specific works, Stonehenge's visual iconography and symbolic power have permeated popular culture in various forms. It is frequently depicted in artwork, photography, and merchandise, capturing its timeless allure and ensuring its presence in the visual landscape. Stonehenge-themed calendars, postcards, and souvenirs further contribute to its cultural presence, allowing people to connect with the monument's essence even from a distance.

Stonehenge's influence in popular culture goes beyond its physical representation. It has become a symbol, an archetype that represents ancient mysteries, spiritual connections, and a link to the past. Its presence in films, literature, and music has helped perpetuate the intrigue and fascination surrounding Stonehenge, making it an enduring subject of artistic exploration and creative interpretation.

In summary, Stonehenge's enigmatic aura and historical significance have made it a prominent presence in popular culture. From films that utilize its ancient majesty as a backdrop, to books that delve into its mysteries, and songs that evoke its power, Stonehenge continues to inspire artists and captivate audiences. Its symbolic resonance and visual iconography ensure its enduring place in the cultural landscape, reflecting its timeless allure and its ability to ignite the imagination of creators and consumers of popular culture.

Stonehenge, with its iconic and awe-inspiring structure, has served as a significant source of inspiration for modern architecture and design. Its unique form, precise alignment, and ancient symbolism have influenced architects, artists, and designers who seek to incorporate elements of its grandeur and mystery into contemporary creations. From architectural structures to interior design and decorative motifs, Stonehenge's influence can be seen in various aspects of modern aesthetics.

In architectural design, the monumental presence and circular form of Stonehenge have inspired the creation of structures that emulate its powerful visual impact. Some modern buildings draw inspiration from the arrangement of stones, utilizing circular or elliptical shapes and incorporating large-scale stone-like elements into their facades. These designs often evoke a sense of timelessness, strength, and connection to the natural world, echoing the enduring appeal of Stonehenge's ancient architecture.

Stonehenge's precise alignment with celestial events, such as the solstices, has also influenced contemporary architectural projects. Some buildings incorporate sun-tracking features that capture and harness the sunlight's movements throughout the day, mimicking the celestial alignments observed at Stonehenge. This integration of astronomical considerations into modern architecture creates dynamic, ever-changing spaces that respond to the natural environment and promote a sense of harmony between the built and natural worlds.

Interior design has also been inspired by Stonehenge's aesthetic qualities. Elements such as stone textures, earthy color palettes, and natural materials are often utilized to create spaces that evoke a sense of ancient mystery and connection to the natural world. Decorative motifs inspired by Stonehenge, such as concentric circles, megalithic shapes, and celestial patterns, can be found in furniture, textiles, and artwork, adding a touch of intrigue and historical significance to modern interiors.

Stonehenge's symbolic and spiritual associations have also influenced contemporary design. Some architectural and decorative elements incorporate ancient symbolism and sacred geometry, seeking to capture the mystical essence associated with the monument. This approach aims to evoke a sense of reverence, connection, and transcendence, drawing inspiration from the spiritual significance attributed to Stonehenge throughout history.

Beyond architectural and interior design, Stonehenge's influence can be seen in various creative disciplines. Artists incorporate Stonehenge-inspired themes and imagery into their paintings, sculptures, and installations, capturing its enigmatic beauty and cultural resonance. Designers create jewelry and accessories that incorporate motifs reminiscent of Stonehenge's ancient symbolism, allowing individuals to carry a piece of its mystique with them.

The influence of Stonehenge on modern architecture and design extends beyond direct imitation. It serves as a reminder of the power of ancient structures to inspire and provoke the imagination, encouraging contemporary creators to draw from the past while exploring new possibilities. Stonehenge's enduring appeal demonstrates the timeless quality of its design principles and the universal fascination with its mysteries, serving as a testament to the ongoing impact of ancient architecture on contemporary creativity.

In summary, Stonehenge's architectural form, celestial alignments, symbolism, and cultural significance have left an indelible mark on modern architecture and design. Its influence can be seen in the use of circular forms, stone textures, and celestial alignments in architectural projects, as well as in the incorporation of ancient symbolism and earthy palettes in interior design. Stonehenge's enigmatic beauty continues to inspire and resonate with contemporary creators, reminding us of the enduring power of ancient structures to shape and inspire the world of design.

BOOK 2

TIMELESS GUARDIANS
EXPLORING THE ENIGMATIC
GOBEKLI TEPE

BY A.J. KINGSTON

Chapter 1: Unveiling the Ancient Wonder

The discovery of Göbekli Tepe has been hailed as one of the most remarkable archaeological findings in recent history. Unearthed in southeastern Turkey, this ancient site has revolutionized our understanding of early human civilization and challenged long-held assumptions about the origins of complex societies.

Göbekli Tepe, meaning "Potbelly Hill" in Turkish, was first discovered in the 1960s by a farmer. However, it was not until the 1990s that its true significance came to light when excavations led by Klaus Schmidt began. What emerged from beneath the earth's surface was a revelation—a complex of monumental stone pillars arranged in circular enclosures, dating back over 11,000 years, predating even the construction of Stonehenge and the Egyptian pyramids.

The sheer scale and intricacy of Göbekli Tepe are astounding. Massive T-shaped pillars, some standing up to 20 feet tall and weighing several tons, dominate the site. Intricate carvings and bas-reliefs adorn the pillars, depicting various animal forms, such as lions, foxes, and birds, as well as abstract symbols and human-like figures. These remarkable sculptures showcase the ancient artisans' skill and artistic expression, offering a glimpse into the cultural and symbolic world of the time.

One of the most remarkable aspects of Göbekli Tepe is its age. Dating back to the Pre-Pottery Neolithic period (c. 9600-7300 BCE), the site predates the advent of agriculture and settled communities. This challenges the prevailing belief that the transition to settled life was driven primarily by agricultural developments. Instead, Göbekli Tepe suggests that monumental construction and complex social organization may have preceded the rise of agriculture, challenging our understanding of the trajectory of human civilization.

The purpose of Göbekli Tepe remains a subject of speculation and debate among archaeologists. Some propose that it served as a religious or ritual site, given the elaborate and symbolic nature of the stone carvings. The circular enclosures and alignment of the pillars with celestial events, such as the solstices, suggest a connection to celestial and seasonal cycles. Others suggest that it may have been a communal gathering place or a center for social and cultural exchange. Regardless of its precise purpose, Göbekli Tepe stands as a testament to the sophisticated social organization, craftsmanship, and shared beliefs of its builders.

The discovery of Göbekli Tepe has had profound implications for our understanding of early human civilization. It challenges the prevailing narrative that the construction of monumental architecture and complex societies developed gradually over time. Instead, it suggests that even hunter-gatherer communities were capable of organizing and building elaborate structures, raising questions about the dynamics and complexities of prehistoric social organization.

Göbekli Tepe's significance extends beyond its archaeological value. It has captured the imagination of the public, drawing visitors and researchers from around the world. Its discovery has sparked renewed interest in the study of early human civilization and has prompted further exploration of other sites in the region. Göbekli Tepe stands as a testament to the resilience and creativity of our ancient ancestors, challenging our preconceived notions and inviting us to reconsider the depth and complexity of early human history.

In summary, the discovery of Göbekli Tepe has unveiled an extraordinary archaeological marvel. Its monumental stone pillars, intricate carvings, and remarkable age have reshaped our understanding of early human civilization. Göbekli Tepe challenges established theories about the origins of complex societies and offers a tantalizing glimpse into the cultural and symbolic world of our ancient ancestors. Its significance as a cultural and historical site cannot be overstated, as it continues to inspire and inform our understanding of the remarkable achievements of early human societies. Excavating the past at Göbekli Tepe has been a journey of unravelling the enigmatic structures that have defied our understanding of ancient civilizations. Situated in southeastern Turkey, this archaeological site has presented researchers with an extraordinary puzzle, revealing a complex and sophisticated society that predates the invention of agriculture. The excavation process at Göbekli Tepe has been meticulously conducted by archaeologists, unveiling an awe-inspiring array of monumental stone pillars arranged in circular enclosures. The sheer scale and precision of these structures have astounded experts, with some pillars standing as tall as 20 feet and weighing several tons. Careful examination and recording of each stone's position have been essential in deciphering the intricate layout of the site.

The significance of Göbekli Tepe lies not only in its impressive architectural features but also in the intricate carvings and bas-reliefs that adorn the pillars. These exquisite sculptures depict a variety of animal forms, including lions, foxes, snakes, and birds, as well as abstract symbols and human-like figures. The artistry and attention to detail exhibited in these carvings offer valuable insights into the culture, symbolism, and spiritual beliefs of the people who constructed Göbekli Tepe. As excavations progress, archaeologists have pieced together the timeline of Göbekli Tepe's construction and use. The site is estimated to have been built in several phases, spanning from approximately 9600 BCE to 7300 BCE, during the Pre-Pottery Neolithic period. This chronology indicates that Göbekli Tepe predates the emergence of settled agricultural communities, challenging the prevailing notion that complex societies were primarily driven by agricultural advancements.

One of the remarkable aspects of Göbekli Tepe is the deliberate burial of the monumental structures. As each phase of construction came to an end, the enclosures were filled with debris, intentionally burying the pillars and preserving them for millennia. This deliberate act of burial has played a crucial role in the preservation of Göbekli Tepe's unique architectural features, allowing us to marvel at the sophistication and craftsmanship of its builders.

The purpose of Göbekli Tepe continues to be a subject of intense speculation and debate. The absence of residential structures or evidence of permanent habitation suggests that it was not a settlement site. Instead, theories propose that Göbekli Tepe served as a ceremonial or ritual center, possibly hosting gatherings, ceremonies, or social events. The alignment of the stone pillars with celestial events, such as the solstices, further supports the hypothesis of a site with a strong connection to astronomical observations and religious or spiritual practices.

The excavation efforts at Göbekli Tepe have not been without challenges. The fragility of the ancient structures and the need for meticulous preservation have required delicate excavation techniques and careful documentation. The restoration and stabilization of the pillars have been essential to safeguarding the site's integrity, ensuring that future generations can continue to explore and study this exceptional archaeological treasure.

Göbekli Tepe's excavation has sparked immense interest and fascination worldwide, drawing researchers, scholars, and curious visitors alike. The significance of this site extends beyond its archaeological value, as it challenges long-held assumptions about the development of early human civilizations. Göbekli Tepe stands as a testament to the ingenuity, craftsmanship, and complex social organization of our ancient ancestors, forever altering our understanding of the human story.

In summary, the excavation of Göbekli Tepe has allowed us to uncover the enigmatic structures that have reshaped our understanding of ancient civilizations. The meticulous excavation process, combined with the exploration of intricate carvings, has shed light on a sophisticated society predating the advent of agriculture. Göbekli Tepe's deliberate burial, its purpose as a ceremonial or ritual center, and its connection to celestial observations continue to intrigue and inspire researchers. Excavating Göbekli Tepe has been an incredible journey of unearthing the past and unraveling the mysteries of an extraordinary ancient site. Understanding the historical context of Göbekli Tepe is crucial to grasping its significance in prehistory. Situated in southeastern Turkey, this ancient site offers a remarkable window into the early stages of human civilization, challenging traditional narratives and providing valuable insights into the development of complex societies.

Göbekli Tepe was constructed during the Pre-Pottery Neolithic period, specifically between approximately 9600 BCE and 7300 BCE. This timeframe places it at a pivotal moment in human history, predating the rise of settled agriculture and the emergence of permanent settlements. The prevailing belief that the advent of agriculture was the primary catalyst for the development of complex societies has been challenged by the discovery of Göbekli Tepe, which suggests that complex social structures and monumental architecture existed even before the transition to agricultural practices.

The construction of Göbekli Tepe's monumental stone pillars and circular enclosures represents a remarkable feat of engineering and organization. The scale, precision, and intricacy of the structures indicate a level of craftsmanship and technical skill that was previously unrecognized in this period of prehistory. The ability to mobilize labor, manage resources, and coordinate the construction of such large-scale projects suggests a highly organized society with sophisticated social structures and collective efforts. Göbekli Tepe's significance lies not only in its architectural achievements but also in its implications for our understanding of early religious, symbolic, and ritual practices. The elaborate carvings and bas-reliefs found on the stone pillars depict a variety of animal forms, abstract symbols, and human-like figures. These artistic representations suggest a complex belief system, perhaps associated with animism or shamanism, and provide valuable insights into the spiritual and symbolic world of the people who inhabited the region during this time.

The intentional burial of Göbekli Tepe's structures raises intriguing questions about the reasons behind this practice. It suggests that the site held profound cultural and symbolic significance, possibly linked to concepts of regeneration, transformation, or the cyclical nature of life and death. The deliberate burial and preservation of the structures also indicate a sense of reverence and respect for the site, highlighting the importance placed on its enduring legacy.

Göbekli Tepe's significance extends beyond its immediate vicinity. Its discovery has prompted scholars to reevaluate other archaeological sites in the region and explore potential connections and influences. The site's architectural and artistic elements have been found to share similarities with other contemporaneous sites in Anatolia, further indicating a network of cultural exchange and interaction during this period. Göbekli Tepe serves as a cornerstone in the understanding of the complex social and cultural dynamics that were taking place in the broader Near Eastern region during the Pre-Pottery Neolithic period.

The excavation and ongoing research at Göbekli Tepe have revolutionized our understanding of prehistoric societies and challenged long-held assumptions about the development of complex civilizations. The site's existence pushes back the timeline of monumental architecture and organized social structures, revealing the existence of complex societies far earlier than previously believed. Göbekli Tepe forces us to reevaluate the trajectory of human history, emphasizing the complexity and sophistication of early societies and the richness of their cultural and spiritual practices.

In summary, Göbekli Tepe's historical context is essential in comprehending its significance in prehistory. Its construction during the Pre-Pottery Neolithic period, its remarkable architecture, intricate carvings, intentional burial, and its pre-agricultural existence challenge conventional narratives about the development of complex societies. The site offers a glimpse into the sophistication, organization, and spiritual beliefs of its builders, providing valuable insights into the dynamics of early human civilization. Göbekli Tepe's impact extends beyond its immediate region, contributing to a broader reevaluation of prehistoric societies and highlighting the complexity and richness of our shared human history.

The preservation and restoration efforts at Göbekli Tepe have been vital in safeguarding this remarkable archaeological site and ensuring its long-term survival. Since its discovery in the 1990s, experts and local authorities have collaborated to protect and maintain the site's integrity, allowing future generations to appreciate and study this invaluable cultural heritage.

Preservation efforts at Göbekli Tepe have involved a range of measures aimed at minimizing damage from natural elements, erosion, and human impact. One of the primary challenges faced by the site is the exposure of the ancient stone pillars to the elements. Weathering, including rainfall, temperature fluctuations, and wind, can potentially erode the delicate carvings and structural stability of the pillars. To mitigate these risks, protective coverings, including specially designed roofs and shelters, have been constructed over the most vulnerable areas, shielding the stone pillars from direct contact with the elements.

Another critical aspect of preservation has been the ongoing monitoring and assessment of the site's stability. Regular inspections are conducted to identify any signs of degradation, erosion, or structural weakness. These observations inform maintenance activities and interventions to prevent further deterioration. Preservation experts work closely with archaeologists to strike a balance between protecting the site and allowing for continued research and exploration.

Restoration efforts at Göbekli Tepe have focused on stabilizing the ancient structures and preserving their original form to the greatest extent possible. This involves meticulous documentation and mapping of the site to ensure accurate reconstruction and replication of any damaged or missing elements. The use of advanced imaging technologies, such as photogrammetry and 3D scanning, has proven invaluable in capturing detailed information about the site's features, aiding restoration efforts and providing a digital record for future reference.

When necessary, damaged or collapsed sections of the stone pillars are carefully repaired, using compatible materials and techniques to maintain the authenticity and integrity of the original construction. Great care is taken to ensure that any interventions are reversible, allowing for future adjustments or modifications based on evolving preservation practices and research findings.

Public awareness and education initiatives play a crucial role in the preservation and appreciation of Göbekli Tepe. Efforts have been made to engage local communities, visitors, and the wider public in understanding the significance of the site and the importance of its protection. Educational programs, guided tours, and interpretive signage provide context and insights into the site's history, architecture, and cultural significance, fostering a sense of stewardship and responsibility among visitors.

International collaboration and support have also contributed to the preservation and restoration of Göbekli Tepe. The site's exceptional value as a cultural heritage site has garnered attention and funding from various organizations, both domestic and international. Partnerships with archaeological institutions, conservation experts, and heritage organizations have facilitated the exchange of knowledge, expertise, and resources, ensuring best practices in preservation and restoration.

The preservation and restoration efforts at Göbekli Tepe serve as a testament to the commitment to protect and celebrate our shared cultural heritage. Through ongoing vigilance, research, and collaboration, the site continues to be preserved for future generations, allowing us to explore and appreciate the rich history and remarkable achievements of our ancient ancestors.

In summary, the preservation and restoration of Göbekli Tepe are of paramount importance in safeguarding this extraordinary archaeological site. Protective measures, ongoing monitoring, and restoration interventions ensure the site's stability, while public engagement and international collaboration foster a sense of responsibility and appreciation. These efforts not only protect Göbekli Tepe's physical integrity but also allow us to delve into the profound insights it offers about our shared human history. The dedication to the preservation and restoration of Göbekli Tepe ensures that its remarkable legacy will endure for generations to come.

Göbekli Tepe has had a profound impact on our understanding of early human civilization, reshaping our perceptions and challenging long-held assumptions about the development of complex societies. This extraordinary archaeological site has provided valuable insights into the sophistication and organization of prehistoric cultures, pushing back the timeline of monumental architecture and revealing a more complex narrative of human history.

One of the most significant contributions of Göbekli Tepe lies in its age. Dating back over 11,000 years, the site predates the invention of agriculture and settled communities, which were previously believed to be the primary drivers of complex societies. Its existence challenges the conventional narrative that the transition to agriculture was a prerequisite for the development of large-scale construction and organized social structures. Instead, Göbekli Tepe suggests that complex societies may have emerged earlier than previously thought and that monumental architecture and communal activities played a crucial role in the early stages of human civilization.

The monumental stone pillars and intricate carvings found at Göbekli Tepe provide evidence of a highly skilled and organized society. The scale, precision, and artistic sophistication of the structures indicate a level of craftsmanship and technical expertise that was previously unrecognized in this period of prehistory. The collaborative effort required to quarry, transport, and erect these massive stones suggests complex social organization, labor specialization, and the ability to mobilize resources on a large scale.

The discovery of Göbekli Tepe has also shed light on the religious and symbolic practices of early human societies. The elaborate carvings and bas-reliefs on the stone pillars depict a rich array of animal forms, abstract symbols, and human-like figures. These artistic representations suggest a complex belief system and a deep connection to the natural world. The alignment of the stone pillars with celestial events, such as the solstices, further supports the hypothesis that Göbekli Tepe served as a ritual or ceremonial center, where communal gatherings and ceremonies took place. This challenges the notion that organized religion emerged much later in human history.

Göbekli Tepe's influence extends beyond its immediate region. The site has prompted researchers to reevaluate other archaeological sites in the Near East, leading to a broader reexamination of early human civilizations and their cultural interactions. It has raised questions about the dynamics of social organization, the development of symbolic language, and the role of communal activities in the emergence of complex societies. By challenging established paradigms, Göbekli Tepe has spurred a reevaluation of prehistoric cultures and enriched our understanding of the diversity and complexity of human civilizations.

Furthermore, the discovery of Göbekli Tepe has ignited public fascination and interest in archaeology and prehistory. It has captured the imagination of people around the world, inspiring curiosity and sparking a sense of wonder about our shared human past. Göbekli Tepe serves as a testament to the ingenuity, creativity, and cultural richness of our ancient ancestors, reminding us of the depth and complexity of human history.

In summary, Göbekli Tepe has had a transformative impact on our understanding of early human civilization. Its age, architectural sophistication, and artistic intricacy challenge traditional narratives and provide evidence for the existence of complex societies before the advent of agriculture. The site's religious and symbolic significance offers valuable insights into the spiritual beliefs and practices of our ancient ancestors. Göbekli Tepe has stimulated further research and reevaluation of prehistoric cultures, inspiring a deeper appreciation of the complexity and diversity of human civilizations. Its influence reaches beyond the academic realm, captivating the public's imagination and fostering a sense of connection to our shared human heritage.

Göbekli Tepe's age and chronology have truly rewritten the history books, challenging long-held assumptions about the development of human civilization. Situated in southeastern Turkey, this extraordinary archaeological site has provided archaeologists with a new perspective on the early stages of human culture and has forced a reevaluation of our understanding of prehistoric societies.

The age of Göbekli Tepe is truly astounding. Excavations and dating methods have revealed that the site dates back over 11,000 years, making it one of the oldest known monumental construction projects in human history. To put this into perspective, Göbekli Tepe predates well-known ancient sites such as Stonehenge in England and the Egyptian pyramids by thousands of years. This revelation has shifted our understanding of the capabilities and achievements of early human societies, suggesting that complex social structures and monumental architecture existed much earlier than previously believed.

The significance of Göbekli Tepe's age goes beyond mere chronological adjustments. Its existence challenges the prevailing belief that the development of agriculture was the driving force behind the rise of complex societies. Traditional theories held that settled agriculture led to the accumulation of surplus resources, the establishment of permanent settlements, and the development of social hierarchies. However, Göbekli Tepe predates the advent of agriculture, suggesting that the impetus for monumental construction and social organization may have originated from other factors, such as communal rituals, shared beliefs, or even a need for social cohesion.

The dating of Göbekli Tepe has been made possible through various scientific techniques, including radiocarbon dating of organic materials found at the site. These methods have provided archaeologists with a chronological framework that challenges existing narratives and forces a reconsideration of the cultural and technological capabilities of prehistoric societies. The remarkable age of Göbekli Tepe highlights the complexity and sophistication of early human cultures and raises intriguing questions about the social dynamics, spirituality, and organization of these ancient communities.

The implications of Göbekli Tepe's age extend beyond the site itself. Its existence prompts a reevaluation of other archaeological sites in the region and their relative chronologies. The discovery of Göbekli Tepe has sparked new research initiatives and collaborations, with archaeologists seeking to identify connections and influences between sites across the Near East. By revising our understanding of the timeline and sequence of events, Göbekli Tepe has reshaped the way we interpret the cultural developments of early human civilizations.

The age of Göbekli Tepe also holds significance in the broader context of human history. It pushes back the timeline of monumental architecture and complex social organization, suggesting that these achievements were not solely the product of later, more technologically advanced societies. Instead, Göbekli Tepe challenges us to recognize the capabilities and innovative spirit of our ancient ancestors, who were capable of conceptualizing and executing grand construction projects and organizing themselves into intricate social structures.

In summary, Göbekli Tepe's age and chronology have had a profound impact on our understanding of human history. Its remarkable antiquity forces a reevaluation of the conventional narrative that attributes the rise of complex societies solely to the development of agriculture. By pushing back the timeline of monumental architecture and social organization, Göbekli Tepe highlights the sophistication and cultural richness of early human civilizations. This remarkable site has rewritten the history books, expanding our knowledge of our ancient past and challenging us to reconsider the capabilities and achievements of our early ancestors.

The engineering marvels of Göbekli Tepe have captivated researchers and historians, shedding light on the sophisticated construction techniques employed by its ancient builders. Situated in southeastern Turkey, this megalithic site showcases the ingenuity and craftsmanship of early human civilizations, challenging conventional assumptions about their technological capabilities.

One of the remarkable aspects of Göbekli Tepe is the massive stone pillars that comprise its circular enclosures. These pillars, some weighing up to 20 tons and standing several meters tall, required a high degree of planning, precision, and engineering expertise to quarry, shape, transport, and erect. The methods employed by the ancient builders have impressed modern researchers, as they reflect a level of sophistication and technical knowledge previously unattributed to this period of prehistory.

The first step in the construction process involved quarrying the stone from nearby sources. The stone used at Göbekli Tepe is primarily limestone, abundant in the surrounding region. The ancient builders carefully selected appropriate blocks, taking into consideration their size, shape, and structural integrity. They likely used a combination of stone hammers, chisels, and other cutting tools to shape the raw stones into the desired forms, often with remarkable precision.

Once shaped, the next challenge was transportation. Moving these massive stones from the quarries to the construction site required ingenious solutions. It is believed that the builders utilized a combination of sledges, wooden rollers, ropes, and possibly even inclined planes to maneuver the stones over varying terrain. The logistics of such operations, including the coordination of labor and the mastery of engineering principles, reveal a high level of organizational skills and collective effort.

Erecting the stone pillars at Göbekli Tepe was a monumental undertaking. Researchers speculate that ramps and levers were used to raise the stones into position. The builders likely employed a combination of wooden scaffolding, ropes, and manpower to carefully maneuver the pillars into place. The precision with which the pillars were aligned and interlocked indicates an advanced understanding of engineering principles, ensuring the stability and longevity of the structures.

An intriguing aspect of the construction at Göbekli Tepe is the deliberate burying of the structures over time. Each phase of construction concluded with the intentional filling of the enclosures, preserving the stone pillars for future generations. The reasons behind this burial practice remain a subject of speculation, but it demonstrates the builders' knowledge of the importance of protecting and preserving their monumental creations.

The engineering techniques employed at Göbekli Tepe highlight the resourcefulness and adaptability of early human civilizations. The meticulous planning, precise shaping of stones, ingenious transportation methods, and precise positioning of the pillars all point to a level of technological sophistication that was previously unrecognized in this period. The construction of Göbekli Tepe stands as a testament to the human ability to conceive, design, and execute ambitious architectural projects, even in the absence of advanced tools or modern construction techniques.

Studying the engineering marvels of Göbekli Tepe not only enhances our understanding of the site itself but also contributes to broader discussions on the technological capabilities of early human civilizations. It challenges assumptions about the linear progression of technological advancements and invites us to reassess the ingenuity and problem-solving abilities of our ancient ancestors. The remarkable construction techniques utilized at Göbekli Tepe emphasize the significance of this site as a testament to human creativity and craftsmanship.

In summary, Göbekli Tepe's engineering marvels showcase the ingenuity and advanced construction techniques of its ancient builders. The quarrying, shaping, transportation, and erection of the massive stone pillars demonstrate a level of sophistication and technological expertise previously unrecognized in this period of prehistory. The deliberate burial of the structures further highlights the builders' understanding of the importance of preservation. The study of Göbekli Tepe's construction techniques deepens our appreciation for the technological achievements of early human civilizations and encourages us to reevaluate our understanding of their capabilities and cultural achievements.

Comparisons between Göbekli Tepe and other megalithic sites around the world have provided valuable insights into prehistoric cultural exchange and the shared practices and beliefs of ancient civilizations. Despite the geographical and temporal distances that separate these sites, there are striking similarities in their construction methods, architectural features, and symbolic representations, pointing to interconnectedness and shared cultural influences.

One notable comparison can be made between Göbekli Tepe and Stonehenge in England. Both sites feature large stone pillars arranged in circular patterns, suggesting a common architectural concept. The precision with which the stones are aligned and the significance of celestial alignments in their positioning demonstrate a shared interest in celestial observations and a potential understanding of astronomical events. These similarities provide evidence of a cultural exchange or a common cultural heritage that transcended vast distances.

Another significant comparison can be drawn between Göbekli Tepe and the megalithic temples of Malta, such as the Ggantija Temples. These temples, like Göbekli Tepe, showcase large stone structures and intricate carvings. The architectural styles and artistic motifs found at both sites share remarkable resemblances, including depictions of animals and abstract symbols. These similarities suggest cultural connections or shared cultural practices, reinforcing the idea of ancient networks of communication and cultural exchange.

Furthermore, Göbekli Tepe's influence can be traced to other megalithic sites in the broader Near East region. Similar architectural features, such as T-shaped pillars, have been found at other contemporaneous sites, including Nevalı Çori and Karahan Tepe in Turkey. These resemblances indicate a shared architectural vocabulary and potentially shared cultural or religious practices. The existence of these commonalities suggests the existence of cultural interactions and exchanges, challenging the notion that prehistoric societies were isolated and insular.

The comparison between Göbekli Tepe and other megalithic sites offers insights into the cosmological and spiritual beliefs of ancient cultures. The presence of carved animals and abstract symbols at Göbekli Tepe mirrors similar motifs found in other megalithic sites worldwide, suggesting a shared symbolic language or a common understanding of the natural world. The focus on natural elements and celestial alignments in the construction and arrangement of megalithic structures underscores the significance of these beliefs in prehistoric cultures.

While the exact mechanisms of cultural exchange between these sites remain speculative, several theories have been proposed. Some suggest the possibility of long-distance trade routes or migratory patterns that facilitated the transmission of ideas, architectural styles, and cultural practices. Others propose that shared belief systems or a collective cultural memory could have been passed down through generations, resulting in the similarities observed in the megalithic sites.

Comparisons between Göbekli Tepe and other megalithic sites highlight the interconnectedness of ancient civilizations and the complex web of cultural exchange that spanned vast distances and extended over thousands of years. The shared architectural elements, artistic motifs, and symbolic representations provide valuable clues about the beliefs, rituals, and cultural practices of our ancient ancestors. By examining these similarities, archaeologists and researchers can piece together a more comprehensive understanding of prehistoric societies and the diverse ways in which humans interacted and shared knowledge across time and space.

In summary, the comparisons between Göbekli Tepe and other megalithic sites reveal significant insights into prehistoric cultural exchange and shared practices. The similarities in architectural design, artistic motifs, and symbolic representations point to interconnectedness and cultural interactions among ancient civilizations. These comparisons challenge the notion of isolated and insular prehistoric societies and highlight the importance of examining these sites collectively to gain a deeper understanding of our shared human heritage. The study of these connections provides valuable insights into the cosmological, spiritual, and cultural beliefs of our ancient ancestors and sheds light on the complex web of cultural exchange that shaped the development of human civilization. Göbekli Tepe has had a profound impact on archaeological and anthropological studies, revolutionizing our understanding of prehistoric cultures and rewriting the narrative of human history. This remarkable site has challenged long-held assumptions, inspired new research avenues, and opened up exciting possibilities for exploring the complexities of early human societies.

One of the most significant contributions of Göbekli Tepe lies in its age. Dating back over 11,000 years, the site predates the invention of agriculture and settled communities, which were previously believed to be prerequisites for the development of complex societies. This challenges the conventional timeline of human cultural evolution and prompts a reevaluation of the factors that led to the emergence of large-scale construction and organized social structures. Göbekli Tepe suggests that the desire for communal gathering places and the practice of ritual activities played a crucial role in the early stages of human civilization, highlighting the importance of social cohesion and shared beliefs.

Göbekli Tepe has also revolutionized our understanding of the sophistication and complexity of prehistoric cultures. The monumental stone pillars, intricate carvings, and precise alignments reveal a level of architectural skill and artistic expression that was previously unrecognized in this period of history. The discovery of such advanced construction techniques challenges the notion that monumental architecture and intricate craftsmanship were later developments, arising only after the advent of settled agriculture and complex societies. Göbekli Tepe suggests that the creative and technical capacities of our ancient ancestors were far more advanced than previously believed, pushing back the timeline of human achievements and challenging the traditional linear models of cultural evolution.

Furthermore, the symbolic and ritualistic elements found at Göbekli Tepe have shed light on the spiritual and social dynamics of prehistoric communities. The intricate carvings of animals, abstract symbols, and humanoid figures hint at a complex belief system and a shared cosmology. The intentional alignment of the stone pillars with celestial events indicates an understanding of astronomy and the significance of celestial bodies in religious or ritualistic practices. These insights into the spiritual world of our ancient ancestors provide valuable clues about their worldview, social structures, and cultural practices.

The impact of Göbekli Tepe extends beyond its immediate archaeological significance. It has inspired new research directions and fostered interdisciplinary collaborations. Scholars from various fields, including archaeology, anthropology, art history, and sociology, have come together to unravel the mysteries of this extraordinary site. The study of Göbekli Tepe has fueled discussions on the origins of complex societies, the role of ritual and belief systems in cultural development, and the interconnectedness of ancient civilizations.

The significance of Göbekli Tepe has also reverberated in the public sphere. Its discovery and ongoing excavations have captured the imagination of people worldwide, creating a sense of wonder and fascination about our ancient past. The site has become a symbol of human creativity, resilience, and ingenuity, resonating with individuals from all walks of life and inspiring a deeper appreciation for our shared human heritage.

In summary, Göbekli Tepe has had a transformative impact on archaeological and anthropological studies. Its age, architectural sophistication, and symbolic richness have challenged traditional narratives, reshaped our understanding of prehistoric cultures, and propelled new research avenues. By pushing back the timeline of monumental architecture, complex social structures, and advanced artistic expression, Göbekli Tepe highlights the ingenuity and complexity of early human societies. Its significance reaches beyond the academic realm, capturing the public's imagination and fostering a deeper connection to our shared human history. The ongoing exploration of Göbekli Tepe continues to unveil new insights into the ancient past and reinforces the importance of interdisciplinary collaboration and the continuous reevaluation of our understanding of the human story. The legacy of Göbekli Tepe is far-reaching, with profound implications for our understanding of human development and the course of our collective history. This extraordinary archaeological site has challenged prevailing theories and reshaped our perspectives on the origins and evolution of human civilization. One of the key implications of Göbekli Tepe is the evidence it provides for the existence of complex social structures and monumental architecture much earlier than previously believed. The site predates the advent of settled agriculture and the establishment of permanent communities, which were traditionally considered essential for the development of such sophisticated cultural achievements. Göbekli Tepe's existence suggests that communal gathering places and shared rituals played a vital role in the early stages of human development, challenging the long-held assumption that agriculture was the primary catalyst for complex societal organization.

The architectural and artistic sophistication of Göbekli Tepe also challenges linear models of cultural evolution. The site showcases advanced construction techniques, intricate carvings, and elaborate symbolism, all of which were traditionally associated with later, more technologically advanced civilizations. This challenges the notion that cultural progress follows a straightforward path of linear advancement and suggests that human creativity and innovation were present much earlier in our history than previously recognized.

Furthermore, Göbekli Tepe raises questions about the mechanisms of cultural transmission and interaction in prehistoric times. The similarities between Göbekli Tepe and other megalithic sites around the world suggest the presence of shared cultural practices, beliefs, or even a network of cultural exchange that spanned vast distances. This challenges the perception of early human societies as isolated and independent entities and suggests a more interconnected and dynamic social landscape.

The site also offers insights into the spiritual and symbolic dimensions of prehistoric cultures. The carved reliefs and T-shaped pillars found at Göbekli Tepe depict a rich array of animal forms, abstract symbols, and human-like figures, suggesting a complex belief system and a deep connection to the natural world. The deliberate alignment of the stone pillars with celestial events suggests a sophisticated understanding of astronomy and a reverence for the celestial realm. This challenges the notion that organized religion emerged much later in human history and suggests that spiritual beliefs were integral to the fabric of early human societies. The legacy of Göbekli Tepe extends beyond academia. It has captured the imagination of the public and inspired a sense of wonder and curiosity about our ancient past. The site serves as a powerful reminder of the intellectual and cultural achievements of our early ancestors and highlights the deep roots of human creativity and ingenuity. It prompts us to question our assumptions and encourages us to explore the complexities of human development with fresh perspectives.

In summary, the legacy of Göbekli Tepe has profound implications for our understanding of human development. It challenges traditional theories, expands our timeline of cultural achievements, and sheds light on the sophisticated social and architectural practices of our ancient ancestors. By demonstrating the existence of complex societies and monumental architecture before the advent of agriculture, Göbekli Tepe forces us to reconsider the factors that contributed to the rise of human civilization. Its impact reaches beyond the academic realm, inspiring a sense of awe and fostering a deeper appreciation for the ingenuity and resilience of early human cultures. The ongoing exploration and study of Göbekli Tepe continue to shape our understanding of the human story and encourage us to explore the depths of our shared past.

Chapter 3: Carvings and Symbolism of Gobekli Tepe

The intricate stone carvings of Göbekli Tepe have captivated researchers and sparked intense curiosity about their meaning and significance. These elaborate reliefs, etched onto the surface of the massive stone pillars at the site, offer glimpses into the symbolic world of our ancient ancestors. Interpreting these carvings is a complex endeavor, requiring a multidisciplinary approach that combines archaeological, anthropological, and comparative analysis.

One of the most striking aspects of the carvings at Göbekli Tepe is the depiction of animals. Various species, including wild boars, foxes, snakes, birds, and more, are intricately carved into the stone. These representations are highly detailed and exhibit a remarkable level of artistry. Some theories suggest that the animals depicted at Göbekli Tepe may have held symbolic or mythological significance, representing different aspects of the natural world or embodying certain cultural or spiritual beliefs. The presence of both predatory and prey animals, as well as their interactions, could be seen as symbolic of the delicate balance and interconnectedness of nature.

In addition to animals, abstract symbols and geometric patterns are also prevalent in the carvings. These enigmatic symbols, ranging from simple geometric shapes to more complex designs, have perplexed researchers for years. Interpretations of these symbols vary, with theories proposing that they may represent celestial bodies, mythical beings, or abstract concepts related to the spiritual or cosmological beliefs of the ancient people who created them. Decoding the meaning of these symbols requires a careful examination of their recurring patterns, possible cultural references, and potential connections to other symbolic systems of the time.

Contextual analysis is crucial in understanding the carvings at Göbekli Tepe. Studying the placement and arrangement of the carvings within the site can provide clues about their intended purpose. For example, the positioning of certain reliefs in relation to the celestial alignments of the site suggests a connection between the carvings and astronomical observations or celestial events. This raises the possibility that the carvings served as a means to convey cosmological or celestial beliefs, providing a visual representation of the ancient people's understanding of the heavens.

Comparative analysis with other contemporary and later cultures can also provide valuable insights into the meaning of the carvings. By examining similar artistic motifs and symbolic representations found in other regions, researchers can draw parallels and uncover potential shared cultural or religious practices. This comparative approach helps to situate Göbekli Tepe within a broader cultural and historical context, shedding light on its potential influences and contributions to the development of human civilization.

While the exact meanings behind the carvings at Göbekli Tepe may never be fully deciphered, their presence attests to the importance of symbolism, art, and spiritual expression in the lives of our ancient ancestors. The intricate nature of the carvings suggests a sophisticated understanding of artistic techniques and a desire to communicate and preserve their beliefs and cultural heritage for future generations.

In summary, the interpretation of the intricate stone carvings at Göbekli Tepe is a complex endeavor that requires careful analysis, interdisciplinary collaboration, and a nuanced understanding of the cultural and historical context. The depictions of animals, abstract symbols, and geometric patterns provide tantalizing glimpses into the symbolic world of our ancient ancestors. Through contextual analysis, comparative studies, and a comprehensive understanding of the site's astronomical alignments, researchers can begin to unravel the meanings and significance of these enigmatic carvings. While some aspects of interpretation remain speculative, the carvings at Göbekli Tepe stand as testament to the artistic, spiritual, and cultural richness of our ancient past.

The art of Göbekli Tepe is replete with symbolism and meaning, offering valuable insights into the spiritual and cultural beliefs of the ancient people who created it. The intricate carvings and reliefs found on the massive stone pillars at the site reveal a rich symbolic language that invites us to explore the depths of their worldview and explore the layers of meaning embedded within their artistic expressions.

One of the prominent features of the art at Göbekli Tepe is the depiction of animals. These carvings exhibit a high level of detail and craftsmanship, capturing the essence and vitality of various creatures. Animals such as wild boars, foxes, snakes, birds, and more are prominently represented. These animal depictions are not merely realistic portrayals but are laden with symbolic significance. They are believed to represent various aspects of the natural world, embodying certain qualities or serving as metaphors for cultural, spiritual, or mythical concepts. For example, the presence of predatory animals may symbolize power, strength, or the forces of nature, while prey animals could represent vulnerability, fertility, or the cyclical nature of life.

Beyond animals, abstract symbols and geometric patterns are recurrent themes in the art of Göbekli Tepe. These enigmatic symbols, often intricately carved and arranged in intricate compositions, convey a sense of complexity and hidden meaning. The interpretation of these symbols remains a subject of ongoing research and debate. Some theories propose that they represent celestial bodies, constellations, or astronomical events, reflecting the ancient people's fascination with the cosmos and their belief in celestial powers. Others suggest that the symbols may convey more abstract concepts related to cosmology, spirituality, or even cultural identities.

The arrangement and positioning of the carvings within the site also hold significance. The deliberate placement of certain symbols or animal depictions in relation to the celestial alignments and architectural elements of Göbekli Tepe suggests an intentional connection between the art and the physical environment. This alignment with celestial events indicates a deep appreciation for the celestial realm and may have been tied to the ancient people's religious or cosmological beliefs.

Interpreting the symbolism and meaning in the art of Göbekli Tepe requires a multidisciplinary approach. Archaeological evidence, comparative studies with contemporary and later cultures, and contextual analysis of the site's layout and function all contribute to unraveling the layers of symbolism. However, it is important to approach interpretation with caution, recognizing that the symbolic meanings may have varied among different communities, and that some aspects of the ancient belief systems may remain elusive to us.

The art of Göbekli Tepe represents a profound expression of the ancient people's understanding of the world and their place within it. It showcases their ability to create intricate and meaningful representations that conveyed their beliefs, cultural values, and spiritual practices. The symbolism and meaning embedded in the art invite us to ponder the mysteries of the past, sparking curiosity and inspiring a deeper appreciation for the creative and spiritual dimensions of our early human ancestors.

In summary, the art of Göbekli Tepe is a testament to the profound symbolism and meaning that infused the ancient culture. The depictions of animals and the use of abstract symbols reveal a rich symbolic language that expressed their understanding of the natural world, their cosmological beliefs, and their cultural identities. The careful arrangement of the art within the site and its alignment with celestial events emphasize the interconnectedness of the physical and spiritual realms. Although the exact meanings may remain elusive, the art of Göbekli Tepe offers a window into the symbolic world of our ancient ancestors, igniting our imagination and prompting us to explore the depths of their beliefs and cultural expressions.

The carvings at Göbekli Tepe hold significant ritual and ceremonial significance, providing valuable insights into the religious and spiritual practices of the ancient people who created and used the site. The intricate artistry and deliberate placement of these carvings suggest that they played a central role in the ritualistic activities and ceremonies that took place at Göbekli Tepe.

One of the key aspects of the carvings is the representation of animals. These depictions are not mere artistic expressions but are believed to have held symbolic and spiritual meaning. Animals have long been associated with religious and mythological beliefs, often representing different qualities, powers, or entities. The inclusion of animals at Göbekli Tepe suggests their significance in the religious and ritual context of the site. These animal depictions may have served as totems or representations of spiritual beings, guiding forces, or even deities. The choice of specific animals may have been influenced by their perceived qualities, associations with natural elements, or mythological narratives within the ancient belief system.

The abstract symbols and geometric patterns present in the carvings also played a crucial role in the ritual and ceremonial practices at Göbekli Tepe. These symbols, with their intricate designs and precise arrangements, are believed to have carried deep symbolic meanings. They may have represented cosmological concepts, sacred geometries, or symbolic representations of deities or spiritual entities. The repetition and uniformity of these symbols across different pillars suggest a consistent and shared symbolic language that was understood and recognized by the ancient community. The presence of such symbols in the religious context of Göbekli Tepe implies their use in sacred rituals, ceremonies, or as markers of sacred spaces.

The positioning and arrangement of the carvings within the site also indicate their ritual significance. The intentional alignment of the stone pillars with celestial events suggests a deep connection between the carvings and astronomical observations. This celestial alignment implies that the carvings were not only decorative but were also an integral part of the rituals and ceremonies that took place at specific times of the year, such as during solstices or equinoxes. The carvings may have been used as focal points for rituals, where the alignment of celestial bodies with specific symbols or animals held profound spiritual meaning and marked important moments within the religious calendar.

Additionally, the presence of communal spaces and large circular structures at Göbekli Tepe further suggests that the carvings played a role in collective ritual activities and ceremonies. The gathering of people within these structures, surrounded by the elaborate carvings, would have created an immersive and spiritually charged environment. The symbolism and imagery of the carvings would have served to evoke a sense of awe, reverence, and connection to the divine or the spiritual realm.

Interpreting the precise details and meanings of the carvings and their role in rituals and ceremonies is a complex task. It requires careful analysis of archaeological evidence, comparative studies with other ancient cultures, and a comprehensive understanding of the cultural context of the time. The study of the carvings at Göbekli Tepe provides invaluable insights into the religious and spiritual beliefs, practices, and rituals of our ancient ancestors, deepening our understanding of their worldview and the role of symbolism in their religious lives.

In summary, the carvings at Göbekli Tepe hold significant ritual and ceremonial significance, representing the religious and spiritual beliefs of the ancient people who used the site. The depiction of animals, the use of abstract symbols, and the intentional celestial alignment all point to their role in guiding and enriching the rituals and ceremonies that took place at Göbekli Tepe. These carvings served as conduits for spiritual connections, markers of sacred spaces, and focal points for communal worship and gatherings. Their intricate artistry and symbolic language offer glimpses into the rich religious and ritual practices of our ancient ancestors, fueling our imagination and expanding our understanding of the complexities of their spiritual lives.

The carvings at Göbekli Tepe provide intriguing insights into the spiritual and religious beliefs of the ancient people who constructed and used the site. Although the precise nature of their belief system remains speculative, the symbolism and imagery found in the carvings suggest connections to ancient cosmologies and religious practices.

One way to approach the interpretation of these carvings is to consider their broader cultural and historical context. Göbekli Tepe was constructed during a time when early human societies were transitioning from hunter-gatherer lifestyles to settled agricultural communities. This period witnessed significant shifts in social organization, economic practices, and the emergence of new belief systems. The carvings at Göbekli Tepe reflect this transitional phase, offering glimpses into the religious and spiritual world of these early communities.

The depictions of animals, such as wild boars, snakes, birds, and foxes, in the carvings suggest connections to animistic or shamanistic belief systems. Animals often held symbolic significance and were seen as intermediaries between the human and spiritual realms. They were believed to possess inherent qualities or powers that could be tapped into through rituals and ceremonies. The presence of these animal depictions at Göbekli Tepe implies a belief in the sacredness of the natural world and a desire to establish a connection with the spiritual forces embodied by these animals.

The abstract symbols and geometric patterns found in the carvings also hold potential religious and spiritual connotations. These symbols may represent cosmological concepts, celestial bodies, or metaphysical ideas related to the ancient people's understanding of the universe. The intricate arrangement and repetition of these symbols suggest a deliberate system of visual communication, possibly conveying complex religious or mythological narratives. Decoding the precise meaning of these symbols requires a careful analysis of their recurrence, potential cultural references, and comparisons with other ancient symbol systems.

The deliberate alignment of the stone pillars at Göbekli Tepe with celestial events indicates an awareness of and reverence for the cosmos in the ancient belief system. This celestial alignment may have been a central component of their rituals and religious practices, tying the earthly realm to the celestial realm. The carvings themselves may have served as markers or visual representations of celestial bodies or celestial events, reinforcing the connection between the human and divine realms.

It is important to approach the interpretation of these carvings with caution, recognizing the inherent challenges of understanding belief systems from the distant past. The ancient people of Göbekli Tepe did not leave behind written records explaining the exact meaning of their carvings, and their worldview may have been vastly different from our own. Therefore, interpretations of their spiritual and religious beliefs must be grounded in careful analysis of the archaeological evidence, comparative studies with other contemporary and later cultures, and an appreciation for the complexity and diversity of ancient belief systems.

In summary, the carvings at Göbekli Tepe offer tantalizing glimpses into the spiritual and religious beliefs of the ancient people who inhabited the site. The depictions of animals, the use of abstract symbols, and the celestial alignments reflect their connections to the natural world, their cosmological understandings, and their efforts to establish a connection with the divine. While the precise meanings and interpretations of these carvings may remain elusive, studying them provides valuable insights into the complex belief systems and religious practices of our ancient ancestors, deepening our understanding of the rich tapestry of human spirituality throughout history.

The carvings at Göbekli Tepe offer valuable glimpses into the cultural and social expressions of the ancient people who inhabited the site. These intricate and carefully crafted carvings were not merely artistic endeavors but served as important vehicles for the expression of cultural beliefs, social identities, and collective experiences.

One of the significant aspects of the carvings is their portrayal of animals. The depiction of various animal species, including wild boars, foxes, snakes, and birds, suggests a close relationship between the ancient people and the natural world. Animals often held symbolic significance in ancient cultures, representing different qualities, attributes, or even deities. The inclusion of animal motifs in the carvings at Göbekli Tepe may have been a way for the ancient community to express their reverence for nature, their reliance on hunting, or their belief in the spiritual significance of certain animals.

In addition to animal depictions, the abstract symbols and geometric patterns found in the carvings indicate a symbolic language that was shared and understood within the community. These symbols may have represented cultural concepts, mythological narratives, or even personal or clan identities. The repetition and uniformity of these symbols across different pillars suggest a collective and shared cultural expression. The use of abstract symbols allowed for a more versatile and enduring means of communication, transcending linguistic or temporal limitations.

The arrangement and positioning of the carvings within the site also reveal aspects of social organization and community interactions. The deliberate placement of certain carvings in specific locations suggests a conscious effort to create a visually cohesive and meaningful environment. It is possible that the carvings were placed strategically to delineate different areas of significance, mark important gathering spots, or establish boundaries within the site. The communal nature of the site is further supported by the large circular structures and the shared experience of engaging with the carvings during rituals, ceremonies, or communal activities.

The carvings at Göbekli Tepe also reflect the collaborative efforts of the ancient community. The precision and intricacy of the carvings required skilled craftsmanship and a shared understanding of the artistic and symbolic traditions. The creation and maintenance of the carvings may have served as a means of fostering social cohesion, reinforcing collective identity, and preserving cultural knowledge across generations. Interpreting the cultural and social expressions found in the carvings at Göbekli Tepe requires careful analysis of archaeological evidence, comparative studies with other contemporary and later cultures, and an appreciation for the dynamic and multifaceted nature of ancient societies. While specific meanings and interpretations may be elusive, studying these carvings allows us to connect with the rich cultural heritage and social dynamics of our ancient ancestors.

In summary, the carvings at Göbekli Tepe are not only artistic masterpieces but also powerful cultural and social expressions. Through their portrayal of animals, their use of abstract symbols, and their intentional arrangement, the carvings provide insights into the ancient people's relationship with the natural world, their shared cultural beliefs, and their communal experiences. The carvings serve as tangible links to the past, allowing us to appreciate the creative endeavors, cultural values, and social dynamics of the ancient community that thrived at Göbekli Tepe.

Chapter 4: The Mysteries of T-shaped Pillars

The enigmatic T-shaped pillars at Göbekli Tepe stand as silent witnesses to a fascinating ancient civilization. These remarkable stone structures, characterized by their distinctive T shape, have captured the attention of researchers, archaeologists, and enthusiasts alike, fueling speculation and curiosity about their purpose and significance.

Göbekli Tepe, located in present-day Turkey, is an archaeological site that dates back over 10,000 years, making it one of the oldest known monumental structures in the world. At the heart of this ancient site are the enigmatic T-shaped pillars, which were meticulously carved and erected by the hands of our early ancestors.

The T-shaped pillars are massive in size, with some reaching heights of up to six meters. Carved from limestone, these pillars exhibit impressive craftsmanship and attention to detail. The top of each pillar is shaped like a capital "T," with broad, flat tops and slender bodies that taper towards the base. The surface of the pillars is adorned with intricate carvings, depicting animals, abstract symbols, and geometric patterns, which add to their enigmatic allure.

The purpose of these T-shaped pillars at Göbekli Tepe continues to be a subject of intense debate and speculation. One prevailing theory suggests that they served as supports for roofs or other structures that are no longer preserved. These massive pillars would have provided stability and structural integrity to the buildings or enclosures that once stood above them. This interpretation aligns with the architectural and engineering achievements demonstrated at the site.

Another intriguing possibility is that the T-shaped pillars held symbolic or religious significance. The carvings on the pillars, depicting animals and abstract symbols, may have represented spiritual beings, mythological narratives, or cosmological concepts within the belief system of the ancient people. The deliberate arrangement of these pillars and their alignment with celestial events suggest a connection to astronomical observations, suggesting a possible link between the T-shaped pillars and ancient rituals or celestial worship.

The significance of the T-shaped pillars is further enhanced by their placement within the larger complex of Göbekli Tepe. The pillars are arranged in large circular or oval enclosures, forming concentric rings. These enclosures may have served as sacred spaces or gathering areas for communal rituals and ceremonies. The presence of the T-shaped pillars within these enclosures would have created a visually striking and spiritually charged environment, providing a focal point for the ancient community's religious and social activities.

While the exact purpose and meaning of the T-shaped pillars at Göbekli Tepe may remain elusive, they serve as tangible reminders of the ingenuity, artistic expression, and cultural sophistication of our early ancestors. Their presence challenges our understanding of early human civilization, pushing back the timeline of monumental architecture and revealing the complexity of ancient societies.

As ongoing excavations and research shed more light on Göbekli Tepe and its T-shaped pillars, we inch closer to unraveling the mysteries of this ancient site. The enigmatic T-shaped pillars continue to captivate our imagination, serving as a testament to the remarkable achievements and enduring legacy of the early humans who carved and raised them. The T-shaped pillars at Göbekli Tepe served important structural and architectural functions within the ancient site, contributing to the stability and durability of the monumental structures that once stood there. Their unique shape and design demonstrate the advanced engineering knowledge and skill of the early builders.

One primary function of the T-shaped pillars was to provide support for the roofs or upper structures that were likely present at Göbekli Tepe. These massive stone pillars were erected in carefully constructed sockets in the ground, anchoring them firmly in place. The broad, flat tops of the pillars would have served as load-bearing elements, distributing the weight of the superstructure evenly and preventing the collapse of the roof or upper levels.

The tapering bodies of the T-shaped pillars were designed to minimize the strain on the pillars and ensure their stability. The gradual reduction in width towards the base helped to distribute the load downwards, reducing the risk of structural failure. This tapering design, combined with the substantial size and weight of the pillars, would have provided the necessary structural integrity to support the roof or upper levels of the buildings.

The placement of the T-shaped pillars within large circular or oval enclosures further enhanced their structural function. The arrangement of multiple pillars in concentric rings created a robust framework, reinforcing the stability and durability of the overall structure. The interlocking nature of the pillars and their connection to the surrounding walls or other architectural elements would have contributed to the overall strength and longevity of the buildings.

Beyond their structural function, the T-shaped pillars also played an important role in the architectural aesthetics of Göbekli Tepe. The impressive craftsmanship and intricate carvings on the pillars added beauty and artistic expression to the site. The elaborate designs, featuring depictions of animals, abstract symbols, and geometric patterns, showcased the artistic skills of the ancient craftsmen and imbued the structures with symbolic and cultural significance.

The careful placement and alignment of the T-shaped pillars within the enclosures at Göbekli Tepe also demonstrate an architectural intention. The arrangement of the pillars would have contributed to the visual impact of the structures, creating a sense of order and symmetry. Their positioning within the circular or oval enclosures may have played a role in defining the sacred space and enhancing the spiritual atmosphere of the site. Overall, the T-shaped pillars at Göbekli Tepe served a dual purpose: they provided essential structural support for the roof or upper structures, ensuring stability and durability, while also contributing to the architectural aesthetics and symbolic significance of the site. Their advanced engineering design and meticulous craftsmanship stand as a testament to the ingenuity and architectural achievements of our ancient ancestors. Studying the T-shaped pillars not only sheds light on the functional aspects of the buildings but also deepens our understanding of the cultural, religious, and artistic dimensions of the ancient society that thrived at Göbekli Tepe. The T-shaped pillars at Göbekli Tepe hold deep symbolic and ritual significance, offering intriguing insights into the religious and spiritual beliefs of the ancient people who constructed and used the site. These remarkable stone structures, with their distinctive shape and intricate carvings, were not just architectural elements but also served as conduits for the expression of cultural and spiritual practices.

One of the key aspects of the T-shaped pillars is their symbolism, which likely held profound meaning within the belief system of the ancient community. The T shape itself has been interpreted in various ways. Some researchers suggest that the shape represents the human form, with the horizontal bar representing arms or shoulders and the vertical pillar representing the body. This interpretation suggests a connection between the pillars and the human presence or perhaps the representation of ancestral or divine beings.

The carvings on the T-shaped pillars further enhance their symbolic significance. The motifs and images depicted on the pillars include animals, abstract symbols, and geometric patterns, each carrying its own symbolic connotations. Animals, such as wild boars, snakes, and birds,

119

may have represented spiritual beings, totems, or mythological creatures. The choice of specific animals may have been influenced by their perceived qualities, associations with natural elements, or their importance in cultural narratives.

Abstract symbols and geometric patterns found on the pillars are also thought to hold symbolic meaning. These symbols may represent cosmological concepts, celestial bodies, or sacred geometries within the ancient belief system. The repetition and consistency of these symbols across different pillars suggest a shared symbolic language understood by the ancient community.

The deliberate arrangement and alignment of the T-shaped pillars within the enclosures at Göbekli Tepe indicate their ritual significance. The circular or oval enclosures, formed by the arrangement of the pillars, likely served as sacred spaces or ceremonial areas. The T-shaped pillars, positioned at specific intervals and aligned in patterns, may have functioned as focal points for rituals and ceremonies. The alignment of the pillars with celestial events, such as solstices or equinoxes, suggests a connection between the human and divine realms, where the positioning of the pillars may have played a role in marking important celestial moments.

The communal nature of the site and the presence of multiple pillars within the enclosures imply that these rituals and ceremonies were likely collective and shared experiences. The pillars, with their symbolism and arrangement, would have created an immersive and spiritually charged environment, evoking a sense of awe, reverence, and connection to the sacred.

Interpreting the precise meanings and rituals associated with the T-shaped pillars at Göbekli Tepe is challenging due to the limited available evidence and the vast temporal and cultural distance between us and the ancient community. However, the combination of their symbolic motifs, intentional arrangement, and alignment with celestial events strongly suggests their central role in religious and ritual practices. The T-shaped pillars would have served as powerful symbols, bridging the earthly and divine realms, facilitating communication with the spiritual forces, and facilitating collective religious experiences.

In summary, the T-shaped pillars at Göbekli Tepe carry deep symbolism and ritual significance. Through their shape, carvings, and alignment, they offer glimpses into the religious and spiritual beliefs, practices, and rituals of our ancient ancestors. The T-shaped pillars served as powerful symbols, markers of sacred spaces, and focal points for communal worship and gatherings. While precise interpretations may remain speculative, studying these pillars allows us to appreciate the spiritual and cultural richness of the ancient community that thrived at Göbekli Tepe and offers insights into the complexities of their belief systems and ritual practices. The purpose of the T-shaped pillars at Göbekli Tepe has been a subject of much speculation and debate among researchers and archaeologists. While the exact function of these enigmatic stone structures remains elusive, several theories have been proposed to explain their purpose within the ancient site.

One prevailing theory suggests that the T-shaped pillars were integral components of ceremonial or ritual structures. The carefully arranged circular or oval enclosures, formed by the placement of the pillars, may have served as sacred spaces where rituals, ceremonies, and communal gatherings took place. The T-shaped pillars, with their prominent presence and symbolic carvings, would have played a central role in these religious or social activities. The positioning and alignment of the pillars may have facilitated specific rituals or served as markers for specific celestial events, such as solstices or equinoxes, connecting the earthly realm to the cosmic forces.

Another theory proposes that the T-shaped pillars were architectural elements supporting roofs or upper structures that are no longer preserved. The massive size and sturdy construction of the pillars suggest their capacity to bear the weight of a substantial superstructure. This interpretation suggests that the T-shaped pillars served as load-bearing elements, contributing to the stability and longevity of the buildings at Göbekli Tepe. The symbolic carvings on the pillars, in this view, would have enhanced the aesthetic and cultural significance of the structures.

Some researchers propose that the T-shaped pillars had a combination of functions, serving both practical and symbolic purposes. The pillars may have provided architectural support while also carrying symbolic and ritualistic meanings. The combination of structural stability and symbolic expression would have contributed to the overall significance of the site and its role within the social and cultural fabric of the ancient community.

It is important to note that these theories are not mutually exclusive, and the purpose of the T-shaped pillars may have been multifaceted, serving various functions simultaneously. The precise intention behind the construction of these pillars may have been influenced by a complex interplay of religious, social, architectural, and symbolic factors.

One challenge in understanding the purpose of the T-shaped pillars lies in the temporal and cultural distance between the ancient builders and contemporary researchers. The belief systems, rituals, and social dynamics of the ancient people at Göbekli Tepe may have been significantly different from our own, making it challenging to decipher their exact intentions and interpretations.

As ongoing research and excavations continue to shed light on Göbekli Tepe, it is possible that new discoveries will provide additional insights into the purpose of the T-shaped pillars. With a comprehensive understanding of the site's architectural, cultural, and social context, future studies may bring us closer to unraveling the mystery and revealing the true significance of these intriguing stone structures.

In summary, the purpose of the T-shaped pillars at Göbekli Tepe remains a subject of speculation and ongoing research. While theories suggest that they played roles in rituals, ceremonies, architectural support, or a combination of these functions, their true purpose may be more complex and intertwined with the religious, social, and cultural practices of the ancient community. Continued archaeological investigations and interdisciplinary studies offer promising avenues for further understanding the enigmatic nature of these T-shaped pillars and their significance within the broader context of Göbekli Tepe. Recent research and ongoing excavations at Göbekli Tepe have provided valuable insights and shed new light on the secrets surrounding the T-shaped pillars. As our understanding of this ancient site deepens, researchers have made significant discoveries that contribute to our knowledge of the purpose and significance of these enigmatic stone structures.

One important development in recent years is the realization that Göbekli Tepe was not simply a solitary and isolated site but part of a broader cultural landscape. Excavations in the surrounding area have revealed the existence of other similar sites, suggesting that the construction of monumental structures and the use of T-shaped pillars were not unique to Göbekli Tepe alone. This discovery challenges previous assumptions and prompts new questions about the shared practices, beliefs, and social networks of these ancient communities.

New insights into the symbolism and iconography of the T-shaped pillars have also emerged. Advanced imaging techniques, such as photogrammetry and three-dimensional scanning, have allowed for detailed analysis of the carvings and intricate patterns on the pillars. Researchers have identified recurring motifs and symbols, such as serpents, spiders, scorpions, and abstract geometric patterns. These findings provide a basis for further investigation into the religious, mythological, and cosmological beliefs of the ancient people who created these carvings.

Additionally, recent research has focused on the relationship between the T-shaped pillars and celestial alignments. Astronomical studies and analysis of the site's geographical orientation have revealed correlations between the positioning of the pillars and astronomical phenomena, particularly solstices and equinoxes. This suggests that the ancient builders of Göbekli Tepe were not only aware of celestial events but also intentionally incorporated them into the design and alignment of the pillars, emphasizing a connection between the earthly and celestial realms.

Archaeologists have also made significant progress in understanding the chronology and development of Göbekli Tepe. By carefully analyzing the stratigraphy and examining the construction sequences, researchers have been able to establish a more accurate timeline for the site's evolution. This chronological framework enables a better understanding of how the T-shaped pillars and other architectural elements were added, modified, and expanded over time, providing insights into the site's growth and the cultural dynamics of its builders.

Furthermore, ongoing interdisciplinary studies, including archaeology, anthropology, and environmental science, are contributing to our understanding of the social organization, economic practices, and environmental context of Göbekli Tepe. By examining the surrounding landscape, investigating subsistence strategies, and analyzing the use of local resources, researchers are gaining valuable insights into the daily lives and societal complexities of the ancient people who inhabited the area.

While these recent research findings have offered tantalizing glimpses into the secrets of the T-shaped pillars, many questions and mysteries still remain. The significance of specific carvings, the precise rituals and ceremonies associated with the pillars, and the broader cultural context of Göbekli Tepe continue to be subjects of ongoing investigation and debate.

As technology advances and new research methods emerge, our understanding of the T-shaped pillars and their role within Göbekli Tepe will undoubtedly continue to evolve. The collaborative efforts of archaeologists, scientists, and scholars from various disciplines provide a promising path towards unraveling the remaining secrets and gaining a deeper appreciation for the ancient civilizations that once thrived at Göbekli Tepe.

The figures and depictions found at Göbekli Tepe offer a fascinating glimpse into the artistic expressions and cultural beliefs of the ancient people who inhabited the site. These intricate and often lifelike representations, carved into the stone pillars and other architectural elements, provide valuable insights into the symbolic, mythological, and ritualistic dimensions of the ancient community.

Animal figures are among the most prominent and frequently depicted at Göbekli Tepe. These include various species such as wild boars, foxes, snakes, birds, and more. The animal depictions exhibit a high level of detail and naturalistic rendering, suggesting a keen observation of the surrounding fauna. Animals likely held significant cultural and symbolic meaning for the ancient people, representing qualities, associations, or perhaps even deities within their belief system. The choice of specific animals may have been influenced by their perceived power, importance in hunting or daily life, or their mythological and spiritual associations.

In addition to animal figures, abstract symbols and geometric patterns are also present at Göbekli Tepe. These symbols include concentric circles, spirals, crescents, nets, and various other shapes. While their precise meanings remain elusive, these abstract symbols likely held symbolic or ritualistic significance within the cultural framework of the ancient community. Some interpretations suggest that these symbols may represent cosmic or celestial concepts, such as the sun, moon, stars, or celestial alignments, while others propose associations with fertility, regeneration, or cultural identity.

Human figures, although less frequent, also make appearances in the carvings at Göbekli Tepe. These depictions include both male and female figures, often portrayed in stylized or schematic forms. Some figures exhibit exaggerated features such as prominent sexual characteristics or elongated limbs. The significance of these human representations is not fully understood, but they may represent ancestral beings, mythical or spiritual figures, or individuals of particular social or religious importance within the ancient community.

The interplay between animal, human, and abstract depictions suggests a complex interweaving of symbolic and cultural elements. The carvings at Göbekli Tepe were likely imbued with layers of meaning, reflecting the cosmological beliefs, mythologies, and social identities of the ancient people. These depictions were not purely artistic expressions but served as powerful visual tools for communication, religious rituals, or communal storytelling.

The placement and arrangement of these figures within the larger architectural context of Göbekli Tepe are also significant. They often appear in specific locations, on specific pillars or within specific enclosures, suggesting intentional choices in their positioning. The spatial relationships between the figures and their architectural surroundings likely played a role in shaping the visual and symbolic impact of the site, creating immersive and spiritually charged environments.

Interpreting the specific meanings and narratives behind the figures and depictions at Göbekli Tepe remains a complex and ongoing task. The limited available evidence, the temporal and cultural distance, and the absence of written records make it challenging to decipher their precise symbolism and intended interpretations. However, the meticulous craftsmanship, attention to detail, and recurring motifs found in these carvings emphasize their cultural significance and provide a window into the rich symbolic world of the ancient community that thrived at Göbekli Tepe.

Continued archaeological research, interdisciplinary studies, and advancements in analytical techniques offer promising avenues for further understanding and unraveling the mysteries of the figures and depictions at Göbekli Tepe. These enigmatic carvings serve as tangible links to our ancient past, providing valuable insights into the artistic, religious, and social dimensions of our early ancestors. The presence of figures and depictions at Göbekli Tepe has sparked fascinating mythological interpretations, suggesting a connection to supernatural beings and mythological narratives within the ancient belief system. While the precise mythological significance of these carvings remains speculative, their portrayal of certain figures and motifs hints at a rich mythological landscape.

One interpretation suggests that the animal figures depicted at Göbekli Tepe may represent mythological or supernatural beings. The lifelike and highly detailed renderings of animals, such as wild boars, snakes, and birds, may indicate their status as mythological creatures or divine entities within the ancient cosmology. These animal figures could have symbolized guardian spirits, totems, or even deities associated with natural forces, hunting, fertility, or other significant aspects of the human experience.

The presence of human figures, albeit less frequent, also invites mythological interpretations. The stylized and schematic representations of human forms may point to mythological or ancestral figures. Some of these figures exhibit exaggerated features, such as prominent sexual characteristics or elongated limbs, suggesting their status as mythical beings or divine ancestors. They could have played roles in creation myths, heroic narratives, or other mythological stories central to the ancient belief system.

Furthermore, the interplay between the animal and human figures suggests a complex mythological narrative. These carvings might represent mythological encounters, interactions, or even transformative processes, revealing a mythology that involved both human and animal realms. These narratives could have addressed themes such as the relationship between humans and the natural world, the origins of life, the cycles of nature, or the balance between earthly and divine realms.

The abstract symbols and geometric patterns found at Göbekli Tepe also hold potential mythological significance. These symbols could represent cosmological concepts or celestial beings within the ancient mythology. Some interpretations suggest connections between these symbols and celestial bodies, such as the sun, moon, or stars, inferring a celestial mythology intertwined with the earthly realm. The geometric patterns might have represented sacred geometries or symbolic representations of cosmic order and balance.

It is important to approach these mythological interpretations with caution, as our understanding of the specific mythologies and belief systems of the ancient people at Göbekli Tepe remains limited. The absence of written records from that time period poses challenges in deciphering the precise mythological narratives associated with the carvings. Nevertheless, the intricate craftsmanship, deliberate positioning, and recurring motifs strongly suggest that these figures and depictions held significant mythological and symbolic meanings for the ancient community.

By exploring the mythological interpretations of the figures and depictions at Göbekli Tepe, we can gain valuable insights into the imaginative and cultural landscape of our early ancestors. These carvings offer tantalizing glimpses into their belief systems, mythologies, and the way they sought to understand and interact with the supernatural realms. As ongoing research and interdisciplinary studies continue to unfold, we may come closer to unraveling the mythological narratives encoded within the remarkable stone carvings of Göbekli Tepe.

The symbolic representations found at Göbekli Tepe suggest a connection to guardianship and protection within the ancient belief system. The presence of certain figures and motifs, along with their positioning and arrangement, alludes to the notion of safeguarding and preserving the sacred space and its associated rituals.

One interpretation suggests that the animal figures depicted at Göbekli Tepe may serve as symbolic guardians. The lifelike and detailed carvings of wild boars, snakes, birds, and other animals imply a sense of protection and watchfulness. These creatures could have been perceived as powerful and protective beings, guarding the sacred site and its inhabitants against malevolent forces or spiritual intrusions. Their presence may have been intended to ensure the sanctity of the rituals and ceremonies conducted at Göbekli Tepe.

The positioning and alignment of the T-shaped pillars themselves also contribute to the idea of guardianship. The deliberate arrangement of these pillars within circular or oval enclosures suggests the creation of defined spaces that may have been considered sacred or ceremonial. The pillars, with their significant size and prominence, may have acted as sentinels, visually and spiritually guarding the sacred space and its activities. Their role as focal points for rituals and their alignment with celestial events could further enhance their perceived guardianship.

The geometric patterns and abstract symbols found at the site may also hold symbolic significance related to protection. Some interpretations propose that these symbols may represent concepts such as boundaries, barriers, or spiritual shields. The repetition and consistency of these patterns across different pillars and enclosures suggest their intentional use in creating a protective environment. These symbols may have been seen as metaphysical or spiritual tools for warding off negative energies or influences.

Furthermore, the human figures depicted at Göbekli Tepe may have embodied the role of guardians or protectors. Although less frequent than animal figures, the stylized human representations may have represented mythological or ancestral figures who served as guardians of the sacred site. Their exaggerated features and distinctive postures may have conveyed a sense of strength and authority, emphasizing their protective role within the ancient belief system.

While these interpretations offer glimpses into the symbolic representations of guardianship and protection at Göbekli Tepe, it is crucial to approach them with caution. The precise meanings and beliefs of the ancient community remain speculative due to the limited available evidence and the temporal gap between us and the builders of the site. As such, further research and interdisciplinary studies are necessary to deepen our understanding of the symbolic significance of the figures and motifs at Göbekli Tepe.

By exploring the symbolic representations of guardianship and protection, we gain insights into the worldview, beliefs, and cultural practices of the ancient people who constructed and used Göbekli Tepe. These symbolic elements highlight the importance of safeguarding the sacred space and maintaining its sanctity within their belief system. They reveal a profound reverence for the spiritual realm and the rituals performed at the site, offering us a fascinating glimpse into the ancient understanding of guardianship and protection within the context of the megalithic temples.

Guardian figures have played a significant role in various prehistoric belief systems around the world, spanning different cultures and time periods. These enigmatic beings, often depicted in art and mythology, served as protectors, intermediaries, and gatekeepers between the human realm and the spiritual or supernatural domains.

In many prehistoric societies, guardian figures were associated with specific sacred sites, such as megalithic temples, burial grounds, or natural landmarks. They were believed to possess supernatural powers and were entrusted with safeguarding these sacred spaces from malevolent forces, ensuring the well-being and spiritual harmony of the community. Guardian figures were thought to have the ability to ward off evil spirits, prevent spiritual intrusions, and maintain the sanctity of the sacred sites.

The representations of guardian figures in prehistoric art varied widely depending on cultural and regional contexts. They could take the form of animal spirits, anthropomorphic beings, or a blend of both. Animals, with their strength, agility, and innate instincts, were often revered as powerful protectors. They embodied qualities such as bravery, wisdom, and ferocity, which were believed to be essential for guarding sacred spaces. Anthropomorphic guardian figures, on the other hand, combined human and animal characteristics, bridging the gap between the earthly and spiritual realms.

The symbolism associated with guardian figures was multifaceted and complex. They were often depicted with attributes or motifs signifying their protective roles. These might include weapons, such as spears or shields, symbolizing their ability to defend against threats. Other symbols, such as geometric patterns, spirals, or abstract designs, could represent spiritual energies, cosmic forces, or the interconnectedness of the human and divine realms.

Guardian figures were not only protectors but also served as intermediaries between humans and the spiritual world. They were believed to have the ability to communicate with deities or ancestral spirits, acting as conduits for prayers, offerings, and rituals. These figures were seen as bridges between the mundane and the divine, facilitating the exchange of spiritual energies and blessings.

The significance of guardian figures extended beyond the physical realm. They played vital roles in the cultural and social fabric of prehistoric societies. The presence of these protective beings provided a sense of security, reinforcing the community's collective identity and spiritual beliefs. They instilled a reverence for the sacred and fostered a sense of connection with the natural world, encouraging the harmonious coexistence between humans and their environment.

Understanding the role of guardian figures in prehistoric belief systems is a complex task, often requiring interdisciplinary approaches that combine archaeological evidence, mythological narratives, and comparative studies across different cultures. While the specifics may vary, the concept of guardianship and the belief in protective beings emerged as a common thread in the spiritual and cultural practices of prehistoric societies.

By studying the representations and symbolism associated with guardian figures in prehistoric art and mythology, we gain valuable insights into the spiritual worldview, belief systems, and the complex relationship between humans and the supernatural realm. These guardian figures embody the deep-rooted human desire for protection, guidance, and connection with forces beyond the material world, leaving an enduring imprint on the ancient cultures that revered them. The artistic and cultural significance of the guardian figures at Göbekli Tepe is a subject of great intrigue and speculation. These enigmatic beings, depicted in the carvings and reliefs found throughout the site, hold a prominent role in the artistic narrative and cultural symbolism of this ancient complex.

The guardian figures at Göbekli Tepe are often represented as anthropomorphic beings with human-like characteristics combined with animalistic features. These hybrid forms suggest a blending of the human and animal realms, symbolizing the connection between the natural and supernatural worlds. The intricate detailing and stylized representations of these figures indicate a sophisticated artistic tradition and a deliberate effort to convey symbolic meaning.

One interpretation suggests that these guardian figures served as protectors of the sacred site and its rituals. Their imposing stature and fierce appearance imply their role as powerful guardians, warding off malevolent forces and preserving the sanctity of the site. They were believed to possess spiritual or supernatural qualities that enabled them to safeguard the rituals, ceremonies, and communal gatherings that took place at Göbekli Tepe.

The positioning and arrangement of the guardian figures within the architectural spaces of Göbekli Tepe further highlight their cultural significance. Many of these figures are located on the monumental T-shaped pillars, which are strategically placed throughout the enclosures. The pillars themselves act as visual markers and focal points, while the guardian figures enhance their spiritual presence and contribute to the overall sacred atmosphere of the site.

The artistic depiction of these guardians at Göbekli Tepe also reflects the broader cultural symbolism and belief systems of the ancient people who created them. The combination of human and animal features suggests a deep reverence for the natural world and the interplay between the human and animal realms. These representations may embody spiritual connections, animistic beliefs, or a mythology that merged human and animal attributes.

The presence of guardian figures at Göbekli Tepe signifies the importance of protection, guardianship, and the spiritual realms within the cultural practices of the ancient community. These figures were not merely artistic creations but held a significant role in the belief system and collective imagination of the people who frequented the site. Their artistic depiction and positioning within the architectural spaces served to heighten the spiritual ambiance and emphasize the sacred nature of the rituals performed at Göbekli Tepe.

While the precise meanings and interpretations of these guardian figures remain speculative, ongoing research and interdisciplinary studies continue to shed light on their cultural and symbolic significance. The careful analysis of the artistic details, comparative studies with other ancient sites, and the examination of associated archaeological evidence contribute to our evolving understanding of the artistic and cultural importance of these guardian figures at Göbekli Tepe.

The guardian figures at Göbekli Tepe stand as enduring testament to the creative abilities and spiritual beliefs of our ancient ancestors. Their presence reflects a profound connection between the human experience, the natural world, and the supernatural realm, providing a glimpse into the artistic and cultural legacy of the early civilizations that thrived at Göbekli Tepe.

Chapter 6: Rituals and Beliefs at the Sacred Site

Sacred rituals held a central place in the ancient ceremonies conducted at Göbekli Tepe, infusing the site with profound spiritual significance. These rituals, performed by the ancient community, involved a range of practices and symbolisms that connected them with the divine, fostered communal bonds, and maintained the harmony between the human and supernatural realms.

The precise details of the ancient ceremonies at Göbekli Tepe remain largely speculative, as written records from that time period are absent. However, the architectural layout and the presence of intricate carvings provide valuable insights into the possible nature of these sacred rituals.

The circular and oval enclosures found at Göbekli Tepe suggest designated spaces for ceremonial activities. These areas, often containing the monumental T-shaped pillars, would have served as focal points for the rituals. The positioning and arrangement of the pillars within the enclosures may have played a role in creating a sacred and visually compelling atmosphere, enhancing the ritualistic experience.

One interpretation proposes that the T-shaped pillars themselves were integral to the rituals. They may have represented deities, ancestral spirits, or mythological figures and acted as intermediaries between the human and divine realms. The carvings and reliefs on the pillars, including depictions of animals and abstract symbols, may have held specific symbolic meanings associated with the rituals performed.

The celestial alignments of Göbekli Tepe also suggest a connection between the rituals and the cycles of the natural world. The careful placement of the site and its alignment with celestial events, such as solstices or equinoxes, indicates an awareness of cosmic forces and their significance within the ritual framework. These celestial alignments may have guided the timing and nature of the ceremonies, marking important moments in the agricultural calendar, celestial observations, or mythological narratives.

Sound and music likely played a significant role in the rituals at Göbekli Tepe. The architectural acoustics of the stone structures and the enclosed spaces may have enhanced the resonance and amplification of sound, creating an immersive auditory experience during the ceremonies. Ritual chants, musical instruments, and rhythmic movements could have been employed to evoke spiritual states, induce trance-like experiences, or communicate with the divine.

The communal aspect of the rituals at Göbekli Tepe is also of great importance. The shared participation in these ceremonies would have fostered a sense of community, reinforcing social bonds and collective identity. The rituals likely served as occasions for storytelling, mythological narratives, and the passing down of cultural traditions from one generation to another.

While the specifics of the ancient ceremonies at Göbekli Tepe may never be fully known, the evidence suggests a complex and spiritually significant ritualistic landscape. These ceremonies acted as conduits for the ancient community to connect with the supernatural, to express their collective beliefs and values, and to reaffirm their place within the natural and cosmic order.

Studying the architectural features, artistic symbolism, and cultural context of Göbekli Tepe provides valuable insights into the ancient rituals and their significance. Ongoing research, interdisciplinary collaborations, and advancements in archaeological techniques continue to deepen our understanding of the sacred rituals that once took place at this remarkable site, offering us a window into the rich and meaningful spiritual lives of our ancient ancestors.

Uncovering the spiritual beliefs of prehistoric societies offers a fascinating glimpse into the ancient faith systems that shaped their worldview. While the specifics of these belief systems vary across different cultures and time periods, common threads can be found in their reverence for natural forces, their connection to ancestral spirits, and their engagement with the supernatural realm.

One prevalent aspect of prehistoric spiritual beliefs is the veneration of natural forces and elements. These early societies recognized the awe-inspiring power and significance of natural phenomena such as the sun, moon, stars, rivers, mountains, and forests. They perceived these natural elements as imbued with spiritual energies or as embodiments of divine entities. Rituals and ceremonies were conducted to honor and seek the blessings of these natural forces, fostering a deep sense of interconnectedness between humans and the natural world.

Ancestor worship and reverence for ancestral spirits were also prominent features of prehistoric faith systems. Ancestors were believed to possess wisdom, guidance, and protective qualities, and were venerated as intermediaries between the human and supernatural realms. Ancestral spirits were honored through rituals, offerings, and commemorative practices, maintaining a connection between the living and the deceased and ensuring the well-being and continuity of the community.

The belief in supernatural beings, such as gods, goddesses, and mythical entities, was another significant aspect of prehistoric faith systems. These divine beings often represented various aspects of the natural world, human experiences, or cosmic forces. They were invoked and propitiated through prayers, rituals, and offerings, as well as through myths and narratives that explained the origins of the world, the creation of humanity, and the moral codes by which people should live.

The practice of shamanism, with its emphasis on spiritual communication, healing, and divination, was prevalent in many prehistoric cultures. Shamanic practitioners, often serving as intermediaries between the human and spirit realms, played crucial roles in guiding individuals and communities through spiritual experiences, performing healing rituals, and offering guidance and wisdom. Shamanism allowed individuals to connect with the spiritual realm, gain insights, and address personal or communal challenges.

Art, symbolism, and ritual objects were integral to the expression of prehistoric spiritual beliefs. Cave paintings, rock art, and the carvings found at sites like Göbekli Tepe and other megalithic structures served as visual representations of the spiritual world. Symbolic motifs, abstract designs, and anthropomorphic or zoomorphic figures conveyed spiritual concepts, mythological narratives, and cosmological beliefs. Ritual objects, such as amulets, charms, and sacred tools, were used in ceremonies to facilitate communication with the divine and invoke spiritual powers.

The precise details and nuances of prehistoric spiritual beliefs are challenging to ascertain due to the scarcity of written records. However, through careful analysis of archaeological findings, comparative studies across different cultures, and the study of oral traditions and myths that have been passed down through generations, scholars continue to shed light on these ancient faith systems.

Uncovering prehistoric faith systems provides valuable insights into the human quest for meaning, the origins of religious and spiritual practices, and the ways in which our early ancestors sought to understand and engage with the world beyond the material realm. It offers us a deeper appreciation for the rich diversity of human spiritual experiences throughout history and invites contemplation on the enduring questions of our place in the cosmos.

The role of shamanism and shamanic practices at Göbekli Tepe, one of the world's oldest known religious sites, is a subject of fascination and speculation. While the exact nature of shamanic practices at Göbekli Tepe remains elusive due to the limited available evidence, the presence of shamanic elements and the site's spiritual significance suggest a possible connection to shamanic traditions.

Shamanism is a spiritual practice that dates back thousands of years and has been practiced by diverse cultures around the world. It involves individuals, known as shamans, who are believed to have the ability to communicate with the spirit world, navigate spiritual realms, and act as intermediaries between humans and the supernatural.

One interpretation proposes that shamanic practices may have played a role at Göbekli Tepe due to the site's architectural layout, symbolic carvings, and the possible ceremonial nature of the site. The circular and oval enclosures, often containing monumental T-shaped pillars, could have served as spaces for shamanic rituals, vision quests, healing ceremonies, or other spiritual practices. These enclosed spaces may have provided an environment conducive to altered states of consciousness and spiritual experiences.

The T-shaped pillars themselves, with their anthropomorphic and zoomorphic carvings, have been associated with shamanic symbolism in various cultures. The T-shape is reminiscent of the human form and is thought to represent a bridge between the earthly and spirit realms. The carvings on these pillars, including animal figures and abstract symbols, may have held spiritual significance and aided in the shamanic journeying or communication with the supernatural.

The role of shamans at Göbekli Tepe may have encompassed various functions. They might have performed healing rituals, divination, or served as guides for individuals seeking spiritual insights. Through the use of rhythmic movements, chanting, music, or the consumption of psychotropic substances, shamans could induce altered states of consciousness and engage with the spirit world to address personal, communal, or cosmological concerns.

The incorporation of sound and music is another aspect that points to possible shamanic practices at Göbekli Tepe. The architectural acoustics of the stone structures and the enclosed spaces may have amplified sound, enhancing the ritualistic experience. Shamanic rituals often involve the use of rhythmic drumming, chanting, or other sonic elements to induce trance-like states, invoke spiritual forces, or facilitate healing.

While the evidence for shamanic practices at Göbekli Tepe remains speculative, the presence of spiritual symbolism, ritualistic spaces, and the architectural features of the site suggest a connection to shamanic traditions. These practices likely played a vital role in the spiritual and communal life of the ancient community, facilitating connections with the supernatural, addressing spiritual needs, and providing guidance and healing.

Further research, interdisciplinary collaborations, and advancements in archaeological techniques will continue to shed light on the role of shamanism at Göbekli Tepe. As our understanding of this ancient site deepens, we may gain further insights into the specific shamanic practices, rituals, and beliefs that were integral to the spiritual experiences of our early ancestors at Göbekli Tepe.

The presence of sacrificial offerings at ancient sites, including Göbekli Tepe, provides intriguing insights into the ritualistic practices and symbolism of prehistoric cultures. While the exact nature and purpose of these offerings at Göbekli Tepe remain speculative, the presence of animal remains and other artifacts suggests the involvement of sacrificial rituals within the spiritual and ceremonial activities of the site.

Sacrificial offerings, throughout human history, have been a way to establish a connection with the divine, seek favor, express gratitude, or appease supernatural forces. In the context of Göbekli Tepe, the animal remains found at the site indicate the involvement of animal sacrifices. The intentional selection and deposition of these animal offerings suggest a deliberate act with spiritual significance.

The animals chosen for sacrificial offerings may have held symbolic meaning and represented various aspects of the natural world, ancestral spirits, or mythological beings. Different animal species might have been associated with specific qualities or attributes, such as strength, fertility, or divinity. The selection of particular animals for sacrifice may have been influenced by the cosmological beliefs and cultural symbolism of the prehistoric community.

The manner in which these sacrificial offerings were made is also significant. The careful arrangement or placement of animal remains within the enclosures or near the monumental structures suggests a deliberate act with ritualistic intent. The positioning of these offerings may have been associated with specific celestial alignments, seasonal cycles, or mythological narratives, further emphasizing their ceremonial significance.

The act of sacrifice itself was believed to facilitate communication with the supernatural realm, forge a connection with the divine, or reinforce the social and spiritual order within the community. It was seen as a means to establish a reciprocal relationship between humans and the supernatural, in which offerings were made in exchange for blessings, protection, or spiritual guidance.

Symbolism played a crucial role in sacrificial rituals at Göbekli Tepe. The act of sacrifice, through its symbolic gestures and actions, expressed the community's devotion, reverence, and submission to the supernatural. The blood or life force of the sacrificial animal was believed to carry spiritual potency and served as a conduit for spiritual communication or appeasement.

The presence of other artifacts, such as stone tools or personal ornaments, alongside the animal remains at Göbekli Tepe, suggests a multifaceted nature to the sacrificial rituals. These offerings may have included both tangible objects and living beings, emphasizing the diverse ways in which the prehistoric community sought to engage with the divine.

While the precise meanings and motivations behind the sacrificial practices at Göbekli Tepe remain elusive, the presence of sacrificial offerings reflects a deep spiritual and ritualistic dimension within the cultural practices of the ancient community. These rituals allowed for a connection with the supernatural, served as expressions of faith and devotion, and reinforced social cohesion and communal identity.

The study of sacrificial offerings at Göbekli Tepe and other ancient sites continues to be a subject of ongoing research and exploration. As our understanding of the archaeological evidence deepens, we gain valuable insights into the spiritual beliefs, ritual practices, and symbolic systems that shaped the worldview of our early ancestors.

In the annals of ancient civilizations, there exist remarkable sites that captivate the imagination and challenge our understanding of human history. Amongst these enigmatic places, Gobekli Tepe stands as an archaeological marvel, shrouded in mystery and steeped in spiritual significance. Situated in modern-day Turkey, this sacred site unravels the secrets of our prehistoric ancestors, revealing a profound connection between spirituality, ritual, and the shaping of human societies.

Gobekli Tepe, meaning "Potbelly Hill" in Turkish, is a hilltop sanctuary that dates back to the Neolithic period, approximately 12,000 years ago. Its discovery in the 1990s sent shockwaves through the archaeological community, challenging prevailing notions of human development and civilization. This meticulously crafted site, with its massive stone pillars arranged in circular enclosures, defied the conventional narrative that attributed such monumental construction to advanced agricultural societies.

The spiritual significance of Gobekli Tepe becomes evident upon closer examination of its architectural design and intricate carvings. The stone pillars, some reaching up to 20 feet in height and weighing several tons, were meticulously crafted and erected with astounding precision. The sheer effort and communal cooperation required to create such monumental structures point to a deeply ingrained spiritual impetus within the prehistoric community.

As one gazes upon the enclosures of Gobekli Tepe, a palpable aura of sanctity permeates the air. The circular and oval-shaped enclosures, carefully constructed and adorned with ornate reliefs, were not mere architectural feats but rather sacred spaces that fostered a profound connection with the divine. These spaces served as the backdrop for rituals, ceremonies, and communal gatherings that defined the spiritual and social fabric of the ancient community.

The carvings and reliefs found at Gobekli Tepe provide a visual tapestry of prehistoric belief systems and cosmological understanding. Intricately carved animal figures, abstract symbols, and enigmatic human-like depictions adorn the stone pillars, depicting a rich tapestry of mythological narratives and spiritual motifs. These carvings offer glimpses into the prehistoric worldview, where the natural world, the animal realm, and the supernatural intermingled in a harmonious and interconnected dance.

The precise meaning and symbolism of these carvings elude definitive interpretation. However, scholars have proposed that they represent celestial entities, mythical beings, ancestral spirits, or the embodiment of natural forces. The placement and arrangement of these carvings within the enclosures suggest a deliberate effort to evoke a sense of cosmic harmony and spiritual resonance, aligning the ancient community with the rhythms of the universe.

Gobekli Tepe's significance extends beyond its physical structure and artistic representations. It serves as a testament to the emergence of complex social structures and the development of organized religious practices. The construction of such an elaborate sanctuary required a cohesive and coordinated effort, suggesting the existence of social hierarchies, specialized labor, and shared belief systems that bound the ancient community together.

The spiritual practices enacted at Gobekli Tepe were a fundamental aspect of the community's worldview and social cohesion. Rituals and ceremonies, infused with symbolism and a deep reverence for the divine, served as a conduit for communication with the supernatural realm. These sacred gatherings brought people together, fostering a sense of communal identity and shared purpose.

Gobekli Tepe's spiritual significance extends beyond its immediate community. It signifies a pivotal moment in human history, marking the transition from small, nomadic groups to settled societies engaged in communal endeavors. The construction of such monumental structures necessitated a shift in societal dynamics, where spiritual beliefs and ritual practices played a central role in organizing and uniting the community.

The legacy of Gobekli Tepe echoes through the corridors of time, reaching into the present day. Its discovery challenges long-held assumptions about the trajectory of human civilization, inviting us to reassess our understanding of prehistoric societies and the origins of organized religion. Gobekli Tepe reminds us of the inherent human inclination towards spirituality and the universal quest for meaning and connection.

As we delve into the depths of Gobekli Tepe's spiritual significance, we encounter an ancient tapestry woven with the threads of faith, ritual, and communal identity. Its monumental architecture and intricate carvings stand as testaments to the spiritual yearnings and creative ingenuity of our prehistoric ancestors. Gobekli Tepe invites us to explore the depths of our shared humanity, inspiring awe and wonder as we navigate the eternal enigma of our spiritual existence.

The excavation of Gobekli Tepe, an extraordinary archaeological site that has captured the attention of scholars and enthusiasts alike, requires meticulous planning, innovative techniques, and a deep respect for the delicate preservation of the ancient remains. The quest to unveil the subterranean secrets of this Neolithic sanctuary presents a unique set of challenges and opportunities, demanding a harmonious interplay between technology, expertise, and historical sensitivity.

The excavation process at Gobekli Tepe begins with a comprehensive survey of the site, employing cutting-edge technologies such as ground-penetrating radar, aerial surveys, and geophysical imaging. These techniques provide a non-invasive means of mapping the subsurface features, identifying potential archaeological structures, and determining the most promising areas for excavation. This initial survey sets the stage for targeted excavations and informed decision-making regarding the allocation of resources and manpower.

The excavation itself requires a delicate balance between preservation and exploration. The ancient structures and artifacts at Gobekli Tepe are incredibly fragile, requiring meticulous handling and documentation to ensure their preservation for future generations. Archaeologists employ a variety of excavation methods, including manual digging, brushes, trowels, and sieving, to carefully remove layers of soil and debris while minimizing the risk of damage to the delicate remains.

As the excavation progresses, each layer of soil and sediment is meticulously recorded and analyzed. This stratigraphic approach allows archaeologists to reconstruct the chronological sequence of human activity at the site, deciphering the layers of history embedded within the earth. By carefully documenting the position and context of each discovered artifact, structural feature, and geological formation, a comprehensive understanding of the site's development and occupation emerges.

The discovery and documentation of artifacts play a vital role in understanding the cultural and historical significance of Gobekli Tepe. Excavators employ a meticulous process of artifact retrieval, employing fine brushes, small tools, and a keen eye for detail. Each artifact is carefully cleaned, photographed, and cataloged, with precise attention given to its location within the site. These artifacts range from intricately carved stone pillars and sculptures to pottery fragments, tools, and personal ornaments, each offering valuable insights into the lives, beliefs, and practices of the ancient community.

In addition to manual excavation techniques, modern technology has revolutionized the exploration of Gobekli Tepe. Remote sensing technologies, such as LiDAR (Light Detection and Ranging), enable archaeologists to create high-resolution digital models of the site, revealing previously hidden details and aiding in the interpretation of the landscape. 3D modeling techniques further enhance the visualization and analysis of the complex architectural features, allowing for a more comprehensive understanding of the site's layout and construction.

Collaboration and interdisciplinary approaches are integral to the excavation process at Gobekli Tepe. Archaeologists, anthropologists, geologists, botanists, and other specialists come together to contribute their unique perspectives and expertise. This multidisciplinary approach enables a holistic understanding of the site, incorporating geological processes, environmental contexts, and social dynamics into the interpretation of the ancient remains.

Preservation of the excavated structures and artifacts is a paramount concern at Gobekli Tepe. To ensure the long-term conservation of the site, meticulous documentation, digital archiving, and protective measures are employed. Conservation experts employ specialized techniques to stabilize and protect the fragile ancient materials, such as applying protective coatings, monitoring environmental conditions, and developing long-term preservation plans.

The excavation of Gobekli Tepe is an ongoing endeavor, continually shedding new light on the remarkable history of this ancient sanctuary. Each excavation season brings forth new discoveries, challenges previous assumptions, and deepens our understanding of the prehistoric cultures that thrived in this region. The careful application of excavation techniques, guided by historical sensitivity and technological innovation, ensures that Gobekli Tepe's subterranean secrets can be unveiled with the utmost care and reverence, opening a window into the distant past and illuminating our shared human heritage.

As the layers of soil are carefully peeled away at Gobekli Tepe, an awe-inspiring picture of human history gradually emerges. The excavation of this ancient sanctuary provides a unique opportunity to delve deep into the chronology of human occupation and unravel the complex layers of time that have shaped the site.

At Gobekli Tepe, the stratigraphic approach serves as the foundation for understanding the sequence of human activity and the development of the site over thousands of years. Each layer of soil, known as a stratigraphic unit, represents a distinct period in the site's history. By meticulously documenting and analyzing these layers, archaeologists can discern the chronological order of construction, modification, and abandonment of the structures at Gobekli Tepe.

The process begins by establishing a detailed stratigraphic profile, which involves carefully recording the position, thickness, and composition of each stratigraphic unit. Excavators use brushes, trowels, and other delicate tools to remove soil layer by layer, paying close attention to any changes in sediment color, texture, or composition. The excavated soil is then sieved to recover any small artifacts or ecofacts that may provide further insights into the site's history.

Once the layers are exposed, archaeologists analyze the artifacts, ecofacts, and structural features found within each stratigraphic unit. Radiocarbon dating, a technique that measures the decay of radioactive carbon isotopes in organic materials, is often employed to obtain precise chronological data. By dating the remains of plant and animal materials, such as charcoal, bone, or seeds, researchers can establish the approximate age of each layer and the activities associated with it.

The stratigraphic analysis at Gobekli Tepe has revealed a fascinating sequence of construction and modification. The earliest layers, referred to as Layer III, date back to around 9600-8800 BCE and consist of circular enclosures with massive T-shaped pillars. These structures represent the oldest known megalithic architecture in the world, pushing back the timeline of monumental construction by thousands of years.

As the excavation progresses through the layers, the complexities of Gobekli Tepe's history become apparent. Successive layers, known as Layers II, I, and Upper Building Level, reveal additional enclosures, pillars, and architectural modifications. These layers provide valuable insights into the evolution of the site, including changes in architectural styles, carvings, and the symbolic significance of the structures.

The excavation of Gobekli Tepe has also uncovered evidence of intentional burial practices. Human remains found within certain layers provide glimpses into the rituals and beliefs surrounding death and the afterlife during different periods of the site's use. These burials, marked by carefully arranged stones or unique burial positions, shed light on the cultural and social aspects of the ancient community.

As the excavation team progresses deeper into the layers, the challenge of interpretation becomes increasingly complex. The combination of architectural changes, varying styles of carvings, and the presence of multiple construction phases within each layer presents a puzzle that requires careful analysis and contextual understanding. Interpreting these layers requires an interdisciplinary approach, integrating archaeological, anthropological, geological, and environmental data to construct a comprehensive narrative.

The stratigraphic analysis at Gobekli Tepe not only sheds light on the timeline of construction and occupation but also provides a glimpse into the social and cultural dynamics of the ancient community. The modifications made to the site over time suggest an ongoing engagement with spiritual practices, communal rituals, and the symbolic transformation of the landscape.

The excavation of Gobekli Tepe continues to uncover new layers of history, deepening our understanding of this ancient sanctuary and its significance in the human story. Each layer holds within it a multitude of stories, waiting to be deciphered and woven into the fabric of our collective past. As archaeologists painstakingly peel back the layers of time, the true magnitude of Gobekli Tepe's chronology becomes increasingly apparent, offering a tantalizing glimpse into the rich tapestry of human existence.

The recovery of artifacts at archaeological sites provides invaluable insights into the lives, beliefs, and cultural practices of our ancient ancestors. At Gobekli Tepe, a treasure trove of artifacts has been unearthed, offering a glimpse into the rich tapestry of the Neolithic communities that once thrived in this sacred sanctuary.

Excavations at Gobekli Tepe have yielded a diverse array of artifacts, each with its own story to tell. Among the most notable discoveries are the intricately carved stone pillars that adorn the enclosures. These T-shaped pillars, standing as high as 20 feet, are adorned with detailed reliefs depicting a variety of animals, including lions, snakes, birds, and foxes. The craftsmanship and artistic expression displayed in these carvings provide a window into the prehistoric community's worldview and their reverence for the natural world.

Another significant category of artifacts recovered at Gobekli Tepe is pottery. Fragments of ceramic vessels, adorned with intricate designs and patterns, offer insights into the technological advancements and artistic skills of the ancient inhabitants. The analysis of pottery sherds provides valuable information about the techniques of pottery production, decorative motifs, and possible functions of the vessels within the social and ritual contexts of the site.

Tools and implements made of stone, bone, and antler have also been discovered, shedding light on the daily lives and activities of the ancient community. Stone tools, such as flint blades and arrowheads, reflect the resourcefulness and ingenuity of the prehistoric people in crafting functional objects for hunting, cutting, and shaping materials. Bone and antler tools, including awls, needles, and harpoons, provide insights into activities such as sewing, fishing, and working with animal materials.

Personal adornments and decorative items, such as beads, pendants, and figurines, offer glimpses into the aesthetic sensibilities and symbolic expressions of the ancient community. These artifacts demonstrate the value placed on personal adornment, self-expression, and possibly social status within the society. The materials used, ranging from stone and bone to shells and minerals, reveal the availability of local resources and possible trade networks.

Furthermore, the recovery of organic materials at Gobekli Tepe has provided unique opportunities for scientific analysis and understanding. Plant remains, including seeds, pollen, and charred grains, have been found, offering insights into the local vegetation, agricultural practices, and subsistence strategies of the ancient community. Animal bones and remains provide evidence of hunting practices, domestication efforts, and dietary patterns.

The analysis and interpretation of these artifacts go beyond their intrinsic value as objects. They serve as tangible links to the past, connecting us to the daily lives, beliefs, and material culture of the ancient inhabitants. The careful study of these artifacts, combined with interdisciplinary approaches and comparative analyses, allows researchers to reconstruct aspects of the ancient community's social structure, economic systems, belief systems, and technological advancements.

Artifacts recovered from Gobekli Tepe also have broader implications beyond the site itself. They contribute to our understanding of the broader cultural and chronological context of the Neolithic period, allowing for comparisons with other contemporary sites and societies. The similarities and differences in artifact assemblages provide insights into regional connections, trade networks, and cultural interactions.

The recovery of artifacts at Gobekli Tepe is an ongoing process, with each new excavation season bringing forth new discoveries and deeper understandings. As researchers continue to unearth and analyze these ancient relics, the mosaic of Gobekli Tepe's past becomes clearer, painting a vivid picture of the cultural richness, artistic expression, and spiritual beliefs of the Neolithic communities who once gathered at this sacred site.

The preservation, study, and interpretation of these artifacts are essential for reconstructing the past, preserving our shared heritage, and nurturing a deeper appreciation for the diverse cultures that have shaped our world. As each artifact is carefully examined and understood within its archaeological context, we gain valuable insights into the human story, enabling us to bridge the gap between the distant past and our present-day understanding of the world.

Preserving the fragile remains of Gobekli Tepe presents a significant challenge for archaeologists and conservators. The ancient structures and artifacts at the site, dating back thousands of years, require meticulous care and conservation to safeguard them for future generations. Various preservation challenges arise due to factors such as environmental conditions, exposure to the elements, and the delicate nature of the materials.

One of the primary challenges faced in preserving Gobekli Tepe is the protection of the exposed stone pillars and structures from weathering and erosion. The site is located in a region prone to extreme weather conditions, including harsh sun, wind, rain, and temperature fluctuations. These environmental factors can accelerate the deterioration of the ancient stone, leading to erosion, surface flaking, and structural instability.

To combat this challenge, protective measures are implemented to shield the exposed stone surfaces from direct exposure to the elements. Coverings, such as specialized fabrics or temporary structures, can be used to provide shade and protection against sunlight. Additionally, treatments with consolidants or coatings are applied to the stone surfaces to reinforce their structural integrity and protect against weathering.

Another crucial aspect of preservation is the prevention of damage from human activity. Gobekli Tepe attracts a significant number of visitors each year, and the constant foot traffic can have a detrimental impact on the fragile remains. Measures such as walkways, barriers, and controlled access areas are implemented to minimize direct contact and accidental damage to the archaeological features.

Awareness and education play a vital role in the preservation efforts at Gobekli Tepe. Visitors are informed about the importance of responsible behavior and the need to respect the site's fragile nature. Interpretive signage, visitor guides, and guided tours contribute to raising awareness about preservation and the significance of Gobekli Tepe's archaeological heritage.

Monitoring and regular assessment of the site's condition are essential components of preservation efforts. This involves regular inspections by archaeologists and conservators to identify any signs of deterioration or damage. Close monitoring allows for timely intervention and the implementation of necessary measures to mitigate potential risks.

The long-term preservation of Gobekli Tepe requires ongoing research and scientific analysis. Collaborations between archaeologists, conservators, scientists, and other experts help develop effective preservation strategies. Research into the properties of the materials, environmental monitoring, and testing of conservation methods contribute to the development of best practices in the field.

International cooperation and coordination also play a crucial role in preserving Gobekli Tepe. Recognized as a World Heritage Site by UNESCO, Gobekli Tepe benefits from international recognition and support. Collaboration between international organizations, governments, and local authorities ensures that preservation efforts align with global standards and expertise.

Capacity building and training programs for local communities and professionals are vital for the sustainable preservation of Gobekli Tepe. By empowering local communities and involving them in the preservation process, a sense of ownership and responsibility is fostered, leading to enhanced care and protection of the site.

Preservation efforts at Gobekli Tepe aim not only to protect the physical remains but also to ensure the site's continued cultural and historical significance. By preserving the integrity of the site and its artifacts, Gobekli Tepe can serve as an enduring source of knowledge and inspiration for future generations.

The preservation challenges at Gobekli Tepe are formidable, requiring constant vigilance, scientific expertise, and collaborative efforts. Through a combination of proactive measures, ongoing research, and responsible stewardship, the fragile remains of this ancient sanctuary can be safeguarded, allowing the world to marvel at the mysteries and insights they hold for centuries to come.

The preservation and conservation of Gobekli Tepe, with its rich archaeological significance, require collaborative efforts involving international teams and conservation projects. Recognizing the global importance of the site, professionals from various disciplines come together to pool their expertise, knowledge, and resources to ensure the long-term safeguarding of this remarkable archaeological treasure.

International collaboration plays a pivotal role in the conservation efforts at Gobekli Tepe. Archaeologists, conservators, scientists, and experts from different countries contribute their specialized skills and perspectives, enriching the preservation process. This collaborative approach fosters a diverse range of ideas, methodologies, and best practices, ensuring that the conservation efforts adhere to the highest standards of expertise and professionalism.

One of the primary collaborative efforts at Gobekli Tepe involves partnerships between international organizations, research institutions, and local authorities. UNESCO, in particular, has played a significant role in coordinating and supporting conservation projects at the site. Its recognition of Gobekli Tepe as a World Heritage Site has provided a platform for international cooperation, funding opportunities, and the sharing of knowledge and resources.

These collaborations extend beyond archaeological and conservation expertise. Multidisciplinary teams work together to address various challenges, such as environmental monitoring, site management, and visitor engagement. Geologists, environmental scientists, engineers, architects, and tourism experts contribute their insights to ensure the sustainable preservation and responsible management of Gobekli Tepe.

Conservation projects at Gobekli Tepe often involve long-term commitments and partnerships. They entail the establishment of field schools, training programs, and workshops, which not only enhance local expertise but also facilitate knowledge exchange between international and local professionals. Through these initiatives, conservation practices are shared, refined, and adapted to suit the specific needs and context of Gobekli Tepe.

Financial support is another crucial aspect of international collaboration. Donor countries, philanthropic organizations, and research funding bodies contribute significant resources to support conservation projects at Gobekli Tepe. This financial backing enables the implementation of preservation strategies, the employment of skilled personnel, and the acquisition of advanced technologies and equipment.

International teams also play a crucial role in research and scientific analysis at Gobekli Tepe. They bring diverse perspectives and methodologies to the study of the site, contributing to a comprehensive understanding of its archaeological, historical, and cultural significance. Through collaborative research, new insights are gained, and the global knowledge base on ancient civilizations is expanded.

Information sharing and dissemination are vital components of international collaboration at Gobekli Tepe. Conferences, symposia, and academic publications provide platforms for researchers and professionals to present their findings, exchange ideas, and engage in scholarly discourse. These knowledge-sharing endeavors contribute to a broader understanding of Gobekli Tepe's significance and inspire further research and conservation efforts.

International collaboration also extends to public engagement and education. Interactive exhibits, public lectures, and educational programs help raise awareness about Gobekli Tepe among local communities, visitors, and the wider public. Through these outreach initiatives, the global community is invited to appreciate the cultural heritage of Gobekli Tepe and recognize the importance of its preservation.

The collaborative efforts of international teams and conservation projects at Gobekli Tepe demonstrate the shared commitment to preserving our ancient heritage and understanding the complexities of our human past. By working together across borders, disciplines, and cultures, we can ensure the sustainable conservation of this extraordinary site and pass on its profound lessons to future generations.

Chapter 8: Gobekli Tepe's Influence on Ancient Civilization

The discovery of Gobekli Tepe, with its magnificent architecture and intricate carvings, has shed new light on the early development of human civilization. One fascinating aspect of this ancient site is its potential influence on neighboring societies and the diffusion of cultural ideas and practices. Tracing Gobekli Tepe's impact on surrounding communities provides valuable insights into the social, religious, and artistic exchanges that took place during the Neolithic period.

Situated in southeastern Turkey, Gobekli Tepe lies within a region that witnessed the emergence of various prehistoric cultures. The site's monumental architecture, monumental T-shaped pillars, and sophisticated carvings suggest a high degree of cultural sophistication and organization. As such, it is reasonable to speculate that Gobekli Tepe served as a significant cultural center, attracting people from neighboring communities and facilitating the exchange of ideas and practices.

One way in which Gobekli Tepe may have influenced neighboring societies is through the spread of architectural styles and construction techniques. The monumental stone architecture seen at Gobekli Tepe is unparalleled in its scale and intricacy for its time. It is possible that neighboring communities were inspired by the site's architectural achievements and incorporated similar elements into their own structures. The presence of T-shaped pillars, although not as elaborate as those at Gobekli Tepe, has been identified in other contemporary sites, suggesting a diffusion of architectural ideas.

Religious and spiritual beliefs could also have been influenced by Gobekli Tepe's practices. The symbolic depictions of animals, including lions, snakes, and birds, found on the stone pillars suggest a complex belief system and the importance of animal symbolism. Neighboring communities may have adopted similar animal representations in their own religious iconography, drawing inspiration from Gobekli Tepe's artistic expressions and mythological motifs.

Furthermore, Gobekli Tepe's ritual practices and ceremonial activities might have served as a model for neighboring communities. The site's large enclosures, likely used for communal gatherings and ceremonies, could have influenced the development of similar gathering spaces in other settlements. The social and religious significance attached to specific locations and the performance of rituals may have spread from Gobekli Tepe to nearby communities.

The diffusion of cultural practices between Gobekli Tepe and neighboring societies could have occurred through various means. Trade networks and interaction between settlements provided opportunities for the exchange of goods, ideas, and knowledge. Gobekli Tepe's central location within the region would have made it a natural hub for cultural exchanges, fostering connections between different communities.

Additionally, human migration and population movements could have played a role in disseminating Gobekli Tepe's cultural influence. As people traveled across the landscape, they likely carried with them not only physical objects but also intangible aspects of their culture, such as religious beliefs, artistic styles, and ritual practices. Gobekli Tepe's prominence and reputation as a sacred site could have attracted pilgrims and visitors from afar, contributing to the diffusion of its cultural impact.

While the precise extent of Gobekli Tepe's influence on neighboring societies is challenging to determine definitively, the similarities observed in the material culture, architectural elements, and religious symbolism of contemporary sites suggest a degree of cultural diffusion. Gobekli Tepe stands as a testament to the interconnectedness of ancient societies and their shared cultural heritage.

Studying the impact of Gobekli Tepe on neighboring communities provides valuable insights into the dynamics of cultural transmission and the spread of ideas in the ancient world. It highlights the interconnected nature of early human societies and their propensity for exchanging knowledge and practices. By tracing Gobekli Tepe's cultural diffusion, we gain a deeper understanding of the social, religious, and artistic connections that shaped the cultural landscape of the Neolithic period.

The study of Gobekli Tepe, one of the world's most remarkable archaeological sites, offers valuable insights into the social organization of prehistoric communities. This Neolithic sanctuary, with its monumental architecture and intricate carvings, provides a glimpse into the complex social structures, communal activities, and cultural practices of our ancient ancestors.

The monumental nature of the structures at Gobekli Tepe suggests the existence of a highly organized and coordinated community. The immense effort required to quarry, transport, and erect the large stone pillars points to a collective endeavor involving the labor and expertise of many individuals. This indicates a level of social cohesion, shared purpose, and collaborative decision-making within the community.

The arrangement and design of the enclosures at Gobekli Tepe also provide clues about the social dynamics of the site. The deliberate planning and alignment of the stone pillars within the circular enclosures suggest the existence of communal spaces for gathering, rituals, and social interactions. The size and layout of the enclosures imply that they may have accommodated significant numbers of people, emphasizing the importance of communal activities and shared experiences.

The presence of elaborately carved stone pillars with intricate reliefs points to a sophisticated division of labor and specialized craftsmanship within the community. It is likely that skilled artisans and craftsmen were responsible for the creation of these remarkable sculptures, reflecting a hierarchical social structure where individuals with specialized skills held prominent roles within the community.

Furthermore, the symbolism and animal depictions found on the stone pillars suggest a shared belief system and the existence of a complex religious or spiritual framework. The presence of common mythological motifs and the emphasis on animal symbolism in these carvings indicate a system of shared beliefs and a collective understanding of the world. The rituals and ceremonies performed at Gobekli Tepe would have played a central role in reinforcing social bonds, reinforcing cultural identity, and maintaining a sense of community cohesion.

Archaeological evidence, such as the presence of storage pits, indicates that Gobekli Tepe was not just a religious or ceremonial site but likely served as a hub for economic activities and resource management. The presence of storage facilities suggests a system of communal resource allocation and management, reflecting the collective effort in sustaining the community's needs.

The organization of Gobekli Tepe's architectural elements and the careful alignment of the stone pillars with celestial phenomena indicate a knowledge of astronomy and a keen awareness of the natural world. This suggests a sophisticated understanding of celestial cycles and their potential significance in marking important events or guiding communal activities.

While the precise social structure and governance system of the Gobekli Tepe community are still subjects of ongoing research and debate, the site provides compelling evidence of the existence of complex social organizations during the Neolithic period. The construction and maintenance of such a monumental sanctuary required a degree of social coordination, cooperation, and leadership.

Gobekli Tepe's significance lies not only in its architectural grandeur but also in the clues it offers about the social dynamics and organization of prehistoric communities. The site invites us to contemplate the complex social networks, shared beliefs, and communal activities that shaped the lives of our ancient ancestors. By studying the social organization of Gobekli Tepe, we gain a deeper understanding of the remarkable achievements and cultural practices of prehistoric societies.

Gobekli Tepe, with its extraordinary architecture and intricate carvings, provides valuable insights into the technological advancements of early human societies. The site's construction techniques, craftsmanship, and artistic achievements demonstrate a level of innovation and skill that challenges our understanding of the capabilities of prehistoric cultures.
One remarkable aspect of Gobekli Tepe's technological achievements is the precision and sophistication of its stone carving. The intricate reliefs on the T-shaped pillars showcase a mastery of stone working techniques. The level of detail, intricacy, and artistry in these carvings suggests advanced craftsmanship and a deep understanding of stone manipulation.
The carving and shaping of the large stone pillars at Gobekli Tepe required advanced stonecutting techniques. Stone tools such as chisels, hammers, and abrasives were likely used to carve the intricate designs into the limestone surfaces. The precise shaping of the pillars and the ability to create detailed and complex reliefs reveal the high level of skill and knowledge possessed by the ancient craftsmen.
The transport and erection of the massive stone pillars at Gobekli Tepe also required innovative techniques. The large size and weight of the pillars indicate a level of engineering expertise in quarrying, transportation, and positioning. It is believed that a combination of sledges, ramps, ropes, and levering mechanisms were employed to move and raise these enormous stones, showcasing the ingenuity and problem-solving abilities of the prehistoric builders.
Furthermore, the architecture of Gobekli Tepe demonstrates a deep understanding of structural stability and load-bearing principles. The circular enclosures with their carefully arranged stone pillars exhibit an understanding of the forces at play and the need for structural integrity. The precise placement and alignment of the pillars suggest an awareness of the need for balance and stability within the architectural design.
The construction methods employed at Gobekli Tepe also reveal early advancements in site planning and organization. The deliberate arrangement of the stone pillars and the layout of the enclosures suggest a systematic approach to construction, with careful consideration given to the overall design and spatial relationships. This indicates a level of

architectural planning and project management that was remarkable for its time.

Gobekli Tepe's contributions to early innovations extend beyond its architecture and stone carving. The site's longevity and preservation are also a testament to the ancient community's knowledge of materials and their durability. The selection of durable limestone for construction and the careful preservation of the site over thousands of years demonstrate an understanding of material properties and long-term preservation strategies.

The technological advancements evident at Gobekli Tepe challenge the traditional view of prehistoric societies as primitive and technologically limited. The site's achievements push back the timeline of human technological development, suggesting that early societies possessed a level of skill, knowledge, and innovation that was previously underestimated.

Studying the technological advancements of Gobekli Tepe not only enhances our understanding of prehistoric cultures but also prompts us to reconsider the complexities of human progress. The site serves as a testament to the ingenuity, resourcefulness, and creative problem-solving abilities of our ancient ancestors. It reminds us that innovation and technological advancement have been fundamental aspects of human development since the earliest stages of civilization.

The discovery of Gobekli Tepe, with its monumental architecture and intricate carvings, has sparked significant interest in the role it may have played in the agricultural revolution—the transition from hunter-gatherer societies to settled farming communities. While the site itself predates the advent of agriculture, its cultural and archaeological context provides valuable insights into the interplay between the rise of farming and the development of complex societies.

Gobekli Tepe is situated in a region that witnessed the transition from a nomadic, hunter-gatherer lifestyle to a more sedentary, agricultural way of life. It is believed to have been constructed during the Pre-Pottery Neolithic period, a time when humans began to experiment with plant cultivation and domestication of animals. The presence of large-scale, permanent stone structures at Gobekli Tepe suggests that settled communities were already emerging, supported by a stable food supply.

One theory posits that Gobekli Tepe served as a ceremonial or ritual center for these early agricultural communities. The site's complex architecture and elaborately carved pillars may have been associated with the religious and spiritual practices that accompanied the transition to farming. The social cohesion and shared beliefs fostered at Gobekli Tepe may have played a crucial role in the successful adoption and spread of agricultural practices in the region.

The carvings at Gobekli Tepe also provide intriguing hints about the relationship between humans and the natural environment during this pivotal period. Depictions of animals, such as wild boars, snakes, and birds, suggest a deep connection between humans and the local fauna. It is possible that these carvings reflect the increasing importance of animal domestication and the recognition of the symbiotic relationship between humans and animals in the agricultural context.

Furthermore, the positioning of Gobekli Tepe within a landscape rich in natural resources is indicative of the significance of the surrounding environment in the development of early farming communities. The site is located near fertile soils, freshwater sources, and areas suitable for cultivation. This suggests that the availability of resources and the favorable environmental conditions played a vital role in attracting and sustaining settled communities engaged in agricultural practices.

The transition from a nomadic lifestyle to settled agriculture was a momentous shift in human history, resulting in profound social, economic, and cultural changes. The establishment of permanent settlements allowed for more intensive food production, surplus storage, and the development of specialized labor roles. This shift, in turn, led to the emergence of complex social structures, increased population densities, and the eventual rise of civilizations.

Gobekli Tepe's importance lies not only in its chronology but also in its cultural and geographical context. It serves as a window into the dynamic processes that contributed to the agricultural revolution. The site's construction and religious significance may have fostered the social cohesion necessary for communities to transition from a mobile lifestyle to settled farming, ultimately shaping the course of human history.

While the precise connection between Gobekli Tepe and the rise of agriculture is still a subject of ongoing research, the site's cultural and archaeological context offers compelling evidence of the intertwined nature of early farming and the development of complex societies. The significance of Gobekli Tepe lies not only in its architectural grandeur but also in its potential role as a catalyst for social and agricultural change.

The study of Gobekli Tepe provides a unique opportunity to unravel the complexities of the agricultural revolution, offering valuable insights into the processes that shaped human societies. It highlights the interplay between technological advancements, social organization, environmental factors, and cultural practices in the transformative shift from a hunter-gatherer lifestyle to settled agriculture. By examining Gobekli Tepe's connection to the rise of farming, we deepen our understanding of the fundamental changes that set the stage for the development of civilization as we know it.

The ancient site of Gobekli Tepe, with its intricate carvings and remarkable iconography, not only offers insights into the beliefs and practices of its Neolithic builders but also provides evidence of the lasting impact it had on later cultures and artistic expressions. The artistic motifs and symbolism found at Gobekli Tepe can be traced through the centuries, influencing the art, iconography, and religious beliefs of subsequent civilizations.

One of the notable features of Gobekli Tepe's iconography is its depiction of animals. The stone pillars bear carvings of various animal species, including lions, snakes, birds, and other creatures. These representations highlight the significance of animals in the belief systems and cultural expressions of the Neolithic people. The reverence for animal symbolism, as evidenced at Gobekli Tepe, became a recurring theme in the art and religious practices of many ancient cultures.

The animal motifs found at Gobekli Tepe seem to have resonated deeply with later civilizations, influencing their artistic traditions and religious iconography. For instance, the depiction of lions at Gobekli Tepe can be linked to the subsequent fascination with lion symbolism in ancient Mesopotamian and Egyptian art. Lions became prominent symbols of power, strength, and royalty in these civilizations, with images of lions adorning thrones, palace walls, and temple facades.

Similarly, the representation of serpents at Gobekli Tepe holds significance in the iconography of numerous cultures throughout history. The serpent's association with wisdom, fertility, and regeneration can be traced back to Gobekli Tepe and is evident in the mythologies and religious beliefs of diverse civilizations, including ancient Mesopotamia, Egypt, Greece, and Mesoamerica. The influence of Gobekli Tepe's serpent iconography can be seen in the serpent motifs of temples, sculptures, and pottery of these civilizations.

Birds, another common motif at Gobekli Tepe, also left their mark on subsequent artistic expressions. The symbolic importance of birds, often representing freedom, spirituality, and divine communication, can be observed in the art and mythology of various cultures, including ancient Egyptian, Greek, and Native American civilizations. The bird imagery found at Gobekli Tepe likely played a role in shaping these later representations.

Furthermore, Gobekli Tepe's emphasis on the interplay between human and animal forms can be seen as a precursor to the concept of therianthropy—the blending of human and animal characteristics—in later mythologies and art. The fusion of human and animal elements in religious and mythological figures became a prevalent theme in ancient civilizations such as Egypt, Greece, and the Near East. Gobekli Tepe's early exploration of these motifs contributed to the development and evolution of such artistic expressions.

The enduring influence of Gobekli Tepe's artistic expressions can also be seen in the realm of religious beliefs. The symbolism and rituals associated with animal worship, celestial alignments, and the interplay between the human and divine realms at Gobekli Tepe left a lasting imprint on subsequent religious systems. The concepts and practices originating at Gobekli Tepe resonated with later civilizations, shaping their religious beliefs, ceremonies, and sacred spaces.

The impact of Gobekli Tepe's artistic expressions extends beyond specific civilizations and regions. As ancient cultures interacted and exchanged ideas through trade, migration, and cultural diffusion, the artistic motifs and religious concepts of Gobekli Tepe traveled across vast distances, permeating the artistic and religious landscapes of different societies.

Gobekli Tepe stands as a testament to the enduring power of artistic expressions and their ability to transcend time and space. The carvings and iconography found at the site influenced the art, religious beliefs, and cultural practices of subsequent civilizations, leaving an indelible mark on the artistic and spiritual legacies of humanity. By studying the influence of Gobekli Tepe's iconography, we gain a deeper appreciation for the interconnectedness of ancient cultures and the enduring nature of artistic inspiration.

Chapter 9: Theories on the Purpose and Function of Gobekli Tepe

The practice of ancestor worship, the veneration and reverence of deceased ancestors, is a phenomenon that has persisted across many cultures throughout human history. It is a belief system rooted in the idea of a continued spiritual connection between the living and the deceased, with rituals and ceremonies aimed at honoring and maintaining the relationship with past generations. The study of burial practices and commemorative rituals at sites like Gobekli Tepe provides valuable insights into the theories surrounding ancestor worship in ancient societies.

The burial practices observed at Gobekli Tepe offer intriguing clues about the role of ancestor worship in Neolithic communities. The presence of burial pits and graves within the vicinity of the site suggests that Gobekli Tepe may have served as a sacred space for funeral rites and the commemoration of ancestors. The deliberate positioning of human remains within the vicinity of the stone structures indicates a deep spiritual connection to the site and its rituals.

One theory posits that Gobekli Tepe's monumental architecture, with its intricately carved pillars and symbolic imagery, served as a means of honoring and memorializing ancestors. The rich iconography found on the stone pillars, including anthropomorphic figures and animal depictions, may have represented specific individuals or ancestral spirits. The rituals and ceremonies performed at Gobekli Tepe would have played a central role in maintaining the spiritual bond between the living and their ancestors.

Another theory suggests that Gobekli Tepe served as a communal gathering place for ancestral worship and remembrance. The circular enclosures and carefully arranged stone pillars created a sacred space conducive to collective ceremonies and rituals. These gatherings would have allowed the community to come together, share stories and memories, and pay homage to their ancestors through prayers, offerings, and commemorative acts.

The practice of ancestor worship is often intertwined with the belief in an afterlife or a continued existence of the spirit beyond death. The construction of monumental structures, such as those found at Gobekli Tepe, may have been motivated by the desire to create a connection between the earthly realm and the realm of the ancestors. The impressive architecture and elaborate carvings were not only a testament to the memory of the deceased but also a means of ensuring their spiritual presence and protection.

Furthermore, the placement of human remains in close proximity to the stone structures at Gobekli Tepe suggests that the site was perceived as a gateway to the spiritual realm. The alignment of the enclosures with celestial events, such as solstices or equinoxes, may have been seen as moments of heightened spiritual connection, reinforcing the belief in the presence and influence of ancestral spirits.

The practice of ancestor worship, as reflected in the burial and commemorative rituals at Gobekli Tepe, highlights the importance of familial and communal bonds in early human societies. Ancestor worship provided a sense of continuity, identity, and guidance to communities, as they sought to maintain a connection with their past and draw upon the wisdom and protection of their ancestors.

The theories surrounding ancestor worship at Gobekli Tepe offer valuable insights into the spiritual beliefs and cultural practices of ancient societies. The site serves as a testament to the enduring human desire to honor and remember our forebears, as well as the role of sacred spaces in facilitating these rituals. By studying the burial and commemorative theories associated with Gobekli Tepe, we gain a deeper understanding of the complex and profound ways in which ancient societies engaged with their ancestors, shaping their worldview, social structures, and religious practices.

The ancient site of Gobekli Tepe, with its remarkable stone pillars and intricate carvings, has sparked intriguing theories about its function as an astronomical observatory. The alignment of the stone structures with celestial events and the incorporation of astronomical symbolism suggest that Gobekli Tepe played a significant role in observing and understanding the movements of the celestial bodies.

One compelling aspect of Gobekli Tepe's potential astronomical function is its orientation and alignment with key celestial events. Several of the stone pillars at the site are positioned in a way that aligns with important astronomical phenomena, such as the solstices and equinoxes. These alignments may have allowed the ancient observers to track the changing seasons, mark significant celestial events, and develop a calendar system based on celestial cycles.

The incorporation of astronomical symbolism in the carvings and reliefs at Gobekli Tepe further supports the notion of its role as an observatory. Depictions of celestial bodies, such as the sun, moon, and stars, are intricately carved into the stone pillars, suggesting a deep understanding and fascination with the cosmos. These representations may have served as visual aids for celestial observations and as a means of imparting astronomical knowledge to future generations.

Furthermore, the circular enclosures at Gobekli Tepe, with their central pillars and surrounding stone walls, have been likened to celestial maps or observatories. The circular shape, reminiscent of celestial bodies, may have symbolized the connection between the earthly and celestial realms. The arrangement of the pillars within the enclosures may have corresponded to specific celestial positions or served as reference points for celestial observations.

The potential astronomical function of Gobekli Tepe raises intriguing questions about the knowledge and capabilities of its ancient builders. The precise alignment of the stone structures with celestial events would have required a deep understanding of astronomy, geometry, and advanced observational techniques. It suggests a level of scientific sophistication that challenges our conventional understanding of prehistoric societies.

The astronomical observations conducted at Gobekli Tepe may have served multiple purposes. They could have facilitated the timing of agricultural activities, such as sowing and harvesting, by tracking the seasonal changes and celestial markers. The knowledge gained from these observations could have contributed to the development of a more accurate calendar system and aided in predicting celestial events.

Moreover, the observation of celestial phenomena at Gobekli Tepe may have had cultural, religious, and symbolic significance. The alignment of the stone structures with celestial events could have been linked to cosmological beliefs and the spiritual connection between the earthly and celestial realms. The understanding and interpretation of celestial patterns may have been intertwined with the religious and mythological narratives of the ancient community.

While the exact purpose of Gobekli Tepe as an astronomical observatory remains speculative, the evidence suggests that it played a vital role in the observation and interpretation of celestial phenomena. The alignment of the stone structures, the incorporation of astronomical symbolism, and the potential cultural and agricultural implications all point to a sophisticated understanding of the cosmos by the ancient builders of Gobekli Tepe.

The investigation into Gobekli Tepe as an ancient observatory not only deepens our understanding of prehistoric astronomy but also highlights the intellectual and scientific achievements of early human societies. It challenges our perception of ancient cultures as primitive and emphasizes their inherent curiosity, intellectual prowess, and desire to comprehend the mysteries of the universe. Gobekli Tepe stands as a testament to the enduring human quest for knowledge and the significance of astronomical observations in shaping our understanding of the cosmos.

Gobekli Tepe, with its awe-inspiring structures and ancient mysteries, has become a pilgrimage destination for those seeking a deeper connection to the past and a spiritual journey to the roots of human civilization. The site's profound historical significance and enigmatic allure have captured the imagination of many, drawing pilgrims from all corners of the globe.

The pilgrimage to Gobekli Tepe is not just a physical journey but also a spiritual quest. It is an opportunity to explore the sacredness of the site and its profound impact on our understanding of human history. As pilgrims embark on this journey, they are guided by a sense of reverence, curiosity, and a longing to connect with the ancient wisdom that Gobekli Tepe holds.

The pilgrimage begins long before reaching the physical site. It starts with the study and contemplation of Gobekli Tepe's significance, its archaeological discoveries, and the theories surrounding its purpose. Pilgrims immerse themselves in the stories and narratives that have emerged from this ancient sanctuary, allowing their minds to wander through the annals of time.

Upon arrival at Gobekli Tepe, pilgrims are greeted by the monumental stone structures that have stood the test of time. The sheer magnitude and intricate carvings of the site evoke a sense of wonder and reverence. The atmosphere is charged with a palpable energy, as if the spirits of the past linger in the air, waiting to be acknowledged and embraced.

As pilgrims navigate the site, they follow in the footsteps of the Neolithic builders, treading on the same sacred ground that witnessed ancient rituals and ceremonies. The stone pillars, with their enigmatic carvings, offer glimpses into the spiritual and cultural practices of our ancestors. Each step taken is an act of communion with the past, a way to forge a connection with the human story that unfolded at Gobekli Tepe.

Pilgrims engage in contemplation and reflection, seeking to unravel the mysteries and symbolism embedded in the site's architecture. They ponder the purpose behind the carefully arranged stone pillars, the significance of the celestial alignments, and the messages conveyed through the intricate carvings. In these moments of introspection, pilgrims connect with the profound wisdom of the ancient world, finding echoes of their own spiritual journeys.

The pilgrimage to Gobekli Tepe is not only a personal quest but also a communal experience. Pilgrims come together, sharing their knowledge, insights, and interpretations of the site. Conversations flow, and bonds are formed as individuals from diverse backgrounds unite in their quest for knowledge and understanding. The collective energy of the pilgrimage enhances the spiritual resonance of the site, creating an atmosphere of shared reverence and mutual exploration.

Beyond the physical structures, the surrounding landscape offers pilgrims an opportunity to connect with nature and its intrinsic spiritual essence. The rolling hills, the whispering wind, and the sense of timelessness envelop the pilgrims, allowing them to attune to the rhythm of the earth and the interconnectedness of all living beings. This communion with nature adds another layer of significance to the pilgrimage, deepening the spiritual experience and fostering a sense of harmony and unity with the natural world.

The pilgrimage to Gobekli Tepe is not confined to a single visit. Its impact lingers long after the physical journey is complete. Pilgrims carry the wisdom and insights gained from the site back into their lives, incorporating them into their personal spiritual practices, creative endeavors, and scholarly pursuits. The experience at Gobekli Tepe becomes a source of inspiration, fueling a lifelong exploration of the human story and the mysteries that lie beyond.

In the pilgrimage to Gobekli Tepe, pilgrims embark on a sacred journey that transcends time and space. It is an opportunity to commune with the ancient world, to reconnect with our roots, and to reflect on the profound journey of human civilization. Gobekli Tepe stands as a testament to the enduring quest for meaning and the eternal human yearning for connection.

Gobekli Tepe, with its remarkable stone structures and intricate carvings, has sparked various interpretations as a ritualistic center and a gathering place for ancient communities. The site's unique architecture and the presence of ceremonial features suggest that Gobekli Tepe played a pivotal role in hosting religious and communal gatherings, serving as a focal point for rituals, ceremonies, and social interactions.

One interpretation posits that Gobekli Tepe functioned as a central gathering place for the surrounding communities. The site's circular enclosures, delineated by stone walls and housing clusters of elaborately carved pillars, provided designated spaces for communal activities. These enclosures could have served as meeting areas where people congregated for various purposes, including religious rites, social events, and collective decision-making.

The placement and arrangement of the stone pillars at Gobekli Tepe suggest a deliberate organization and purpose. The central positioning of larger pillars within the enclosures, often adorned with intricate carvings and anthropomorphic figures, may have symbolized the presence of significant individuals or spiritual entities. These pillars would have served as focal points for rituals and ceremonies, drawing people together in reverence and collective engagement.

The communal nature of Gobekli Tepe's architecture is further supported by the presence of communal structures, such as benches or raised platforms, within the enclosures. These features may have provided spaces for seating, performances, or communal feasting, facilitating social interactions and fostering a sense of community cohesion. The benches could have served as spaces for communal meals, gatherings, or storytelling sessions, fostering a sense of shared identity and reinforcing social bonds.

The symbolism embedded in the stone carvings at Gobekli Tepe also points to its role as a ritualistic center. The depictions of animals, anthropomorphic figures, and abstract symbols suggest a rich tapestry of religious and symbolic meanings. These carvings may have served as visual representations of cosmological beliefs, ancestral spirits, or deities, invoking a sense of the sacred and creating a spiritual atmosphere within the enclosures.

The religious and ritualistic significance of Gobekli Tepe is further supported by the presence of offering pits and the deliberate placement of human remains within the site. These archaeological findings suggest that Gobekli Tepe was a site of ritual practices and commemoration of the deceased. The offerings and burial practices conducted at the site signify a deep connection to the spiritual realm and the belief in the continuation of life beyond death.

The seasonal nature of the site's use is also an important aspect of its interpretation as a gathering place. The alignment of the stone structures with celestial events, such as solstices and equinoxes, indicates a possible connection to agricultural and astronomical cycles. It is plausible that Gobekli Tepe served as a site for seasonal rituals and celebrations, marking the transitions of the agricultural calendar and honoring the natural forces that sustained the community.

The interpretation of Gobekli Tepe as a ritualistic center and gathering place highlights the vital role of community cohesion, religious practices, and social interactions in the lives of ancient societies. The site provided a physical and symbolic space for communal activities, fostering a sense of shared identity, spiritual connection, and collective memory. It served as a hub for social, cultural, and religious exchanges, shaping the worldview and social fabric of the communities that utilized it.

The study of Gobekli Tepe's architecture, carvings, and archaeological findings continues to shed light on its interpretation as a ritualistic center and gathering place. As researchers uncover more evidence and refine our understanding of the site, the significance of Gobekli Tepe as a nexus of communal and spiritual life becomes increasingly apparent. It stands as a testament to the importance of ritual practices, social cohesion, and the quest for meaning in the human experience.

Gobekli Tepe, with its enigmatic stone structures and intricate carvings, has given rise to speculations about its role as a repository of ancient wisdom and sacred knowledge. The site's remarkable architecture and the symbolism embedded within its pillars have fueled theories that Gobekli Tepe served as a custodian of ancient wisdom, preserving and transmitting knowledge across generations.

One speculation suggests that Gobekli Tepe was a center for esoteric knowledge, where spiritual teachings, cosmological beliefs, and sacred rituals were passed down through oral tradition. The carvings and reliefs found on the stone pillars may have served as visual aids in the transmission of this knowledge, encapsulating the wisdom of the ancients and ensuring its preservation over time.

The intricate symbolism present in the carvings at Gobekli Tepe has led some to believe that the site held deep insights into the mysteries of the universe, including cosmology, astronomy, and the interplay between the spiritual and natural realms. The depictions of celestial bodies, constellations, and geometric patterns suggest a sophisticated understanding of the cosmos, conveying profound knowledge about the order and interconnectedness of the universe.

Furthermore, the alignment of Gobekli Tepe's stone structures with celestial events, such as solstices and equinoxes, adds to the speculation that the site was a repository of astronomical knowledge. It is possible that Gobekli Tepe served as an observatory, enabling ancient observers to track celestial movements, study celestial cycles, and make connections between celestial events and earthly phenomena.

The idea of Gobekli Tepe as a repository of sacred knowledge is also tied to the concept of initiation rites and secret societies. It is speculated that the site may have been a place where select individuals underwent initiation rituals, gaining access to esoteric knowledge and becoming custodians of ancient wisdom. The knowledge imparted at Gobekli Tepe could have included spiritual teachings, healing practices, and insights into the nature of the human existence.

Additionally, the presence of burial pits and the deliberate placement of human remains within the site suggest a connection to ancestral wisdom and the belief in a continued relationship between the living and the deceased. It is possible that Gobekli Tepe served as a sacred space where ancestral spirits were honored, and communication with the spiritual realm was sought. The rituals conducted at the site may have been a means of connecting with the wisdom and guidance of the ancestors.

While these speculations about Gobekli Tepe as a repository of ancient wisdom are intriguing, they remain subject to ongoing research and interpretation. The study of the site's carvings, alignments, and archaeological context continues to shed light on its possible functions and significance. As new discoveries are made and our understanding deepens, the role of Gobekli Tepe as a custodian of sacred knowledge may become clearer.

Regardless of the exact nature of Gobekli Tepe's function as a repository of ancient wisdom, the site stands as a testament to the intellectual and spiritual achievements of our ancient ancestors. It represents a tangible link to the past, inviting us to contemplate the depth of human knowledge and the timeless quest for understanding. Gobekli Tepe serves as a reminder that the pursuit of wisdom and the reverence for ancient knowledge have been integral to the human experience throughout history.

Chapter 10: Gobekli Tepe's Significance in Archaeology and History

Gobekli Tepe, with its astonishing discoveries and enigmatic nature, has had a transformative impact on our understanding of prehistoric societies and has forced a paradigm shift in the field of archaeology. The site's exceptional age, intricate architecture, and intricate carvings have challenged long-held assumptions and shed new light on the complexity and sophistication of early human civilizations.

One of the most significant impacts of Gobekli Tepe has been its dating, which pushes back the timeline of human civilization by thousands of years. Previously, the prevailing belief was that complex social and architectural structures emerged after the advent of agriculture. However, Gobekli Tepe, predating the development of agriculture, demonstrates that sophisticated monumental construction and communal gathering places were already present in the pre-agricultural era. This discovery challenges traditional narratives and calls for a reevaluation of the timeline and factors that led to the rise of complex societies.

Furthermore, the elaborate and precise stone carvings found at Gobekli Tepe defy earlier assumptions about the capabilities and artistic expressions of early humans. The intricate depictions of animals, abstract symbols, and anthropomorphic figures exhibit a level of skill and sophistication that was previously believed to have developed much later in human history. Gobekli Tepe forces us to reconsider the intellectual and artistic capabilities of prehistoric societies, expanding our understanding of human creativity and symbolic expression.

Another significant impact of Gobekli Tepe is its implications for social organization and communal dynamics in prehistoric communities. The monumental scale and elaborate design of the site suggest a level of cooperation, social cohesion, and shared purpose that challenges previous notions of early human societies as primarily nomadic or lacking complex social structures. Gobekli Tepe presents evidence for organized labor, long-term planning, and communal efforts that indicate a more complex social organization than previously believed.

Moreover, Gobekli Tepe has stimulated new avenues of research and exploration in fields such as archaeoastronomy, symbolism, and ritual studies. The precise alignments of the stone structures with celestial events and the symbolism embedded in the carvings hint at the importance of cosmology, astronomy, and ritualistic practices in the lives of the site's builders. This has opened up new avenues for understanding the spiritual, cultural, and intellectual lives of prehistoric communities and has led to interdisciplinary collaborations to unravel the mysteries of Gobekli Tepe.

The impact of Gobekli Tepe extends beyond the realm of academia. It has captured the public imagination and sparked curiosity about our shared human origins. The site's mysterious allure and its ability to challenge preconceived notions have generated widespread interest and have prompted public engagement with prehistoric studies. Gobekli Tepe serves as a potent reminder that our understanding of the past is constantly evolving and that there is much more to discover about the richness and complexity of early human civilizations.

In summary, Gobekli Tepe has revolutionized our understanding of prehistoric societies and has triggered a paradigm shift in archaeological research. Its dating, architecture, artwork, and implications for social organization have upended previous assumptions and called for a reevaluation of our knowledge of early human history. Gobekli Tepe's impact reaches beyond the confines of academia, inspiring a broader fascination with our ancient origins and a deeper appreciation for the intellectual and cultural achievements of our early ancestors. It stands as a testament to the ongoing quest to unravel the mysteries of our past and provides a gateway to a more nuanced understanding of the complexities of human civilization.

Gobekli Tepe, with its remarkable discoveries and unprecedented antiquity, has had a profound influence on our understanding of human history. The site's existence challenges the prevailing chronological framework and forces a reassessment of the trajectory of human development. By pushing back the timeline of complex societies and monumental architecture, Gobekli Tepe has transformed our perception of prehistoric civilizations and our place within the tapestry of human history.

The most significant impact of Gobekli Tepe lies in its dating, which places its construction at a time when conventional wisdom held that humans were predominantly nomadic hunter-gatherers. The site's age, dating back over 12,000 years, predates the emergence of agriculture and challenges the long-held assumption that settled agricultural communities were a prerequisite for the construction of monumental structures. Gobekli Tepe's existence compels us to reconsider the traditional narrative of human progress and raises fundamental questions about the drivers and complexities of social and cultural development.

The discovery of Gobekli Tepe also calls into question the traditional view of the Neolithic period as a time of gradual progression from simple to complex societies. The site's sophistication and intricacy suggest that there were sudden leaps in human cultural and social achievements, challenging the notion of linear cultural evolution. It implies that human societies possessed a level of knowledge, organizational skills, and artistic expression that was previously underestimated or unrecognized. Gobekli Tepe presents an alternative narrative of human history, one characterized by bursts of innovation and cultural complexity that occurred earlier than previously thought.

Gobekli Tepe's influence extends beyond its chronological revisions. The site provides valuable insights into the religious and spiritual beliefs of our early ancestors. The elaborate stone carvings depict animals, mythical creatures, and abstract symbols, hinting at a rich mythological and cosmological worldview. The presence of communal gathering spaces, alignments with celestial events, and evidence of ritual practices suggest the importance of spiritual and ceremonial activities in the lives of the site's builders. Gobekli Tepe offers a glimpse into the profound spiritual and symbolic dimensions of prehistoric societies, challenging the notion that such cultural expressions emerged only in later, more complex civilizations.

The impact of Gobekli Tepe reverberates throughout the fields of archaeology, anthropology, and history. Scholars and researchers are engaged in ongoing investigations, seeking to decipher the meaning of the site's intricate carvings, unravel the social dynamics of its builders, and explore its connections to other contemporary and subsequent cultures. The interdisciplinary nature of Gobekli Tepe studies highlights the site's significance in reshaping our understanding of human history and underscores the need for collaboration across disciplines to unlock its secrets.

Moreover, Gobekli Tepe's influence extends to popular culture, captivating the imagination of people worldwide. The site's enigmatic nature, ancient origins, and connection to our shared human past have captured the public's fascination, leading to increased interest in archaeology and a deeper appreciation for the mysteries of our ancient origins. Gobekli Tepe serves as a potent reminder that human history is a tapestry woven with countless threads, and our understanding of it is a constant work in progress.

In summary, Gobekli Tepe has revolutionized our understanding of human history by challenging established chronologies and introducing a more nuanced perspective on the development of complex societies. Its dating, intricate carvings, and cultural implications have reshaped our understanding of prehistoric civilizations, prompting a reevaluation of human achievements and cultural complexity in earlier periods. Gobekli Tepe's impact extends far beyond academia, sparking curiosity and igniting a renewed appreciation for the depth and richness of our shared human heritage. It stands as a testament to the ongoing quest for knowledge and the transformative power of archaeological discoveries.

Gobekli Tepe, with its awe-inspiring structures and remarkable antiquity, has compelled scholars to reevaluate the timeline of societal development and reconsider the patterns of cultural evolution. The site's existence challenges traditional notions of human progress, prompting a reimagining of the stages and pace at which societies have evolved throughout history.

Prior to the discovery of Gobekli Tepe, the prevailing view held that the development of complex societies and monumental architecture was closely tied to the advent of agriculture. However, the site's extraordinary age, dating back over 12,000 years, predates the emergence of agriculture by several millennia. This revelation forces a reconsideration of the relationship between agricultural practices and the rise of complex societies. It suggests that the origins of social complexity and architectural sophistication are more nuanced and multifaceted than previously believed.

Gobekli Tepe challenges the notion that settled agriculture was the primary catalyst for the development of complex societies. Instead, it suggests that social and cultural complexity can emerge in the absence of agriculture, pushing back the timeline of human societal evolution. The construction of monumental structures at Gobekli Tepe, without the reliance on agriculture, indicates that factors beyond food production played a significant role in societal development. This challenges the long-held assumption that agriculture was the singular driving force behind the rise of civilization.

The discovery of Gobekli Tepe also highlights the potential for sudden and dramatic shifts in human cultural and social development. The site's elaborate architecture and intricate stone carvings imply a level of craftsmanship, organization, and communal effort that was previously thought to have emerged gradually over time. Gobekli Tepe suggests that bursts of innovation and cultural complexity can occur unexpectedly, challenging linear models of cultural evolution.

Furthermore, the significance of Gobekli Tepe extends beyond its implications for the timeline of societal development. It offers valuable insights into the cultural, religious, and symbolic practices of prehistoric societies. The intricate carvings and symbolism present at the site suggest a complex belief system and a rich mythological framework. Gobekli Tepe challenges the notion that such sophisticated cultural expressions emerged only in later, more advanced civilizations, indicating that the roots of complex cultural systems may extend much further back in time.

The reimagining of the timeline of societal development prompted by Gobekli Tepe has profound implications for our understanding of human history and cultural evolution. It emphasizes the need for a more nuanced and flexible approach to studying societal development, one that recognizes the multifaceted factors that contribute to the rise of complex societies. Gobekli Tepe reminds us that human cultural and social evolution is a dynamic and intricate process influenced by various interconnected factors, including environmental, social, technological, and ideological dimensions.

The impact of Gobekli Tepe extends beyond the realm of academic discourse. It has captured the imagination of people worldwide, sparking a renewed fascination with the origins of human civilization and the complexities of cultural evolution. The site serves as a potent reminder that our understanding of the past is continuously evolving, and that there are still countless mysteries waiting to be unraveled.

In summary, Gobekli Tepe's existence challenges conventional notions of societal development and calls for a reimagining of the timeline and patterns of cultural evolution. Its remarkable age and sophisticated architecture indicate that social complexity and monumental construction can precede the advent of agriculture. Gobekli Tepe prompts us to reconsider the factors driving societal development and highlights the potential for sudden bursts of cultural innovation. It invites us to embrace a more flexible and multidimensional understanding of cultural evolution, enriching our appreciation for the diversity and complexity of human history.

Gobekli Tepe, with its intricate carvings and awe-inspiring architecture, has made significant contributions to our understanding of ancient beliefs, symbolism, and ideology. The site's elaborate stone pillars, adorned with detailed depictions of animals, abstract symbols, and anthropomorphic figures, provide valuable insights into the rich tapestry of ancient belief systems.

The symbolism embedded in the carvings at Gobekli Tepe offers a window into the spiritual and ideological perspectives of our ancient ancestors. The depictions of animals, such as lions, bulls, snakes, and birds, suggest a reverence for the natural world and a belief in its spiritual significance. These animal representations may have symbolized power, fertility, or specific mythological beings. The repetition of certain motifs across different pillars hints at the existence of shared symbolic meanings and the presence of a cohesive belief system among the site's builders.

The abstract symbols found at Gobekli Tepe present a unique challenge for interpretation. Geometric patterns, spirals, and other enigmatic symbols are scattered throughout the site, inviting speculation about their meaning and purpose. Some researchers propose that these symbols could represent celestial bodies, cosmic forces, or cosmological concepts. Others suggest they may have served as markers of clan or tribal identities, encoding information about social structure and cultural affiliation. The precise meaning of these symbols remains elusive, but their presence underscores the importance of abstract symbolism in ancient belief systems.

The anthropomorphic figures depicted at Gobekli Tepe introduce another layer of complexity to our understanding of ancient ideology. These humanoid representations, often shown with arms, hands, and elaborate clothing or jewelry, raise questions about the role of human-like beings in the belief systems of the time. They may represent deities, ancestors, or mythological figures, embodying spiritual or mythic narratives significant to the community. The presence of these anthropomorphic figures suggests a belief in supernatural beings with human-like qualities and the potential for divine intervention in human affairs.

One of the most intriguing aspects of Gobekli Tepe's symbolism is its potential connection to cosmological beliefs. The alignments of the site's stone structures with celestial events, such as solstices and equinoxes, suggest an understanding of astronomical phenomena and their relationship to religious or spiritual practices. It is plausible that Gobekli Tepe served as an observatory, allowing ancient observers to track celestial movements, mark important astronomical events, and align their rituals and ceremonies with the celestial calendar. The integration of celestial symbolism into the site's carvings further emphasizes the significance of cosmological beliefs in the worldview of the builders.

While the exact meaning of the symbolism at Gobekli Tepe may never be fully deciphered, its presence underscores the profound spiritual and ideological dimensions of ancient cultures. The site provides tangible evidence of the human quest to comprehend the mysteries of the world and establish a connection with the divine. Gobekli Tepe challenges the notion that complex belief systems emerged only in later, more advanced civilizations, revealing the depth and sophistication of ancient spiritual and ideological traditions.

The study of Gobekli Tepe's symbolism has far-reaching implications for our understanding of ancient beliefs and the evolution of human spirituality. It highlights the universal human impulse to find meaning in the world and establish a connection with the sacred. Gobekli Tepe stands as a testament to the enduring power of symbolism and ideology in shaping human thought, providing invaluable insights into the spiritual and intellectual lives of our ancient ancestors. Its symbolism invites us to reflect on our own symbolic systems, encouraging a deeper appreciation for the intricate tapestry of human belief across time and cultures.

Gobekli Tepe, with its profound archaeological significance and unparalleled antiquity, has left a lasting legacy in the field of archaeology and continues to be a focal point of research and exploration. The site's discovery has revolutionized our understanding of prehistoric civilizations and has opened up new avenues for studying the complexities of human history. Gobekli Tepe's enduring importance in archaeological research can be seen through its contributions to various aspects of the field.

First and foremost, Gobekli Tepe has transformed our knowledge of early human civilization by pushing back the timeline of complex societies. The site's age, dating back over 12,000 years, predates the advent of agriculture and challenges long-held assumptions about the prerequisites for societal development. Gobekli Tepe's existence indicates that sophisticated social and architectural structures emerged earlier than previously thought, prompting a reevaluation of the factors that contributed to the rise of civilization.

The architectural marvels and intricate carvings found at Gobekli Tepe have provided valuable insights into the artistic and technical capabilities of our ancient ancestors. The site's monumental stone pillars and elaborate symbolism showcase the sophisticated craftsmanship and engineering skills of prehistoric communities. Gobekli Tepe has broadened our understanding of early human artistic expression and has led to a reevaluation of the creative and intellectual capacities of ancient societies.

Moreover, Gobekli Tepe has sparked new avenues of research and interdisciplinary collaborations. Its significance extends beyond traditional archaeological approaches, attracting scholars from various fields, such as anthropology, art history, astronomy, and mythology. The complexity of the site's carvings, alignments with celestial events, and intricate symbolism have prompted multidisciplinary investigations to unravel its mysteries. These collaborations have resulted in a more holistic and comprehensive understanding of Gobekli Tepe and its broader cultural context.

The site's enduring importance is also evident in its impact on our understanding of social and religious practices in prehistoric communities. Gobekli Tepe's architecture and symbolism suggest the existence of complex belief systems and communal rituals, challenging earlier notions of prehistoric societies as primarily nomadic or lacking in social complexity. The site has shed light on the spiritual and symbolic dimensions of early human culture, providing valuable insights into the worldview and social dynamics of our ancient ancestors.

Gobekli Tepe's legacy extends beyond academia and has captured the imagination of the public. The site's enigmatic nature, ancient origins, and profound cultural significance have garnered widespread interest and public engagement. Gobekli Tepe serves as a powerful reminder of the richness and complexity of our shared human heritage, inspiring curiosity and a deeper appreciation for the mysteries of the past.

In summary, Gobekli Tepe's enduring importance in archaeological research is evident in its transformative impact on our understanding of early human civilization, its contributions to the study of art and engineering in prehistoric societies, and its role in fostering interdisciplinary collaborations. The site's revelations have challenged long-held assumptions, broadened our knowledge of ancient beliefs and practices, and sparked public interest in our collective human history. Gobekli Tepe stands as a testament to the enduring significance of archaeological discoveries, reminding us of the profound insights they can provide into the complexities of our shared human past.

BOOK 3

THE FORGOTTEN GIANTS JOURNEY TO THE GGANTIJA TEMPLES OF MALTA

BY A.J. KINGSTON

Chapter 1: Rediscovering the Giants of Malta

The temples of Ggantija, nestled on the picturesque Maltese island of Gozo, stand as silent witnesses to a forgotten era of human history. These magnificent megalithic structures, shrouded in mystery and steeped in antiquity, have long captured the imagination of explorers, scholars, and historians alike. The lost legacy of Ggantija beckons us to unravel its secrets and uncover the profound significance of these ancient temples.

The origins of the temples of Ggantija are lost in the mists of time. Built during the Neolithic period, a time when agriculture was taking root and sedentary communities were emerging, the temples represent an astonishing feat of construction. The sheer scale and complexity of the architecture defy the limitations of the era, leaving us awestruck by the ingenuity and skill of the temple builders.

The temples consist of two main structures, known as Ggantija South and Ggantija North, both constructed with immense limestone blocks. The stones, some weighing over fifty tons, were meticulously carved, transported, and fitted together without the aid of modern tools or machinery. The precision of the craftsmanship and the mastery of engineering techniques leave no doubt that the builders possessed a level of knowledge and skill that surpasses the expectations of their time.

The purpose and function of the Ggantija temples have long been subjects of speculation and debate. The absence of written records from the Neolithic period leaves us with little direct insight into the beliefs and rituals of the temple builders. However, the sheer scale and grandeur of the temples suggest that they held great religious and symbolic significance. The colossal size of the stones used in their construction, coupled with intricate carvings and architectural features, point to a profound spiritual purpose.

Some scholars propose that the temples of Ggantija were centers of fertility cults or goddess worship, given the presence of statuettes and figurines associated with fertility found in the vicinity. Others suggest that the temples served as communal gathering places for rituals, ceremonies, and social exchange. The absence of formal written records compels us to rely on archaeological evidence, architectural analysis, and comparative studies to piece together the puzzle of Ggantija's purpose.

The cultural and historical context surrounding the Ggantija temples offers further clues to their significance. The Maltese archipelago, with its strategic location in the Mediterranean, has been a crossroads of civilizations throughout history. The temples of Ggantija bear witness to the interactions and cultural exchanges between the early inhabitants of Malta and neighboring Mediterranean cultures. The similarities between Ggantija and other megalithic sites in the region, such as Stonehenge and the temples of Malta's main island, suggest a shared cultural and religious heritage.

The passage of time has not been kind to the temples of Ggantija. Centuries of exposure to the elements, as well as human intervention and neglect, have taken their toll on these ancient structures. Yet, despite the ravages of time, the temples retain an aura of majesty and an air of mystery. Efforts have been made to preserve and restore the temples, ensuring that future generations can appreciate their grandeur and gain insights into the beliefs and practices of our ancient forebears.

The legacy of Ggantija extends beyond its physical presence on the Maltese landscape. Its discovery and ongoing study have shed light on the cultural, architectural, and spiritual dimensions of prehistoric Malta. The temples of Ggantija stand as a testament to the ingenuity and creativity of our ancient ancestors, challenging our perceptions of their capabilities and accomplishments. They remind us of the enduring power of human ambition and the thirst for spiritual connection that transcends time and place.

In summary, the lost temples of Ggantija captivate our imaginations and beckon us to embark on a journey of discovery. Their construction, purpose, and cultural significance remain shrouded in mystery, yet their enduring legacy serves as a testament to the achievements of our ancient forebears. The study of Ggantija opens a window into the rich tapestry of human history and inspires us to unravel the forgotten narratives of our past. As we strive to understand the temples' secrets, we honor the memory of those who came before us and seek to reclaim a piece of our collective heritage.

The journey of rediscovery at Ggantija, the enigmatic megalithic temples of Gozo, has captivated the hearts and minds of archaeologists, historians, and explorers alike. This extraordinary site, nestled on the rugged landscape of the Maltese island, has revealed a rich tapestry of human history, challenging our understanding of ancient civilizations and igniting a fervor for unraveling its secrets.

The story of Ggantija's rediscovery is a testament to the persistence and dedication of those who sought to unearth its hidden treasures. In the early 19th century, explorers and scholars, drawn by tantalizing tales of monumental stone structures, embarked on expeditions to Gozo in search of the fabled temples. These intrepid individuals faced numerous challenges, from navigating treacherous terrain to overcoming the obstacles posed by centuries of neglect and abandonment.

It was the tireless efforts of early archaeologists, such as Sir Themistocles Zammit, that laid the foundation for Ggantija's rediscovery. Zammit's groundbreaking excavations in the early 20th century unearthed the colossal stone blocks and intricate carvings that had been concealed beneath layers of earth and vegetation for millennia. These discoveries sparked a renewed interest in Ggantija and set the stage for further exploration and study.

As excavations continued over the years, the true magnitude of Ggantija began to emerge. The temples, consisting of two main structures known as Ggantija South and Ggantija North, stood as awe-inspiring testament to the architectural prowess of their builders. The sheer size and weight of the limestone blocks used in their construction defied explanation, leaving researchers astounded by the engineering feats achieved by the ancient civilization that called Ggantija home.

The meticulous nature of the excavations at Ggantija revealed a wealth of artifacts and insights into the lives of the temple builders. Intricate pottery, stone tools, and decorative objects shed light on the daily lives, craftsmanship, and artistic expressions of the ancient inhabitants. The presence of statuettes and figurines associated with fertility hinted at the importance of ritual practices and beliefs in the community.

With each new discovery, the puzzle of Ggantija's purpose and significance began to take shape. The grandeur and complexity of the temples suggested a profound spiritual and ceremonial role. The careful arrangement of stones, the intricate carvings depicting animals and human-like figures, and the alignment with celestial events all pointed to a site of great religious and cultural importance. Ggantija was more than a mere architectural marvel; it was a sacred space that connected the ancient inhabitants with the divine.

The journey of rediscovery at Ggantija continues to this day. Ongoing excavations, conservation efforts, and scientific analysis provide fresh insights into the site's history and significance. Advanced techniques and technologies, from 3D mapping to radiocarbon dating, enable researchers to unravel the mysteries of Ggantija with unprecedented precision.

Ggantija's rediscovery has not only enriched our understanding of the ancient past but also fostered a deep appreciation for the resilience and ingenuity of our ancestors. It stands as a testament to human ambition and creativity, challenging our perceptions of what was possible in the distant past. Ggantija reminds us that behind the weathered stones and fragmented artifacts lie the stories of a thriving civilization, a testament to the enduring legacy of those who came before us.

The journey of rediscovery at Ggantija is an ongoing quest to unlock the secrets of our shared human history. With each excavation, each new artifact, and each scientific breakthrough, we move closer to piecing together the puzzle of this remarkable site. Ggantija invites us to delve into the mysteries of the past, to connect with our ancient roots, and to appreciate the profound cultural heritage that has shaped us as a species.

In summary, the journey of rediscovery at Ggantija stands as a testament to human curiosity and perseverance. It has provided a window into the ancient civilization that flourished on the Maltese island of Gozo, challenging our understanding of the past and inspiring a deeper appreciation for the wonders of human achievement. Ggantija's temples, with their colossal stones and intricate carvings, serve as a reminder of the timeless human quest for meaning, connection, and spiritual expression. As we continue to unravel Ggantija's mysteries, we honor the legacy of the ancient builders and connect with our shared cultural heritage.

The preservation and restoration efforts at Ggantija, the awe-inspiring megalithic temples of Gozo, stand as a testament to our commitment to safeguarding our shared cultural heritage. These monumental structures, dating back thousands of years, have weathered the passage of time, facing the relentless forces of nature and the impact of human activity. Yet, through dedicated conservation and preservation initiatives, we strive to ensure that the giants of Ggantija continue to inspire awe and reverence for generations to come.

The conservation of Ggantija presents unique challenges. The temples, constructed with immense limestone blocks, have endured the effects of weathering, erosion, and the gradual decay of the stone. The preservation efforts require a delicate balance between maintaining the authenticity and integrity of the ancient structures while protecting them from further deterioration. This delicate task demands the expertise of skilled conservationists, archaeologists, engineers, and other specialists who work diligently to ensure the long-term survival of Ggantija.

One of the primary objectives of restoration at Ggantija is stabilizing the structures and preventing further deterioration. This involves meticulous assessments of the stability of the stone blocks, identifying areas of weakness or vulnerability, and implementing measures to reinforce and protect them. Various techniques, such as stone consolidation, consolidation of foundations, and structural reinforcements, are employed to ensure the structural stability of the temples.

Another crucial aspect of the restoration process is the meticulous cleaning and conservation of the stone surfaces. Layers of dirt, vegetation, and pollutants accumulated over centuries are gently removed to reveal the original textures and details of the ancient stonework. This process requires meticulous care and expertise to avoid damaging the delicate carvings and surfaces of the temples.

Additionally, extensive research and analysis are conducted to understand the original appearance of the temples and the pigments and coatings that adorned them. By studying ancient pigments, residues, and historical accounts, researchers can make informed decisions regarding the application of protective coatings and the recreation of original colors, enabling visitors to glimpse the temples' original splendor.

The preservation efforts at Ggantija extend beyond the physical structures themselves. The surrounding environment, including the landscape and vegetation, plays a vital role in the overall conservation and presentation of the site. Measures are taken to maintain the ecological balance and minimize any adverse impact on the temples. The site's accessibility and visitor management strategies are carefully planned to ensure a sustainable balance between conservation and public engagement.

Education and public awareness are integral components of the restoration process at Ggantija. Efforts are made to engage local communities, visitors, and stakeholders, raising awareness about the significance of the site and fostering a sense of stewardship. Educational programs, guided tours, and interpretive displays help visitors understand the historical, cultural, and archaeological importance of Ggantija, inspiring a deeper appreciation and respect for the site.

Collaboration and international partnerships play a crucial role in the restoration efforts at Ggantija. Sharing knowledge, expertise, and resources among archaeologists, conservators, and heritage organizations from around the world enables a comprehensive approach to preservation. Through collaborative efforts, best practices in conservation and restoration can be applied, ensuring the highest standards in the protection and presentation of Ggantija.

The restoration and preservation efforts at Ggantija are an ongoing endeavor. The giants of Ggantija continue to inspire awe and fascination, drawing visitors from all corners of the globe. The commitment to their preservation ensures that future generations will have the opportunity to marvel at these ancient structures, fostering a deeper understanding and connection with our shared human history.

In summary, the conservation and preservation efforts at Ggantija demonstrate our dedication to safeguarding and celebrating our cultural heritage. By employing advanced techniques, interdisciplinary collaboration, and community engagement, we strive to restore and preserve the majestic megalithic temples for future generations. The giants of Ggantija, once at risk of being lost to time, now stand as testament to the resilience and ingenuity of our ancient ancestors, inspiring wonder and appreciation for their remarkable achievements.

The rediscovery of Ggantija, the enigmatic megalithic temples of Gozo, has offered a remarkable glimpse into the fascinating world of Neolithic civilization. As archaeologists meticulously excavated the site, unearthing the remnants of this ancient settlement, they embarked on a journey of discovery, seeking to understand the lives, beliefs, and cultural practices of the people who once inhabited this extraordinary place.

The Neolithic period, often referred to as the "New Stone Age," marked a significant turning point in human history. It was a time of profound change, as our ancestors transitioned from a nomadic lifestyle to settled communities, cultivating the land and domesticating animals. Ggantija stands as a testament to this transformative era, revealing the ingenuity and cultural sophistication of its Neolithic inhabitants.

The excavation of Ggantija has uncovered a wealth of artifacts and features that shed light on the daily lives of the people who called this place home. Stone tools, pottery fragments, and traces of domestic activities provide valuable insights into their subsistence strategies, craftsmanship, and social organization. The discovery of grinding stones, querns, and storage pits suggest a reliance on agriculture and food storage, indicating a shift towards a more settled way of life.

One of the most striking aspects of Ggantija is the monumental architecture that defines the site. The temples, composed of massive limestone blocks, exhibit a level of craftsmanship and engineering skill that defies expectations for the time. The precise fitting of the stones, the intricate carvings, and the overall design of the temples speak to a society that possessed advanced knowledge of construction techniques and a strong communal spirit.

The purpose and function of the temples at Ggantija have long intrigued researchers. The colossal scale of the structures, along with the presence of intricate carvings and symbolic elements, suggests that they held deep religious and ceremonial significance. Some scholars propose that the temples were centers of communal gatherings, where rituals, ceremonies, and cultural exchanges took place. Others speculate that they were places of worship, dedicated to deities or ancestral spirits.

The artistry found at Ggantija provides further insights into the spiritual and cultural beliefs of its inhabitants. Intricate carvings depicting animals, human figures, and abstract symbols hint at a complex belief system and a rich mythological tradition. These representations offer glimpses into the cosmology and worldview of the Neolithic people, revealing their connections with the natural world and their reverence for ancestral spirits.

The discovery of human remains and burial sites at Ggantija offers poignant glimpses into Neolithic funerary practices. The presence of collective burials and elaborate grave goods suggests that the deceased were laid to rest with care and reverence, possibly reflecting beliefs in an afterlife or the veneration of ancestors. These burial practices provide invaluable insights into the social and cultural aspects of Neolithic society, illuminating their attitudes towards death and the role of the deceased within the community.

The rediscovery of Ggantija has not only advanced our understanding of Neolithic civilization but also prompted us to reevaluate our preconceived notions about the capabilities and achievements of our ancient ancestors. The monumental architecture, artistic expressions, and social organization exhibited at Ggantija challenge the notion that complex societies emerged only in later periods of human history. Instead, it reveals the remarkable intellectual and creative capacities of Neolithic communities.

The ongoing research and excavation at Ggantija continue to deepen our understanding of this Neolithic civilization. Scientific techniques, such as radiocarbon dating and DNA analysis, offer unprecedented opportunities to unravel the intricate tapestry of their lives and heritage. As archaeologists meticulously sift through the layers of history at Ggantija, they strive to reconstruct the stories of the people who lived here, their aspirations, beliefs, and contributions to the development of human civilization.

In summary, the rediscovery of Ggantija has opened a window into the fascinating world of Neolithic civilization. Through careful excavation, analysis, and interpretation, archaeologists have revealed a thriving society that possessed remarkable architectural, artistic, and cultural achievements. Ggantija stands as a testament to the ingenuity, creativity, and communal spirit of our Neolithic ancestors, reminding us of the richness and diversity of human history. It invites us to marvel at their accomplishments and ponder the enduring legacy they have left behind.

The uncovering of Ggantija, the awe-inspiring megalithic temples of Gozo, has revealed not only the physical remains of an ancient civilization but also the profound cultural significance that this extraordinary site held for its inhabitants. Through careful excavation, analysis, and interpretation, archaeologists and historians have pieced together a captivating narrative of a society that left behind a rich legacy of beliefs, rituals, and social practices.

Ggantija's cultural significance becomes apparent when one considers the monumental scale of its architecture and the meticulous craftsmanship of its stone structures. The temples, composed of colossal limestone blocks, stand as a testament to the technical prowess and engineering capabilities of the builders. The precise fitting of the stones, the intricate carvings, and the harmonious layout of the temples reflect a society that possessed advanced knowledge of construction techniques and a deep reverence for the sacred.

The temples of Ggantija were not simply architectural marvels; they served as focal points for communal gatherings, religious ceremonies, and social interactions. These monumental structures represented the physical embodiment of the community's collective identity and beliefs. It is believed that the temples played a central role in the cultural, spiritual, and social fabric of the society, acting as spaces where individuals could connect with the divine, seek guidance, and partake in communal rituals.

The symbolic significance of Ggantija is evident in the intricate carvings and engravings found within the temples. These include depictions of animals, human figures, abstract motifs, and other symbolic representations. Such imagery likely held deep meaning for the ancient inhabitants, conveying narratives, myths, and cosmological beliefs that were central to their worldview. The artistry and symbolism of Ggantija reflect a complex belief system, where the natural world, ancestral spirits, and celestial forces were intertwined in a holistic understanding of the universe.

Ritual practices were a fundamental aspect of Ggantija's cultural life. The temples served as sites for various ceremonies, including offerings, processions, and communal gatherings. The careful alignment of the temples with celestial events, such as solstices and equinoxes, suggests a deep reverence for the cycles of nature and the interconnectedness of the human and divine realms. These rituals fostered a sense of community, reinforced social bonds, and reinforced the spiritual connection between the people and their gods.

The cultural significance of Ggantija extends beyond the temples themselves. The site's surroundings, such as burial sites, domestic structures, and agricultural features, provide further insights into the daily lives and social organization of the community. The presence of elaborate burials and grave goods indicates the importance placed on ancestral veneration and the afterlife. The remnants of domestic spaces and agricultural practices reveal the intricacies of their subsistence strategies, resource management, and societal divisions.

Ggantija's cultural significance is not limited to its ancient past; it continues to resonate in contemporary society. The site serves as a powerful reminder of the enduring legacy of our ancestors and the connections between past and present. It has inspired artists, writers, and scholars, who have sought to capture its mystique and unravel its secrets. Ggantija's cultural significance is also recognized at a global level, as it has been designated as a UNESCO World Heritage Site, acknowledging its universal value and the importance of its preservation for future generations.

The ongoing research, conservation efforts, and public engagement at Ggantija ensure that its cultural significance remains vibrant and accessible. Educational programs, visitor centers, and interpretive displays provide opportunities for individuals to engage with the site's history, symbolism, and cultural context. By understanding and appreciating the cultural significance of Ggantija, we gain a deeper understanding of our shared human heritage and the rich tapestry of beliefs, traditions, and expressions that have shaped our collective identity.

In summary, the uncovering of Ggantija has revealed its profound cultural significance as more than just a physical monument. It was a center of spiritual and communal life, a place where rituals were performed, and where the community forged its collective identity. The intricate carvings, symbolic representations, and alignment with celestial events all speak to the depth of their cultural beliefs and worldview. Ggantija's cultural significance extends beyond its ancient past, resonating with us today as a testament to human creativity, spirituality, and the enduring power of cultural expression.

The impressive structures of Ggantija, the megalithic temples of Gozo, stand as a testament to the architectural grandeur and technical prowess of their Neolithic builders. These awe-inspiring monuments, constructed over 5,000 years ago, continue to captivate the imagination and leave visitors in awe of their monumental scale, intricate craftsmanship, and enigmatic beauty.

The temples of Ggantija are among the oldest freestanding stone structures in the world, predating the pyramids of Egypt and Stonehenge by several centuries. Composed of immense limestone blocks, some weighing up to 50 tons, the temples exhibit a level of construction mastery that is astounding considering the limited tools and resources available to the ancient builders. The precision fitting of the stones, without the use of mortar, showcases their meticulous attention to detail and their deep understanding of structural stability.

The sheer size of the temples is awe-inspiring. The South Temple, the larger of the two, spans approximately 36 meters in length and rises to an impressive height of 6 meters. The North Temple, though slightly smaller, is still an imposing structure, stretching over 28 meters in length. These monumental dimensions, coupled with the massive stone blocks, create a sense of awe and wonder, leaving observers marveling at the immense effort required to construct such imposing edifices.

The craftsmanship displayed at Ggantija is remarkable. The stone blocks, carefully shaped and fitted together, create seamless walls that have withstood the test of time. The precision-cut openings, including doorways, windows, and apses, showcase the builders' mastery of architectural design. Intricate carvings and decorations adorn the temple walls, depicting animals, spirals, and other abstract motifs, revealing the artistic sensibilities and cultural expressions of the ancient builders.

The construction techniques employed at Ggantija demonstrate an advanced understanding of engineering principles. The massive stones were hewn from quarries, transported over considerable distances, and positioned with remarkable precision. The use of ramps, sledges, and ingenious levering systems facilitated the movement and placement of these enormous blocks. The builders' knowledge of weight distribution, balance, and structural stability allowed them to create enduring structures that have withstood the ravages of time.

The temples' architecture also reflects a sophisticated understanding of acoustics and light manipulation. The circular apses, designed to capture and amplify sound, create an ethereal ambiance within the temple chambers. The intentional placement of openings and roof slabs allows sunlight to penetrate the interiors at specific times, creating dramatic lighting effects and emphasizing the sacredness of the space. These architectural features demonstrate the builders' awareness of the interplay between architecture, natural elements, and the spiritual experience.

The monumental temples of Ggantija were not mere functional structures; they were sacred spaces of great spiritual and communal significance. The temples' layout, with multiple chambers and interconnected spaces, suggests a complex architectural plan that served a variety of ceremonial and ritual purposes. The presence of altars, niches, and platforms within the temple complexes indicates that they were centers for religious and communal gatherings, where offerings, prayers, and other sacred rituals took place.

The enduring legacy of Ggantija's architectural grandeur is not confined to the physical structures themselves. It has inspired architects, archaeologists, and scholars, who have sought to unravel the mysteries of their construction and understand their cultural significance. The magnificent temples of Ggantija continue to be a source of fascination and admiration, reminding us of the remarkable achievements of our ancient ancestors and their ability to create enduring architectural marvels.

In summary, the architectural grandeur of Ggantija's temples stands as a testament to the ingenuity, craftsmanship, and spiritual vision of their Neolithic builders. These massive stone structures, with their precise fitting, intricate carvings, and sophisticated design, inspire awe and reverence, offering a glimpse into the cultural and architectural achievements of our ancient past. Ggantija's temples continue to captivate the imagination and remind us of the remarkable human capacity to create enduring works of architectural magnificence.

The construction techniques and feats achieved at Ggantija, the megalithic temples of Gozo, are nothing short of exceptional. These ancient structures, dating back over 5,000 years, display a level of engineering mastery that continues to astound scholars and visitors alike. From the quarrying and transportation of massive stone blocks to the precise fitting and stability of the temple walls, Ggantija stands as a testament to the ingenuity and technical skill of its Neolithic builders.

One of the most remarkable aspects of Ggantija's construction is the quarrying and transportation of the immense stone blocks used in its construction. The limestone used for the temples was sourced from nearby quarries, and it is believed that the builders employed a combination of stone hammers, chisels, and wooden levers to shape and extract the stones. The transportation of these colossal blocks, some weighing several tons, remains a mystery. Theories range from the use of sledges and wooden rollers to the implementation of advanced pulley systems. Whatever the method, it required meticulous planning, organization, and the collaboration of a skilled workforce.

The precision fitting of the stones without the use of mortar is another testament to the builders' engineering prowess. The walls of Ggantija's temples consist of massive stone blocks stacked atop one another with remarkable precision. The stones were shaped and smoothed to ensure a tight fit, creating a stable and durable structure. The mastery of stonecutting techniques allowed for the creation of intricate doorways, windows, and apses, showcasing the builders' attention to detail and their understanding of structural integrity.

The stability of Ggantija's structures is a remarkable engineering achievement. Despite the passage of millennia and the exposure to the elements, the temple walls still stand strong. The builders demonstrated an understanding of load-bearing principles, using the massive stone blocks to distribute weight evenly and create a stable foundation. The careful placement of stones, along with the integration of corbelling and buttressing techniques, ensured the structural integrity of the temples and their resistance to external forces.

Another remarkable aspect of Ggantija's construction is the incorporation of roof slabs, which form the ceilings of the temple chambers. These slabs, some weighing several tons, were precisely cut and positioned to create a secure and weather-resistant covering. The interlocking design of the slabs, along with the use of supporting walls and corbelling, contributed to the structural stability of the roofs. The engineering ingenuity required to create such impressive roofing systems speaks to the builders' advanced knowledge of materials and construction techniques.

The advanced engineering techniques displayed at Ggantija are even more astonishing when one considers the limited tools and resources available to the Neolithic builders. Without the aid of modern machinery, they achieved feats that continue to impress scholars and researchers to this day. The construction of Ggantija required meticulous planning, meticulous craftsmanship, and a deep understanding of architectural principles.

The exceptional engineering exhibited at Ggantija not only testifies to the skill and knowledge of the Neolithic builders but also raises intriguing questions about their motivation and cultural aspirations. The immense effort invested in the construction of these temples suggests a deep reverence for the sacred, a desire to create enduring structures that would stand as testaments to their beliefs and cultural identity.

In summary, the construction techniques and feats achieved at Ggantija are a testament to the exceptional engineering capabilities of its Neolithic builders. From quarrying and transporting massive stone blocks to the precise fitting and stability of the temple walls, the construction of Ggantija showcases the remarkable ingenuity, craftsmanship, and architectural understanding of its creators. The enduring legacy of Ggantija's engineering marvels continues to inspire awe and admiration, reminding us of the remarkable achievements of our ancient ancestors and their ability to create enduring architectural wonders.

The awe-inspiring artistry displayed in the carvings and decorations of Ggantija, the megalithic temples of Gozo, is a testament to the remarkable artistic skill and creative expression of its ancient builders. These intricate and captivating designs, etched into the massive limestone blocks, offer a glimpse into the cultural and symbolic world of the Neolithic inhabitants and reveal a profound understanding of aesthetics, symbolism, and craftsmanship.

The carvings found at Ggantija encompass a wide range of subjects, from animals and human figures to abstract motifs and geometric patterns. Animals, such as bulls, goats, and birds, are depicted with great attention to detail, capturing their distinctive characteristics and movement. These animal representations likely held significant symbolic meanings, connecting the spiritual realm with the natural world and reflecting the beliefs and cosmology of the ancient builders.

Human figures are also prominently featured in the carvings, displaying a range of postures, gestures, and attire. These figures may represent deities, ancestors, or important individuals within the community. Their presence suggests a deep reverence for the human form and the belief in the interconnectedness of the human and divine realms. The stylized depictions and intricate detailing of these figures demonstrate the artistic skill and creativity of the ancient artisans.

Abstract motifs and geometric patterns are another fascinating aspect of the carvings at Ggantija. Spirals, zigzags, chevrons, and other intricate designs adorn the temple walls, creating visually captivating patterns that seem to dance across the stone surfaces. These geometric motifs likely held symbolic meanings, representing concepts such as eternity, cosmic order, and the cyclical nature of life. They showcase the ancient builders' understanding of pattern, proportion, and visual harmony.

The craftsmanship involved in creating these carvings is exceptional. The ancient artisans utilized simple stone tools, such as chisels and abrasives, to meticulously shape and engrave the limestone blocks. The precision and skill with which the carvings were executed demonstrate a deep mastery of the medium and an acute sensitivity to form, proportion, and detail. The use of different depths and angles in the carvings creates a sense of depth and dimensionality, further enhancing their visual impact.

The artistry of Ggantija extends beyond the carvings themselves. The temple architecture itself serves as a canvas for artistic expression, with ornate decorations and intricate details adorning the walls, doorways, and apses. These architectural embellishments, such as moldings, friezes, and niches, demonstrate a commitment to creating aesthetically pleasing and visually engaging spaces. They transform the temples into immersive artistic experiences, where every surface is an opportunity for creative expression.

The significance of the carvings and decorations at Ggantija extends beyond their artistic beauty. They provide valuable insights into the cultural, religious, and social practices of the ancient inhabitants. The intricate carvings likely conveyed narratives, myths, and historical events, serving as visual representations of the community's collective memory and cultural identity. The artistry of Ggantija played a vital role in communicating and preserving their beliefs, traditions, and values.

The preservation and study of the carvings and decorations at Ggantija continue to shed light on the artistic and cultural achievements of the Neolithic period. Through careful documentation, analysis, and interpretation, researchers and scholars strive to unravel the meanings and symbolism embedded within these ancient artworks. The ongoing research ensures that the artistic legacy of Ggantija remains alive, offering us a glimpse into the rich tapestry of human creativity and expression.

In summary, the carvings and decorations of Ggantija are a testament to the awe-inspiring artistry and craftsmanship of its ancient builders. These intricate and captivating designs reflect a profound understanding of symbolism, aesthetics, and cultural expression. The carvings bring to life the ancient beliefs, mythologies, and artistic sensibilities of the Neolithic inhabitants, serving as a visual portal into their world. The artistry of Ggantija continues to inspire wonder and admiration, reminding us of the enduring power and beauty of human artistic expression across the ages.

The layout and architecture of the Ggantija temples, situated on the island of Gozo, provide valuable insights into the planning, design, and spiritual significance of these ancient structures. Dating back over 5,000 years, the temples are among the world's oldest freestanding stone buildings and are renowned for their remarkable scale, intricate construction, and enigmatic symbolism.

The Ggantija temples consist of two separate but interconnected structures, referred to as the North Temple and the South Temple. Each temple has a distinct layout, yet they share common architectural features and a similar spiritual purpose.

The North Temple, the larger of the two, is characterized by a more complex and multi-chambered layout. It consists of a series of interconnected rooms, including a central corridor flanked by several side chambers. These chambers are accessed through imposing doorways, adorned with decorative elements and symbols. The central corridor leads to a central apse, which serves as the focal point of the temple. The apse is a semicircular recess with intricate carvings and symbolic representations, likely associated with religious and ceremonial activities.

The South Temple, although smaller, shares a similar layout and architectural style with the North Temple. It consists of a central corridor with smaller side chambers, leading to a central apse. The proportions and dimensions of the South Temple mirror those of its larger counterpart, highlighting the deliberate symmetry and balance employed by the ancient builders.

The temples' layout suggests a well-planned and carefully organized architectural design, with each chamber and corridor serving a specific purpose within the religious and ritualistic context. The multiple chambers and interconnected spaces likely facilitated various ceremonies, gatherings, and communal activities. The distinct areas within the temples may have been dedicated to specific deities, ritual practices, or community functions.

The purpose and function of the temples' individual chambers have been the subject of much speculation and interpretation. Some chambers may have been used for ceremonial offerings, while others could have served as spaces for communal gatherings, religious ceremonies, or even as burial chambers. The precise meanings and uses of these spaces continue to be a topic of investigation and debate among archaeologists and researchers.

The architectural elements of the Ggantija temples, such as doorways, windows, and apses, are decorated with intricate carvings and symbolic motifs. These carvings depict animals, spirals, geometric patterns, and other abstract designs. The symbolism and significance of these carvings are still being deciphered, but they likely held religious, spiritual, and cultural meanings for the ancient inhabitants. They may have represented deities, mythological narratives, cosmological concepts, or tribal identities.

The temples' architecture also showcases a remarkable understanding of acoustics and natural lighting. The intentional placement of openings, such as windows and roof slabs, allowed for the manipulation of sunlight and the creation of dramatic lighting effects within the temple chambers. The careful design and acoustic properties of the temples' architecture likely enhanced the spiritual and sensory experiences of the rituals and ceremonies conducted within.

The layout and architecture of the Ggantija temples serve as a testament to the sophisticated understanding of spatial organization, symbolism, and sacred geometry among their Neolithic builders. The deliberate arrangement of chambers, corridors, and apses reflects a careful consideration of the temples' spiritual and communal functions. The intricate carvings and decorative elements demonstrate a deep artistic sensibility and a desire to create visually striking and spiritually resonant spaces.

In summary, the layout and architecture of the Ggantija temples provide valuable insights into the planning, design, and spiritual significance of these ancient structures. The interconnected chambers, central corridors, and symbolic apses reflect a well-thought-out and purposeful architectural design. The intricate carvings and decorative elements within the temples offer glimpses into the religious, symbolic, and cultural beliefs of the Neolithic inhabitants. The layout and architectural features of the Ggantija temples continue to inspire wonder and fascination, inviting us to explore the ancient world and unravel the mysteries of these awe-inspiring monuments.

Unveiling the religious and ritualistic practices of Ggantija, the megalithic temples of Gozo, provides a fascinating glimpse into the spiritual world and ceremonial activities of its Neolithic builders. While much of the precise nature of their beliefs and rituals remains shrouded in mystery, the architectural features, carvings, and archaeological evidence offer valuable clues about the religious and ritual practices that took place within these sacred structures.

The sheer scale and grandeur of the Ggantija temples suggest that they held great importance in the religious and social life of the ancient community. The temples served as centers of communal gathering and were likely the focal points of religious ceremonies, rituals, and social interactions. These ceremonies and rituals played a vital role in the spiritual and social fabric of the community, connecting them to their beliefs, ancestors, and the divine.

The presence of multiple chambers within the temples suggests that different rituals and ceremonies may have taken place in various designated spaces. Each chamber may have served a specific purpose, whether for offerings, prayers, communal feasts, or other religious practices. The architectural layout of the temples, with their central corridors, side chambers, and apses, likely facilitated the flow of people and activities during these rituals, ensuring a structured and meaningful experience.

The carvings found throughout the Ggantija temples provide valuable insights into the religious and mythological beliefs of the Neolithic community. These carvings depict various animals, human figures, abstract symbols, and geometric patterns, each potentially holding symbolic significance within their belief system. The carvings may have represented deities, ancestral spirits, mythical narratives, or cosmological concepts. They acted as visual aids, enabling the participants in rituals to connect with the spiritual realm and invoke divine presence.

The temples' central apses, often adorned with intricate carvings and decorative elements, likely served as focal points for religious ceremonies and offerings. These apses may have housed sacred objects, ritual implements, or representations of deities. They provided a designated space for the performance of sacred rituals, where the community could commune with the divine and seek blessings, guidance, or protection.

The presence of altars and stone benches within the temples suggests the performance of rituals involving offerings, libations, or ceremonial feasting. These activities would have fostered a sense of communal bonding, reinforcing social cohesion and shared spiritual experiences. The presence of hearths and fire installations within the temples further suggests the importance of fire in their rituals, serving as a symbol of purification, transformation, and connection to the divine.

The alignment of the Ggantija temples with astronomical phenomena, such as the rising and setting of the sun during solstices and equinoxes, indicates a profound connection between their religious practices and celestial observations. These alignments may have served as a means to mark and celebrate significant celestial events, symbolizing the cyclical nature of life, the seasons, and the cosmic order. The observation of these celestial events may have been integral to their religious calendar and the timing of specific rituals.

It is important to note that our understanding of the religious and ritual practices at Ggantija is based on interpretations and speculation, as no written records from that time have survived. However, the architectural features, carvings, and material remains offer tantalizing glimpses into the spiritual and ceremonial world of its builders.

In summary, Ggantija's religious and ritual practices were an integral part of the Neolithic community's belief system and social fabric. The temples served as sacred spaces for communal gatherings, religious ceremonies, and ritual activities. The architectural features, carvings, and alignments within the temples suggest a deep connection to the divine, ancestral spirits, and the natural world. Unraveling the religious and ritual practices of Ggantija deepens our understanding of the spiritual lives of our ancient ancestors and highlights the enduring quest for meaning and connection that transcends time.

Legends and myths surrounding Ggantija, the ancient megalithic temples of Gozo, are woven into the fabric of folklore and imagination. These tales, passed down through generations, offer fascinating glimpses into the mythical origins and significance of these enigmatic structures.

One prevalent myth tells of giants who supposedly built the temples, hence the name "Ggantija," which means "Giant's Tower" in Maltese. According to legend, these mighty beings possessed supernatural strength and abilities, allowing them to move the enormous stones that make up the temples. The giants, it is said, had a deep connection to the divine and constructed the temples as a testament to their power and as sacred spaces for worship.

Another popular myth linked to Ggantija involves a fertility goddess known as "Sanna," who is believed to have been worshipped within the temples. According to the legend, Sanna had the ability to bring abundant harvests, fertile lands, and prosperity to the people. The temples, dedicated to her worship, were seen as gateways to the realm of the goddess, where offerings and rituals were conducted to appease her and ensure the blessings of abundance and fertility.

In addition to these tales, Ggantija is also associated with stories of love and romance. One such myth involves a forbidden love affair between a mortal and a divine being. It is said that the mortal was transformed into one of the stone pillars of Ggantija, forever commemorating their eternal love. This myth highlights the deep emotional and spiritual connections that people have attributed to these ancient temples throughout the ages.

The mythical origins of Ggantija also find resonance in the broader cultural landscape of the Maltese islands. Malta itself has a rich tapestry of myths and legends, interwoven with the island's history and folklore. These stories often intertwine with tales of other ancient sites and figures, further enriching the narrative surrounding Ggantija and its place in the collective imagination.

While these legends and myths provide colorful narratives, it is important to note that they are products of oral tradition and cultural storytelling. They reflect the human desire to imbue ancient structures with a sense of wonder, mystery, and divine significance. Such myths serve to evoke a sense of awe and reverence for these monumental temples, preserving their place in the cultural consciousness and fostering a deeper connection to the past.

As with many ancient sites, the true origins of Ggantija remain shrouded in the mists of time. Archaeological research and scientific inquiry continue to uncover valuable insights into the temples' construction, purpose, and cultural context. While the mythical origins offer intriguing narratives, it is through the combined efforts of historical analysis, archaeological evidence, and scientific study that we can unravel the true stories of Ggantija and gain a deeper understanding of their significance in human history.

In summary, the legends and myths surrounding Ggantija provide a rich tapestry of folklore, symbolism, and imagination. These mythical tales, passed down through generations, connect the temples to the realms of giants, goddesses, and timeless love. They serve as cultural touchstones, shaping our perception of these ancient structures and infusing them with a sense of wonder and enchantment. While the myths may not reveal the historical truths of Ggantija, they illuminate the enduring fascination and deep spiritual connection that these remarkable megalithic temples continue to evoke.

The megalithic temples of Ggantija, situated on the island of Gozo, hold profound spiritual and symbolic significance. These ancient structures, dating back over 5,000 years, are not mere architectural marvels but repositories of spiritual beliefs, sacred narratives, and symbolic expressions of the Neolithic community.

At the heart of Ggantija's spiritual significance lies the belief in a divine realm and the connection between the earthly and the divine. The temples are seen as portals or conduits through which humans can interact with the spiritual realm, commune with deities, and seek divine blessings and guidance. The scale, grandeur, and meticulous construction of Ggantija serve as tangible expressions of the community's reverence and devotion to the divine.

Symbolism plays a vital role in the spiritual narrative of Ggantija. The architecture, carvings, and decorative elements are imbued with symbolic meanings, representing the cosmological order, the cyclical nature of life, and the interconnectedness of the natural and spiritual realms. Animals, such as bulls, birds, and snakes, depicted in the carvings, may symbolize fertility, vitality, and the divine forces present in the natural world. Spirals, concentric circles, and geometric patterns found throughout the temples may represent the interconnectedness of all things and the eternal cycles of existence.

The use of stone in the construction of Ggantija holds deep symbolic significance. Stone is often associated with endurance, permanence, and stability, reflecting the divine qualities that the community sought to honor and emulate. The massive megaliths were carefully chosen, shaped, and placed, embodying the community's belief in the transformative power of the sacred stones.

Ggantija also bears witness to the importance of ancestral reverence and the role of ancestors in the spiritual worldview of the Neolithic community. The temples may have served as ancestral sanctuaries, places of veneration and remembrance where the wisdom, guidance, and protection of past generations were sought. The inclusion of burial chambers within the temple complex further suggests the connection between the living and the deceased, as well as the belief in an afterlife and the continuity of the ancestral lineage.

Rituals and ceremonies conducted within the temples were central to the spiritual life of the community. These rituals may have involved offerings, prayers, dances, music, and communal feasts, serving to honor the divine, seek divine intervention, celebrate significant life events, and strengthen social bonds. The shared experience of participating in these rituals fostered a sense of communal identity, belonging, and collective spirituality.

The seasonal cycles, celestial observations, and natural phenomena also played a crucial role in the spiritual and symbolic practices at Ggantija. Alignments with solstices, equinoxes, and celestial events are believed to have held profound significance, reflecting the community's understanding of the cosmic order and the rhythms of nature. These alignments may have marked important agricultural, calendrical, and mythological events, reinforcing the community's connection to the cycles of life and the divine forces that governed them.

The spiritual and symbolic significance of Ggantija continues to captivate and intrigue scholars, archaeologists, and visitors alike. It offers a window into the spiritual and cultural beliefs of an ancient community, revealing their profound reverence for the divine, their deep connection to the natural world, and their quest for meaning, transcendence, and communal harmony.

In summary, Ggantija's spiritual and symbolic significance is woven into its very fabric. The temples serve as sacred spaces where the earthly and the divine intersect, offering a glimpse into the spiritual beliefs, narratives, and practices of the Neolithic community. Through architectural design, carvings, symbolism, and rituals, Ggantija invites us to explore the profound connections between the human and the divine, the natural and the supernatural, and the enduring quest for transcendence and meaning that transcends time and culture.

Ggantija, the ancient megalithic temples of Gozo, are steeped in folklore and cultural beliefs that have been passed down through generations. These stories and beliefs add depth and meaning to the enigmatic structures, connecting them to the cultural identity and imagination of the Maltese people.

One prevalent folklore surrounding Ggantija revolves around the giants who are said to have built the temples. According to the tales, these giants possessed immense strength and stature, capable of moving the massive stones that make up the temples with ease. The folklore often attributes supernatural abilities to these giants, portraying them as beings of great wisdom, power, and connection to the divine. Their involvement in constructing the temples is seen as a testament to their importance in the mythical landscape of Malta.

The giants of Ggantija also find their place in local legends and origin stories. Some folktales suggest that the temples were constructed by giants as a place of worship and spiritual connection with the divine. The enormous scale and intricate construction of Ggantija are seen as evidence of the giants' exceptional abilities and their desire to create a lasting monument to their faith.

These tales of giants are intertwined with the cultural identity of the Maltese people. They serve as a reminder of a mythical past, igniting the imagination and reinforcing a sense of wonder about the ancient origins of their land. The presence of giant-related folklore and beliefs surrounding Ggantija adds to the allure and fascination surrounding these impressive structures.

Ggantija is also associated with legends of fertility and abundance. Some folktales speak of a fertility goddess or a deity linked to the temples, who brings prosperity, bountiful harvests, and fertility to the land. It is believed that offerings and rituals performed at Ggantija were dedicated to this goddess, seeking her blessings for abundant crops, healthy livestock, and prosperity for the community.

In addition to these legends, Ggantija has been linked to various folk beliefs and practices. Some people believe that the temples possess mystical and healing powers. It is said that walking through the ancient chambers and touching the stones can bring good luck, fertility, and protection from harm. Others consider Ggantija to be a site of spiritual energy and connection to the divine, making it a destination for those seeking spiritual experiences or a deeper connection to their heritage.

These folklore and cultural beliefs associated with Ggantija highlight the enduring impact of the temples on the cultural consciousness of the Maltese people. They add layers of meaning, mystery, and enchantment to the already awe-inspiring structures, allowing the imagination to weave stories of giants, gods, and mystical powers. These legends and beliefs reflect the deeply rooted connection between the people and their ancient heritage, preserving a sense of wonder and fascination for generations to come.

While folklore and cultural beliefs provide a lens through which we can explore the cultural significance of Ggantija, it is important to approach them with a sense of appreciation for their storytelling and symbolic value. They enrich our understanding of the deep cultural connections to the temples and invite us to delve into the realms of myth, imagination, and the human desire to weave narratives that give meaning and context to our ancient past. Legends surrounding the construction of Ggantija, the ancient megalithic temples of Gozo, capture the imagination and curiosity of those seeking to unravel the mysteries of these magnificent structures. The legends offer captivating narratives about the builders and their remarkable feats, intertwining myth and history to create a vivid tapestry of folklore.

According to local folklore, Ggantija was built by a race of giants, thus giving the temples their name, which means "Giant's Tower" in Maltese. These giants were said to be immensely powerful beings, possessing strength and stature beyond that of ordinary humans. They were believed to possess supernatural abilities, enabling them to transport and arrange the massive stone blocks that make up the temples.

Legends describe the giants as divine or semi-divine beings, with a direct connection to the gods or an ancient race of celestial entities. Their purpose in constructing Ggantija is often attributed to their desire to create a place of worship and commune with the divine forces that governed their lives. The giants' mastery of advanced construction techniques, their ability to shape and move enormous stones, and their dedication to creating a sacred space demonstrate their awe-inspiring capabilities.

Some legends suggest that the giants acquired their immense strength and knowledge from celestial beings, who imparted their wisdom and divine gifts upon them. Others propose that the giants themselves were the offspring of gods and mortals, embodying a unique blend of power and humanity. These tales imbue the builders of Ggantija with a sense of mythic grandeur and divine ancestry.

The legends of the giants and their involvement in constructing Ggantija are deeply rooted in the cultural identity of the Maltese people. These stories are passed down through generations, fostering a sense of wonder and pride in their ancient heritage. They evoke a world of giants and gods, bridging the realms of myth and history to create a captivating narrative that resonates with the human fascination for the extraordinary.

It is worth noting that while these legends provide captivating tales, they are products of folklore and imagination rather than historical documentation. They reflect the desire to ascribe awe-inspiring origins to monumental structures such as Ggantija, attempting to comprehend the extraordinary efforts required for their construction. The legends serve as a testament to the enduring impact of Ggantija on the cultural consciousness, igniting the imagination and reinforcing a sense of wonder about the ancient builders and their extraordinary accomplishments.

In summary, the legends surrounding the construction of Ggantija offer enchanting narratives that blend myth and history. The giants who supposedly built the temples embody the aspirations and admiration of a culture seeking to explain the remarkable achievements of their ancestors. These legends provide a lens through which we can explore the cultural significance and enduring fascination with Ggantija, inviting us to contemplate the extraordinary capabilities of the ancient builders and the mythical origins of these awe-inspiring temples. Ggantija, the ancient megalithic temples of Gozo, hold a significant place in the mythology and folklore of Malta. These majestic structures have captured the imagination of the Maltese people for centuries, inspiring tales that weave myth, history, and cultural beliefs into a rich tapestry of folklore.

In Maltese folklore, Ggantija is often associated with the legends of giants, who are believed to have inhabited the islands in ancient times. According to the tales, these giants possessed immense strength and power, capable of performing remarkable feats. Ggantija's name itself, meaning "Giant's Tower," is a testament to this belief. The legends describe the giants as mighty beings who constructed the temples as places of worship, using their supernatural abilities to move the massive stone blocks and shape them into the awe-inspiring structures that stand to this day.

The legends of the giants at Ggantija also find resonance in other folklore and mythology of Malta. Stories of giants are prevalent in Maltese folklore, with many tales describing their encounters with humans and their involvement in shaping the landscape of the islands. These stories serve as a reminder of a mythical past, invoking a sense of wonder and fascination with the ancient origins of the land.

Ggantija is also associated with the goddess Sanna, a deity of fertility and abundance. According to the folklore, Ggantija was dedicated to the worship of Sanna, and the temples were seen as sacred spaces where rituals and offerings were performed to seek her blessings for bountiful harvests and prosperity. The presence of Sanna in the folklore highlights the deep connection between Ggantija, the land, and the cycles of fertility and abundance that were vital to the livelihood of the community.

Furthermore, Ggantija is often linked to the broader cultural beliefs and practices of Malta. It is seen as a place of spiritual power, where the boundaries between the human and divine realms are blurred. The temples are considered gateways to the supernatural, and various rituals and ceremonies are believed to have taken place within their sacred walls.

The mythology and folklore surrounding Ggantija serve to reinforce the cultural identity and heritage of the Maltese people. They provide a lens through which the community connects with its ancient past, evoking a sense of pride, wonder, and reverence for the monumental structures and the beliefs associated with them. These stories continue to be passed down through generations, preserving the folklore and keeping the spirit of Ggantija alive.

While the legends and folklore offer imaginative narratives, it is important to approach them with an appreciation for their symbolic and cultural significance. They reflect the human desire to ascribe meaning, wonder, and a sense of the extraordinary to ancient monuments like Ggantija. Through the lens of mythology and folklore, Ggantija becomes more than just a physical structure; it becomes a living entity, woven into the collective consciousness and cultural fabric of the Maltese people.

In summary, Ggantija's mythology and folklore form an integral part of Malta's cultural heritage. The tales of giants, goddesses, and sacred rituals associated with the temples enrich the narrative surrounding these ancient structures, inviting us to delve into the realm of myth, imagination, and the deep connection between the human spirit and the mysteries of the past. They reflect the enduring fascination and reverence for Ggantija, preserving its legacy as a symbol of Malta's ancient heritage and captivating the hearts and minds of all who encounter its timeless presence.

Chapter 4: Architecture and Engineering Feats

The Ggantija temples of Gozo stand as remarkable examples of ancient engineering, showcasing the innovative construction techniques employed by the Neolithic builders. These engineering wonders offer insights into the skill, ingenuity, and resourcefulness of the ancient craftsmen who created these monumental structures.

One of the most astounding construction techniques utilized at Ggantija is the process of quarrying and transporting the massive limestone blocks. These blocks, weighing several tons, were extracted from nearby quarries and then transported to the temple site. The builders demonstrated their mastery by carefully cutting and shaping the stones, ensuring they fit seamlessly into the overall structure. The ability to quarry, shape, and transport these colossal stones reflects the resourcefulness and advanced knowledge of the Neolithic builders.

The placement and alignment of the stones at Ggantija also reveal the builders' engineering expertise. The large megaliths were precisely positioned to create stable and durable structures without the use of mortar. The builders meticulously calculated the weight distribution and stability of each stone, carefully interlocking them to form robust walls and chambers. The precision of their placement is evident in the seamless joints and tight fits, which have allowed the temples to withstand the test of time.

The corbelled arches used in the construction of Ggantija are another engineering marvel. The builders employed this technique to create impressive dome-like ceilings in the temple chambers. The corbelled arches were constructed by gradually projecting inward layers of stone, forming a self-supporting structure. This method not only showcased the builders' understanding of architectural stability but also allowed for the creation of spacious interior spaces. The elegant and sturdy corbelled arches at Ggantija reflect the builders' mastery of structural engineering.

The utilization of trilithons, composed of two upright stones supporting a horizontal lintel, is yet another engineering achievement at Ggantija. These trilithons can be found in the entranceways and chambers of the temples, serving both structural and aesthetic purposes. The careful fitting of the lintels onto the upright stones ensured stability and strength while adding a sense of grandeur to the overall design. The builders' ability to create and position these massive stone structures showcases their understanding of weight distribution and architectural balance.

Additionally, the Ggantija temples feature sophisticated drainage systems, which are evident in the carefully designed channels and cavities within the stone construction. These drainage features ensured that rainwater would be efficiently channeled away from the interior of the temples, preserving their structural integrity over time. The incorporation of such drainage systems demonstrates the builders' attention to practical engineering considerations.

The construction techniques employed at Ggantija reveal a deep understanding of engineering principles and a remarkable level of craftsmanship. The ability to quarry and transport massive stones, the precision placement and alignment, the construction of corbelled arches and trilithons, and the incorporation of drainage systems all attest to the advanced engineering knowledge possessed by the Neolithic builders.

The engineering wonders of Ggantija not only speak to the technical skill of the builders but also reflect the cultural and societal aspirations of the Neolithic community. These magnificent structures were not merely utilitarian in nature but were also monumental expressions of their beliefs, rituals, and social identity.

In summary, the construction techniques employed at Ggantija stand as extraordinary engineering feats. The mastery of quarrying, shaping, and transporting massive stones, the precise placement and alignment, the creation of corbelled arches and trilithons, and the implementation of drainage systems all contribute to the enduring legacy of these Neolithic temples. The engineering wonders of Ggantija serve as a testament to the remarkable abilities and innovation of the ancient builders, leaving us in awe of their architectural achievements.

The Ggantija temples of Gozo are renowned for their precise stonework and the monumental blocks that make up their impressive structures. These megalithic wonders bear witness to the incredible craftsmanship and engineering skill of the Neolithic builders who constructed them.

One of the remarkable features of Ggantija is the precise cutting and shaping of the stones. The builders carefully worked the limestone blocks to ensure a seamless fit, creating tight joints between the stones without the use of mortar. This level of precision is evident in the walls, doorways, and chambers of the temples, where the stones are seamlessly interlocked, forming solid and stable structures.

The monumental size of the stones used at Ggantija adds to their awe-inspiring nature. Some of these blocks weigh several tons and required meticulous planning and engineering to move and position them. The builders demonstrated an incredible understanding of balance, weight distribution, and leverage, allowing them to manipulate these colossal stones with remarkable accuracy.

The monumental blocks found at Ggantija also showcase the Neolithic builders' resourcefulness and ingenuity. They sourced the limestone from nearby quarries and transformed them into the massive blocks that form the temples. The process of quarrying, shaping, and transporting these immense stones would have required extensive labor and the use of rudimentary tools, such as stone hammers and chisels. The builders' ability to work with such large and unwieldy materials is a testament to their skill and determination.

The craftsmanship displayed in the stonework of Ggantija is further highlighted by the intricate carvings found on some of the stones. These carvings depict various symbols, patterns, and motifs, adding a decorative element to the temples' architectural design. The precision and attention to detail exhibited in these carvings reflect the builders' artistic sensibilities and the cultural significance attached to the embellishment of the sacred spaces.

The monumental blocks of Ggantija not only serve as structural components but also contribute to the temples' overall aesthetic impact. Their size and weight convey a sense of grandeur and permanence, creating an imposing presence that commands reverence and admiration. These monumental stones stand as testaments to the Neolithic builders' ambition and their desire to create enduring structures that would endure the passage of time.

The precise stonework and monumental blocks of Ggantija are a testament to the extraordinary skills of the Neolithic builders. The seamless fitting of the stones, the mastery of balance and weight distribution, and the intricate carvings all exemplify the builders' meticulous attention to detail and their ability to transform raw materials into architectural marvels.

In summary, the precise stonework and monumental blocks of Ggantija stand as remarkable achievements of the Neolithic era. These architectural wonders exemplify the mastery of stonecraft and the engineering prowess of the builders. The precision, size, and artistry displayed in the stonework contribute to the enduring legacy of Ggantija, captivating the imagination and admiration of visitors and scholars alike.

The design and layout of the megalithic temples of Ggantija on the island of Gozo reveal a meticulous and purposeful approach to architectural planning. These ancient structures, dating back over 5,000 years, display a unique layout that sets them apart from other megalithic sites of the time.

The temples of Ggantija are composed of multiple chambers, interconnected to form complex architectural arrangements. Each temple consists of two main structures, referred to as the North and South Temples. The North Temple is the larger of the two, featuring a central corridor flanked by multiple chambers on either side. The South Temple is slightly smaller but shares similar characteristics, with a central corridor and chambers branching off from it.

The central corridor of the temples is an important architectural element, serving as a focal point and connecting the various chambers. It is believed that this corridor played a significant role in the rituals and ceremonies conducted within the temples, acting as a processional pathway for worshipers. The design of the corridor suggests a deliberate emphasis on movement and progression, heightening the ceremonial experience for those who traversed it.

The chambers of Ggantija's temples are distinctive in their layout and purpose. They are characterized by trilithons—massive stone structures composed of two upright stones supporting a horizontal lintel. These trilithons form the entranceways and partitions within the temples, creating separate spaces for specific activities or rituals. The placement and arrangement of the chambers suggest a deliberate organization, potentially dedicated to different deities or ceremonial practices.

The overall layout of Ggantija's temples suggests a highly planned and structured design, likely driven by religious or societal considerations. The symmetry and proportionality in the placement of chambers and corridors imply a meticulous approach to spatial arrangement, emphasizing balance and harmony. This intentional layout is indicative of the importance placed on creating a sacred and meaningful environment.

Another notable aspect of Ggantija's design is its orientation in relation to the surrounding landscape. The temples are situated to take advantage of the natural features and topography of the site. They are positioned on an elevated platform, commanding views of the surrounding countryside. This deliberate placement may have had symbolic significance, aligning the temples with the natural elements and reinforcing their connection to the spiritual realm.

The megalithic construction techniques employed at Ggantija also influenced the design and layout of the temples. The massive stone blocks, carefully fitted together without the use of mortar, dictated the scale and structure of the chambers and corridors. The builders' ability to manipulate these colossal stones played a crucial role in shaping the overall architectural form and spatial arrangement.

In summary, the design and layout of Ggantija's megalithic temples showcase a sophisticated and purposeful approach to architectural planning. The intricate interplay of corridors, chambers, and trilithons creates a harmonious and meaningful environment for religious and ceremonial activities. The intentional orientation and placement of the temples within the landscape further enhance their spiritual significance. The design and layout of Ggantija's temples stand as testament to the advanced architectural understanding and the cultural and religious aspirations of the Neolithic community that built them.

The megalithic temples of Ggantija on the island of Gozo boast remarkable innovations in construction methods that set them apart from other ancient structures of their time. These innovations reflect the advanced skills and ingenuity of the Neolithic builders who created these monumental edifices.

One notable innovation in the construction of Ggantija is the use of corbelling. Corbelling is a technique in which stones are progressively stacked in a slightly projecting manner, creating an arch or dome-like structure. This technique was employed in the construction of the temples' ceilings, resulting in impressive and sturdy vaulted chambers. The corbelling technique not only added strength and stability to the structures but also allowed for the creation of spacious interior spaces without the need for additional support structures.

The precise fitting of the stones is another noteworthy innovation at Ggantija. The builders displayed a remarkable level of skill in shaping the limestone blocks and fitting them together with remarkable precision. The absence of mortar or any other binding material indicates that the stones were meticulously selected and carefully positioned to create interlocking joints. This technique not only enhanced the structural integrity of the temples but also contributed to their aesthetic appeal.

The transportation and placement of the massive limestone blocks at Ggantija required innovative methods. The builders had to overcome the logistical challenges of moving stones weighing several tons from the quarries to the temple site. It is believed that sledges, wooden rollers, and possibly ropes were used to transport the stones, utilizing the power of human labor and ingenuity to move these colossal masses. The builders' ability to transport and position such massive stones demonstrates their mastery of engineering and their understanding of leverage and weight distribution.

The builders of Ggantija also demonstrated resourcefulness in their use of local materials. The limestone used in the construction of the temples was sourced from nearby quarries, reflecting the builders' knowledge of the available resources and their ability to adapt to the local environment. By utilizing the natural resources at hand, they reduced the need for long-distance transportation of building materials, further showcasing their practicality and efficiency.

The incorporation of trilithons, consisting of two upright stones supporting a horizontal lintel, is another innovative aspect of Ggantija's construction. These trilithons not only served structural purposes but also added architectural grandeur to the temples. The precise fitting and positioning of the trilithons required careful planning and execution, highlighting the builders' expertise in working with massive stone blocks.

The construction methods employed at Ggantija indicate a level of technical proficiency and engineering knowledge that was highly advanced for its time. The builders' ability to manipulate massive stones, create vaulted ceilings, achieve precise fittings, and transport materials over long distances reflects their ingenuity and problem-solving skills.

In summary, the megalithic temples of Ggantija demonstrate remarkable innovations in construction methods. The use of corbelling, precise fitting of stones, transportation of massive blocks, resourceful utilization of local materials, and incorporation of trilithons all contribute to the uniqueness and sophistication of Ggantija's construction techniques. These innovations are a testament to the advanced skills, engineering prowess, and ingenuity of the Neolithic builders who left their mark on this extraordinary architectural achievement.

Chapter 5: A Glimpse into Neolithic Life

The megalithic temples of Ggantija provide valuable insights into the Neolithic society and culture that flourished on the island of Gozo during ancient times. These temples, dating back over 5,000 years, offer a glimpse into the beliefs, practices, and social organization of the people who built and utilized these remarkable structures.

One of the key aspects of Neolithic society at Ggantija is the religious and spiritual significance attached to the temples. The immense effort and resources invested in constructing these monumental edifices suggest the importance placed on religious beliefs and rituals. The temples served as sacred spaces where the community would gather for ceremonies, worship, and possibly ancestral veneration. The presence of altars, figurines, and other artifacts associated with ritualistic practices indicates a strong connection to the spiritual realm and a belief in the supernatural.

The construction of the temples required the cooperation and coordination of a large number of individuals, reflecting a communal and organized society. The sheer scale of the construction projects suggests a high degree of social organization, with different individuals or groups likely assigned specific tasks and responsibilities. The collaboration required for such endeavors would have fostered a sense of collective identity and shared purpose among the Neolithic inhabitants of Ggantija.

The temples also serve as evidence of the Neolithic society's ability to mobilize resources and engage in long-term planning. The quarrying of limestone, transportation of massive stones, and construction of the temples required extensive labor, time, and expertise. This suggests that the community had developed systems for resource management, organization, and skill acquisition. Such complex endeavors would have required a social structure that supported specialization, cooperation, and the transmission of knowledge from one generation to the next.

The presence of decorative elements and artistic expressions at Ggantija indicates the cultural significance attached to creativity and aesthetics. Intricate carvings, sculptures, and symbolic representations found within the temples reveal the Neolithic people's artistic sensibilities and their desire to beautify their surroundings. These artistic expressions may have served both religious and social purposes, enhancing the ambiance of the temples and reinforcing communal bonds.

The existence of burial sites in the vicinity of Ggantija suggests a reverence for ancestors and a belief in the continuity of life beyond death. The placement of burial grounds in close proximity to the temples may indicate a connection between the spiritual realm, the ancestors, and the living community. This suggests a belief system that integrated the past, present, and future, emphasizing the importance of ancestral lineage and the continuation of cultural traditions.

The agricultural practices of the Neolithic inhabitants of Ggantija also played a significant role in their society and culture. The temples were likely located in close proximity to fertile agricultural land, reflecting the importance of agriculture in sustaining the community. The ability to cultivate crops and domesticate animals would have provided the necessary resources for survival and allowed for the development of settled communities.

In summary, the megalithic temples of Ggantija offer valuable insights into the Neolithic society and culture that thrived on the island of Gozo. The religious significance, communal collaboration, resource mobilization, artistic expressions, ancestral veneration, and agricultural practices all reflect the values, beliefs, and social organization of the Neolithic inhabitants. The temples stand as testaments to their ingenuity, spirituality, and collective efforts, providing a glimpse into a rich and fascinating ancient civilization.

Exploring the daily life and practices of the inhabitants of Ggantija offers a fascinating glimpse into the Neolithic lifestyle on the island of Gozo. While much of their daily routines and specific customs have been lost to time, the archaeological evidence provides valuable insights into their daily activities, social organization, and cultural practices.

One of the key aspects of daily life at Ggantija was likely centered around subsistence activities such as farming and animal husbandry. The fertile land surrounding the temples would have provided an ideal environment for cultivation. Archaeological remains, including stone tools and grain storage pits, suggest that the Neolithic inhabitants engaged in agricultural practices, growing crops such as wheat, barley, and legumes. They likely domesticated animals such as sheep, goats, and pigs, which would have provided them with meat, milk, and other valuable resources.

Food preparation and cooking were essential components of daily life. Excavations at Ggantija have revealed grinding stones and stone ovens, indicating the processing and cooking of grains. The inhabitants would have utilized these tools to grind grains into flour for baking bread or making porridge. Cooking methods likely involved open fires or simple clay ovens.

The community at Ggantija would have relied on various crafts and industries to fulfill their material needs. Stone tools, pottery fragments, and evidence of textile production suggest the presence of skilled artisans within the community. The production of tools and pottery would have been essential for everyday tasks, while textile production would have provided clothing and other fabric-based items. These crafts would have required specialized knowledge and craftsmanship, passed down through generations.

Social interaction and communal activities played an important role in Neolithic society at Ggantija. The temples themselves served as gathering places for religious ceremonies, communal rituals, and likely social events. These communal activities would have fostered a sense of unity and belonging among the inhabitants, reinforcing social bonds and cultural identity.

The role of gender within Neolithic society is a subject of speculation and ongoing research. While specific details are not known, it is believed that there was a division of labor based on gender. Men may have been primarily engaged in activities such as hunting, farming, and construction, while women would have played crucial roles in food preparation, textile production, and possibly child-rearing. However, it is important to note that the specifics of gender roles may have varied among different communities and regions.

The worship and veneration of deities and ancestors likely played a significant part in daily life. The temples of Ggantija were sacred spaces where religious ceremonies and rituals took place. These rituals may have involved offerings, prayers, and other forms of devotion to the spiritual realm. The presence of altars and figurines within the temples suggests a belief system that integrated the divine into daily life.

In terms of housing, the exact nature of Neolithic dwellings at Ggantija is not fully understood. However, it is believed that the inhabitants lived in simple structures made of perishable materials such as wood, reeds, and clay. These structures may have been temporary in nature, requiring regular maintenance and reconstruction.

In summary, the daily life of the inhabitants of Ggantija was likely centered around subsistence activities, crafts, communal rituals, and a close connection with the spiritual realm. Farming, animal husbandry, food preparation, and skilled crafts would have formed the backbone of their material existence. Social interaction, community gatherings, and religious practices would have fostered a sense of identity, unity, and cultural cohesion. While specific details of their daily routines and customs may remain elusive, the archaeological evidence offers valuable insights into the Neolithic way of life at Ggantija.

Burials and funerary rituals were significant aspects of the cultural practices at the Ggantija temples, providing insight into the beliefs and spiritual traditions of the Neolithic inhabitants. Excavations have revealed the presence of burial sites in the vicinity of the temples, shedding light on the reverence for the deceased and the rituals associated with death and the afterlife.

The burials at Ggantija primarily consisted of inhumations, where the deceased individuals were interred within the ground. The exact burial practices varied, with some individuals buried in simple pits and others in more elaborate graves. The position of the body within the burial pit varied as well, with some individuals lying on their side, curled in a fetal position, or extended.

The presence of grave goods and offerings within the burials suggests a belief in an afterlife or a continuation of the individual's journey beyond death. These grave goods included pottery vessels, stone tools, ornaments, and occasionally, animal remains. These offerings were likely meant to accompany the deceased in the afterlife or provide comfort and sustenance for their journey.

The location of the burials in close proximity to the temples suggests a connection between the spiritual realm and the realm of the living. It is possible that the temples were considered sacred spaces where rituals and ceremonies were conducted to honor and commemorate the deceased. The proximity of the burials to the places of worship reflects the belief in a spiritual continuity and a relationship between the living and the ancestors.

The presence of multiple individuals within some burial sites suggests the existence of family or communal burials, further highlighting the importance of kinship and community bonds in Neolithic society. The collective interment of individuals within a shared burial site suggests a sense of communal identity and a belief in the importance of community ties, even in death.

The selection of burial locations and the presence of burials in the vicinity of the temples also indicate a belief in the sanctity of the landscape. The choice to bury the deceased near the temples suggests a connection between the sacredness of the site and the spiritual journey of the departed.

Funerary rituals and ceremonies likely accompanied the burials, although the specific details of these practices are not known. It is reasonable to speculate that these rituals involved mourning, offerings, and perhaps communal gatherings to honor and remember the deceased. The temples themselves may have been used as ceremonial spaces during these rituals, further emphasizing the spiritual significance of the site.

In summary, the burials and funerary rituals at the Ggantija temples provide valuable insights into the beliefs and practices of the Neolithic inhabitants. The presence of burials near the temples, the inclusion of grave goods, and the proximity of the burials to places of worship all suggest a belief in the afterlife, the importance of ancestral reverence, and a strong connection between the spiritual realm and the realm of the living. These burial practices demonstrate the cultural and spiritual significance attached to death, reflecting the beliefs and values of the Neolithic society at Ggantija. Neolithic agriculture and subsistence strategies played a crucial role in the development and sustainability of human societies during this period. The transition from a nomadic, hunter-gatherer lifestyle to settled agricultural communities marked a significant shift in human history. The Neolithic inhabitants of various regions around the world, including the Mediterranean, the Near East, and Europe, developed innovative agricultural practices that laid the foundation for the growth of civilizations.

One of the primary subsistence strategies of the Neolithic era was the domestication of plants and animals. The cultivation of crops provided a stable and reliable food source for communities, leading to a more sedentary lifestyle. Wheat, barley, lentils, peas, and flax were among the crops cultivated during this period. The domestication of animals such as sheep, goats, cattle, and pigs provided additional sources of food, as well as materials for clothing, tools, and transportation.

Agricultural practices during the Neolithic period involved various techniques, including land clearance, planting, harvesting, and storage. Neolithic farmers developed methods for clearing land by burning vegetation or using primitive tools to remove obstacles such as trees and shrubs. They then prepared the soil for planting, often using simple digging sticks or primitive plows to turn the earth. Planting and harvesting were done manually, with seeds sown by hand and crops harvested with sickles or similar tools. The development of storage facilities, such as granaries or underground pits, allowed for the preservation of surplus crops, ensuring a stable food supply during leaner times.

The shift to agriculture not only provided a more stable food supply but also had social and cultural implications. The establishment of settled communities led to the development of permanent dwellings and the formation of larger social groups. It facilitated the division of labor, as different members of the community specialized in various tasks related to agriculture, craftsmanship, or trade. This division of labor allowed for the growth of complex societies and the development of specialized skills and technologies. The advent of agriculture also had significant environmental consequences. Neolithic farmers cleared land for cultivation, which led to the expansion of agricultural fields and the transformation of natural landscapes. The domestication of animals also had an impact on the environment, as grazing practices and herd management influenced the composition of plant communities and ecosystems.

In addition to providing food, agriculture influenced the development of cultural practices, technology, and social structures. Surplus food production allowed for the emergence of craft specialization, with artisans producing tools, pottery, textiles, and other goods for trade and exchange. The development of more permanent settlements led to the construction of dwellings, communal buildings, and eventually, monumental structures like the megalithic temples found at sites such as Ggantija and Stonehenge.

The transition to agriculture during the Neolithic period marked a significant milestone in human history. It transformed human societies from small, mobile groups of hunter-gatherers to settled communities engaged in agriculture, trade, and the development of complex social structures. The knowledge and innovations in agriculture laid the groundwork for the growth of civilizations and set the stage for the development of modern society as we know it today. Trade and exchange played a vital role in the Neolithic society of Ggantija, facilitating the flow of goods, ideas, and cultural interactions among different communities. Although the specifics of trade networks during this period are not fully known, the presence of exotic materials and artifacts at Ggantija suggests that long-distance trade was a significant aspect of their society.

One of the key resources that was likely traded was obsidian, a volcanic glass used for making sharp-edged tools and weapons. Ggantija, located on the island of Gozo, did not have natural sources of obsidian. Therefore, the presence of obsidian artifacts at the site indicates that it was obtained through trade networks. The origins of the obsidian used at Ggantija have been traced to sources in the Mediterranean region, such as Sicily and Lipari.

The exchange of goods would have involved a network of trade routes connecting Ggantija with neighboring communities. These routes may have been established along land or sea routes, allowing for the transportation of goods over varying distances. It is likely that trade was facilitated by the use of watercraft, such as boats or rafts, enabling coastal and maritime connections.

In addition to obsidian, other materials would have been traded, including precious stones, shells, pottery, and perhaps even specialized tools or crafted items. The trade of these materials would have fostered connections and relationships between different communities, leading to cultural exchange, the spread of ideas, and the emergence of regional networks. The exchange of goods in Neolithic societies was not solely driven by economic considerations but also had social and cultural significance. Trade and exchange would have served as mechanisms for establishing alliances, negotiating social relationships, and reinforcing communal ties. The interaction between different communities through trade would have allowed for the sharing of knowledge, traditions, and cultural practices, contributing to the diversity and richness of Neolithic societies.

It is important to note that the scale and complexity of trade during the Neolithic period were likely different from the extensive trade networks seen in later civilizations. Trade may have been conducted on a smaller scale, primarily involving local and regional exchanges. However, the presence of exotic materials at Ggantija indicates that long-distance trade did occur, even if it was not as extensive as in later periods.

The exact mechanisms and dynamics of trade in Ggantija's Neolithic society are subjects of ongoing research and exploration. The study of artifacts, the analysis of isotopes and trace elements, and the examination of archaeological contexts contribute to our understanding of trade networks and the extent of social and cultural interactions during this period.

In summary, trade and exchange played a significant role in the Neolithic society of Ggantija, facilitating the movement of goods, ideas, and cultural interactions. The acquisition of materials such as obsidian from distant sources indicates the existence of trade networks connecting Ggantija with neighboring communities. Trade not only provided access to necessary resources but also fostered social connections, cultural exchange, and the emergence of regional networks. The study of trade in Ggantija's Neolithic society contributes to our understanding of the complexity and interconnectedness of early human societies.

Chapter 6: The Mysteries of Ggantija's Purpose

The purpose of Ggantija's megalithic temples has been a subject of ongoing debate and speculation among archaeologists, historians, and researchers. The enigmatic nature of these impressive structures has fueled various theories regarding their function and significance within Neolithic society.

One prevailing theory suggests that the temples served as religious or ceremonial centers. The grandeur and intricacy of their construction, along with the presence of ritualistic features such as altars and carved stone objects, point to their possible use for communal worship, religious rituals, or spiritual practices. The temples may have been sacred spaces where important ceremonies, offerings, and gatherings took place, reinforcing social cohesion and providing a locus for communal identity and belief systems.

Another theory proposes that the temples were monumental tombs or burial complexes. The presence of human remains within or in close proximity to the temples supports this notion. The intricate construction and elaborate design of the temples may have served as a symbolic tribute to the deceased, highlighting the importance and social status of the individuals or groups interred there. The temples could have functioned as commemorative sites, honoring ancestors or revered figures, and facilitating ongoing rituals and remembrance.

Some researchers argue that the temples had multiple functions, serving as multifaceted community centers. These structures may have been gathering places for social, economic, and cultural activities. They could have hosted trade fairs, religious festivals, communal feasts, or other social events that brought people together from different regions. The temples may have functioned as hubs for exchange, fostering connections and interactions among neighboring communities and promoting cultural exchange.

The unique architectural features of the temples, such as the elaborate corbelled construction and massive stone blocks, have led to speculation about their potential defensive function. The monumental nature of the temples, along with their elevated positions and strategic locations, may have served as symbols of power and authority, or even as defensive structures during times of conflict. However, this theory remains speculative, as evidence for defensive purposes is limited.

It is crucial to acknowledge that the purpose of Ggantija's megalithic temples may have evolved and changed over time, and different temples within the complex may have had distinct functions. The evolving nature of the temples' use, combined with their rich symbolism and intricate design, suggests that they played a multifaceted role in the social, religious, and cultural fabric of Neolithic society.

In summary, the exact purpose of Ggantija's megalithic temples remains elusive, and various theories have been put forth to explain their function. Whether they served as religious centers, burial complexes, community gathering places, defensive structures, or a combination of these roles, the temples played a significant role in the social, cultural, and spiritual life of Neolithic communities. Further research, archaeological discoveries, and interdisciplinary investigations are essential to unraveling the mysteries surrounding the purpose and function of these extraordinary megalithic temples.

Ritualistic practices played a crucial role in the religious and social fabric of Ggantija's Neolithic society, providing insights into their spiritual beliefs, cultural practices, and communal identity. Although the specific details of these ceremonies and beliefs are not fully known, the archaeological evidence and the architectural features of Ggantija's temples offer valuable clues about the ritualistic practices that took place within these sacred spaces.

The temples themselves, with their impressive size, intricate design, and carefully constructed features, suggest a high level of reverence and importance attached to the rituals performed within them. The presence of carved stone altars, platforms, and niches indicate specific areas designated for offerings, symbolic actions, or ceremonial activities. These features provide evidence of the rituals and ceremonies that were conducted, although their exact nature and purpose remain speculative.

The orientation and alignment of the temples with celestial events, such as the rising or setting of the sun or the position of stars, suggest a possible astronomical significance in the rituals performed. It is plausible that these alignments were used to mark important dates or seasonal changes, allowing the Neolithic community to synchronize their rituals with natural cycles. These celestial connections may have played a role in their agricultural practices, fertility rites, or other spiritual observances.

The presence of carved stone objects, including statuettes, animal figures, and geometric motifs, within the temples suggests a symbolic and ritualistic purpose. These objects may have represented deities, spirits, or mythological beings, and their use during ceremonies could have invoked their presence or invoked certain powers or blessings. The symbolism of these objects likely held deep cultural and spiritual significance for the Neolithic community.

The rituals performed at Ggantija may have encompassed various aspects of life, including rites of passage, fertility rituals, seasonal celebrations, or communal gatherings. These ceremonies could have involved chanting, dancing, music, offerings, or other performative acts that brought the community together in shared experiences and heightened spiritual connections. The temples would have provided a focal point for these rituals, serving as spaces where individuals could connect with the divine, commune with their ancestors, or seek guidance and blessings.

It is important to consider the broader cultural and social context in interpreting the ritualistic practices at Ggantija. The Neolithic period was marked by the transition from hunter-gatherer societies to settled agricultural communities, and rituals played a crucial role in maintaining social cohesion, reinforcing beliefs, and fostering a sense of collective identity. The rituals conducted at Ggantija likely played a part in solidifying community bonds, reinforcing hierarchical structures, and ensuring the prosperity and well-being of the community as a whole.

However, the specifics of these rituals and the beliefs underlying them remain elusive, as the Neolithic culture of Ggantija did not leave behind written records. The interpretation of the archaeological evidence requires careful analysis and collaboration among experts from various disciplines.

In summary, the rituals and ceremonies at Ggantija were central to the spiritual and social fabric of the Neolithic society. The temples served as sacred spaces where individuals and the community as a whole could engage in ritualistic practices, connect with the divine, and strengthen communal bonds. While the exact nature and purpose of these rituals may never be fully known, the archaeological evidence and contextual clues provide a glimpse into the beliefs and practices of Ggantija's ancient inhabitants. Further research and interdisciplinary collaboration are essential to deepening our understanding of these ritualistic practices and their significance within Neolithic society.

The purpose and use of Ggantija's temples have been subjects of extensive study and investigation by archaeologists seeking to unravel the mysteries surrounding these remarkable structures. While the precise details may never be fully known, the archaeological clues and evidence provide valuable insights into their purpose and use within the Neolithic society.

One key aspect that has emerged from the archaeological research is the presence of human burials within and around the temples. These burials indicate that Ggantija's temples were likely used as funerary complexes or sacred spaces associated with death and ancestor worship. The presence of multiple burial chambers and the careful arrangement of skeletal remains suggest a reverence for the deceased and the belief in an afterlife. The temples may have served as places for honoring and communing with ancestors, as well as for conducting rituals and ceremonies related to death and the journey of the soul.

The architectural features of Ggantija's temples also provide insights into their possible use. The massive stone walls, corbelled roofs, and intricate construction techniques indicate that these structures were built with great care and precision. The temples' imposing size and unique design suggest that they served as prominent and symbolic religious or ceremonial centers. The layout and organization of the temples may have facilitated specific rituals or acted as focal points for communal gatherings and celebrations.

The presence of carved stone altars, niches, and platforms further supports the idea of ritualistic activities taking place within the temples. These features may have been used for making offerings, performing ceremonies, or conducting spiritual practices. The placement and positioning of these ritual elements within the temple complex may have held symbolic meaning, reflecting the beliefs and cosmological understanding of the Neolithic community.

Additionally, the alignment of the temples with celestial events, such as the rising or setting of the sun, suggests an astronomical significance. The precise orientation of the temples may have allowed for the observation and tracking of celestial phenomena, which in turn could have played a role in determining specific times for rituals, agricultural activities, or seasonal festivities. The celestial alignments may have been seen as a connection between the earthly realm and the divine, enhancing the spiritual significance of the temples.

The artifacts discovered within and around Ggantija's temples also shed light on their purpose and use. These include pottery vessels, stone tools, ornaments, and symbolic objects. The presence of such items suggests that the temples were not only used for religious or ceremonial purposes but also as centers of social and economic activities. They may have served as places for trade, exchange, and communal gatherings,

214

fostering social cohesion and interaction among the Neolithic community.

It is important to note that the purpose and use of Ggantija's temples may have evolved over time and varied among different periods within the Neolithic era. The temples may have served different functions and held different meanings at different stages of their existence. Additionally, the interpretation of the archaeological evidence requires careful analysis, considering the limitations and biases inherent in studying ancient structures and artifacts.

In summary, while the precise purpose and use of Ggantija's temples may remain partially speculative, the archaeological evidence provides valuable insights into their significance within the Neolithic society. The presence of human burials, architectural features, celestial alignments, and ritualistic artifacts suggests that the temples served as centers for death rituals, ancestor worship, religious ceremonies, and communal gatherings. The study of Ggantija's temples continues to contribute to our understanding of the beliefs, practices, and social dynamics of the ancient Neolithic communities in Malta.

Ggantija holds significant cultural importance as one of the most remarkable megalithic temple complexes of the Neolithic period. Its role in Neolithic society extends beyond its architectural grandeur, offering valuable insights into the beliefs, social organization, and cultural practices of the people who built and used it.

One aspect of Ggantija's cultural significance lies in its construction. The immense effort and resources invested in building the temples demonstrate the high level of social organization, labor mobilization, and communal collaboration within the Neolithic community. The construction of such monumental structures required careful planning, sophisticated engineering techniques, and a shared vision among the builders. This suggests the existence of a cohesive social structure capable of mobilizing resources and labor for large-scale communal projects.

The temples also provide evidence of the religious and spiritual beliefs of the Neolithic community. The grandeur and intricacy of Ggantija's architecture, along with the presence of ritualistic features and burial practices, indicate the centrality of religious beliefs and practices in the daily lives of the people. The temples may have been seen as sacred spaces, where individuals could connect with the divine, seek spiritual guidance, and engage in communal rituals. They likely played a role in shaping the Neolithic community's worldview, cosmology, and understanding of their place in the universe.

Ggantija's cultural significance extends beyond its religious and spiritual aspects. The temples likely functioned as important centers for social interaction, cultural exchange, and community cohesion. They may have served as gathering places for festivals, trade, or other social events, facilitating connections between different groups and fostering a sense of collective identity. The presence of communal spaces within the temple complex suggests that they were hubs for social activities, where individuals could come together, share knowledge, and strengthen social bonds.

Furthermore, Ggantija's cultural significance is reflected in its influence on later societies and their cultural practices. The temples have left a lasting legacy in the collective memory of the Maltese people and have become an emblematic symbol of their cultural heritage. The architectural techniques, artistic motifs, and religious symbolism found at Ggantija can be seen echoed in subsequent periods of Maltese history, demonstrating the enduring impact of the Neolithic culture on the island.

The study of Ggantija also contributes to our understanding of the broader cultural and social dynamics of the Neolithic period. It offers insights into the transition from hunter-gatherer societies to settled agricultural communities, the development of specialized crafts and trades, the emergence of social hierarchies, and the establishment of religious and ritual practices. The study of Ggantija allows us to glimpse into the complexity and diversity of Neolithic cultures and their contributions to human history.

In summary, Ggantija's cultural significance lies in its architectural splendor, its role in religious and spiritual practices, its function as a center for social interaction, and its influence on subsequent cultural developments. The temples provide valuable insights into the beliefs, social organization, and cultural practices of the Neolithic community that built and used them. The study of Ggantija contributes to our understanding of the Neolithic period, shedding light on the rich and complex cultural heritage of ancient Malta.

The purpose of Ggantija, one of Malta's most extraordinary megalithic temple complexes, has been the subject of much scholarly debate and evolving theories. Various perspectives have emerged over the years, each offering unique insights and interpretations regarding the purpose and function of this enigmatic archaeological site.

One prevalent theory suggests that Ggantija served as a religious or ceremonial center. The impressive size and intricate architectural features of the temples, along with the presence of ritualistic elements such as altars and niches, indicate their role in facilitating religious practices. The temples may have been sacred spaces where the Neolithic community gathered to engage in rituals, ceremonies, and communal worship. The alignment of the temples with celestial events, such as the rising sun during the equinoxes, further supports the notion of their religious significance and possible astronomical connections.

Another perspective posits that Ggantija functioned as a social and communal hub. The temples' layout, with multiple chambers and communal spaces, suggests that they served as gathering places for communal activities, social interaction, and trade. These spaces may have fostered connections among different groups, facilitating the exchange of ideas, goods, and cultural practices. The presence of communal areas also implies that the temples played a role in community cohesion and identity formation, serving as spaces where individuals came together for shared experiences and collective endeavors.

Furthermore, Ggantija has been associated with ancestral worship and funerary practices. The presence of burials within and around the temples suggests a connection to death rituals and the veneration of ancestors. The temples may have been seen as sacred spaces where the Neolithic community paid homage to their forebears, sought their guidance, or believed they maintained a spiritual presence. The elaborate construction and careful arrangement of human remains within the temples highlight the reverence and importance placed on ancestral connections.

Additionally, some theories propose that Ggantija had a practical function related to resource management or defense. The monumental size and robust construction of the temples may have served as symbols of power, authority, or territorial control. They could have functioned as markers of communal identity and status, reinforcing social hierarchies within the Neolithic society. The presence of defensive features, such as the massive boundary walls surrounding the temples, suggests that Ggantija may have also served a defensive purpose, providing protection for the community in times of conflict.

It is important to note that these theories are not mutually exclusive, and Ggantija may have served a multifaceted role in the lives of the Neolithic community. The site's purpose may have evolved over time, influenced by cultural, social, and environmental factors. It is also crucial to consider the limitations of interpreting archaeological evidence, as our understanding of the past is inevitably shaped by the available data and the biases of researchers.

In summary, the purpose of Ggantija remains a subject of ongoing scholarly investigation, with evolving theories offering different perspectives on its significance. Whether as a religious center, social hub, site of ancestral worship, or a combination of these functions, Ggantija undoubtedly played a vital role in the lives of the Neolithic people who built and used it. Continued research, interdisciplinary collaboration, and the exploration of new evidence will further enhance our understanding of this remarkable archaeological site and its place in human history.

Chapter 7: Preservation and Restoration Efforts

The conservation and restoration efforts at Ggantija, one of Malta's most important archaeological sites, have played a vital role in preserving its ancient glory and ensuring its longevity for future generations. The significance of these efforts goes beyond mere preservation; they contribute to our understanding of the site, provide insights into the construction techniques employed by the Neolithic people, and help us appreciate the cultural and historical value of Ggantija.

The restoration work at Ggantija has been carried out with utmost care and precision, taking into consideration the unique challenges posed by the site's age and delicate state. The main goal has been to stabilize the structures and prevent further deterioration while maintaining their authenticity. This has required a combination of scientific analysis, technical expertise, and a deep understanding of the original construction methods.

One aspect of the restoration process has involved addressing structural issues to ensure the stability of the temples. Measures such as consolidating the stonework, reinforcing the foundations, and implementing appropriate drainage systems have been taken to safeguard the integrity of the structures. These interventions aim to prevent further deterioration caused by natural elements and human activity, ensuring that Ggantija remains standing for future generations to appreciate.

Preserving the architectural features and artistic elements of Ggantija has also been a key focus of the restoration efforts. This includes the meticulous cleaning and conservation of the stone surfaces, the careful reconstruction of fallen or damaged elements, and the protection of intricate carvings and reliefs. By preserving and restoring these features, the unique beauty and craftsmanship of Ggantija are brought to life, allowing visitors to appreciate the skill and artistry of the Neolithic builders.

Additionally, the restoration work at Ggantija has provided an opportunity for further research and archaeological investigation. As the structures are studied and analyzed during the restoration process, new insights into the construction techniques, materials used, and the original appearance of the temples can be gained. This information contributes to our understanding of the Neolithic period and enhances our knowledge of the cultural and technological achievements of the ancient inhabitants of Malta.

Moreover, the restoration efforts at Ggantija have contributed to the development of best practices in heritage conservation. The experience gained from working on such a significant site has informed conservation approaches used not only in Malta but also in other parts of the world. The knowledge and expertise acquired through the restoration work at Ggantija have been shared with professionals in the field, facilitating the preservation of other ancient sites and monuments worldwide.

It is important to note that the restoration efforts have been carried out with a commitment to preserving the authenticity and integrity of Ggantija. The aim is not to create a pristine replica but to ensure that the site's historical and cultural value is protected while allowing visitors to experience and appreciate its ancient atmosphere.

In summary, the conservation and restoration efforts at Ggantija have been crucial in safeguarding the site's ancient glory. By stabilizing the structures, preserving the architectural features, and advancing our understanding of the site, these efforts contribute to our knowledge of the Neolithic period and allow us to connect with the rich cultural heritage of Malta. Ggantija stands as a testament to the ingenuity and craftsmanship of its builders, and through ongoing conservation, its ancient magnificence continues to inspire and educate generations to come. The conservation of Ggantija's megalithic temples poses numerous challenges due to the site's age, complexity, and vulnerability to natural and human factors. Safeguarding these ancient structures requires a comprehensive approach that balances preservation with accessibility and public engagement. Let us explore some of the key challenges involved in the conservation of Ggantija.

One significant challenge is the impact of weathering and erosion. Over thousands of years, exposure to wind, rain, temperature fluctuations, and other environmental elements has taken its toll on the megaliths. The soft limestone used in their construction is particularly susceptible to erosion. Efforts to mitigate these effects involve monitoring and managing water runoff, applying protective coatings to the stone surfaces, and implementing drainage systems to prevent excessive moisture accumulation. These measures help slow down the rate of deterioration and extend the longevity of the structures.

Another challenge is the preservation of fragile and intricate carvings. The elaborate reliefs and decorative elements at Ggantija are susceptible to damage from human touch, pollution, and the passage of time. Balancing the desire for visitor access and engagement with the need to protect these delicate features is a constant challenge. Protective barriers, controlled access, and educational programs play a crucial role in minimizing direct contact with the stone surfaces and raising awareness about the importance of responsible visitation.

The threat of vandalism and theft poses additional challenges to the conservation of Ggantija. Despite the site's significance and legal protection, instances of vandalism and unauthorized removal of artifacts have occurred. Ensuring site security, implementing surveillance systems, and promoting public awareness about the consequences of such actions are essential in deterring vandalism and safeguarding the integrity of the temples.

Furthermore, the presence of vegetation and biological growth on the stone surfaces can impact the stability and preservation of the megaliths. Roots from nearby trees or plants can penetrate the cracks in the stone, exacerbating structural instability and accelerating deterioration. Regular monitoring and maintenance of vegetation around the site are necessary to prevent further damage and preserve the structural integrity of the temples.

Sustainable management of visitor impact is another significant challenge in the conservation of Ggantija. Balancing the desire for public access and educational opportunities with the need to minimize foot traffic and potential damage to the site is crucial. Implementing visitor management strategies such as guided tours, designated pathways, and visitor capacity limits can help reduce the impact of visitation on the fragile archaeological remains.

Funding is a perpetual challenge in the conservation of Ggantija. The cost of ongoing monitoring, maintenance, and preservation efforts can be significant. Securing funding from governmental bodies, private organizations, and international collaborations is crucial to sustain conservation initiatives and ensure the long-term preservation of the site.

Finally, striking a balance between preservation and interpretation is essential in conserving Ggantija. While preserving the site's integrity is of utmost importance, it is equally important to provide interpretive information and educational resources for visitors to understand the historical, cultural, and archaeological significance of the temples. Creating a visitor experience that is both engaging and respectful of the site's integrity requires careful planning and collaboration among conservationists, archaeologists, and interpretive specialists.

In summary, the conservation of Ggantija's megalithic temples faces numerous challenges, including weathering and erosion, fragile carvings, vandalism, vegetation growth, visitor impact, funding, and interpretation. Addressing these challenges requires a comprehensive and multidisciplinary approach that combines scientific research, responsible visitor management, ongoing monitoring, and adequate funding. By safeguarding Ggantija's ancient structures, we can ensure that future generations can continue to appreciate and learn from this remarkable archaeological site. Preserving the ancient structures of Ggantija requires the implementation of various techniques and strategies to ensure their long-term stability and protection. These preservation techniques encompass a range of activities, from regular monitoring to targeted interventions. Let us explore some of the strategies used in maintaining the integrity of Ggantija's megalithic temples. Regular monitoring plays a fundamental role in preserving the structures of Ggantija. Close observation and documentation of any changes, deterioration, or vulnerabilities allow conservationists to identify and address potential issues in a timely manner. This includes visual inspections, photographic documentation, and the use of advanced technologies such as laser scanning and remote sensing to monitor the condition of the temples.

Consolidation and stabilization techniques are employed to reinforce the structural integrity of Ggantija's megalithic stones. This involves identifying areas of instability or decay and implementing measures to strengthen them. Techniques such as grouting, injection of consolidants, and the use of stainless steel dowels or rods can be employed to reinforce fragile or damaged sections of the stone.

Protective coatings are applied to the surfaces of the megaliths to shield them from environmental factors and mitigate deterioration. These coatings act as a barrier, protecting the stone from moisture, pollutants, and biological growth. Careful consideration is given to the selection of appropriate coatings that are compatible with the original materials and do not negatively impact the aesthetics or long-term preservation of the structures.

Drainage systems are crucial in managing water infiltration and preventing moisture-related issues. Excessive moisture can accelerate deterioration, promote biological growth, and compromise the stability of the megaliths. The implementation of effective drainage systems, including the installation of gutters, downspouts, and drainage channels, helps redirect water away from the structures and prevents water buildup.

Vegetation management is an important aspect of preserving Ggantija. Vegetation, such as trees, shrubs, and grasses, can pose risks to the structures by exerting pressure on the stones, causing root intrusion, and facilitating the growth of moss or lichens. Regular trimming, pruning, and the selective removal of vegetation around the site are carried out to mitigate these risks and ensure the long-term stability of the temples.

Conservation cleaning is performed to remove accumulated dirt, debris, and biological growth from the surfaces of the megaliths. Careful and meticulous cleaning methods, using soft brushes, low-pressure water sprays, or specialized cleaning agents, are employed to avoid causing any damage to the delicate stone surfaces. The aim is to maintain the aesthetic integrity of the structures while respecting their historical and archaeological significance.

Educational initiatives and public outreach programs are essential in fostering a sense of responsibility and awareness among visitors. Informative signage, guided tours, and visitor codes of conduct help promote the importance of respectful visitation and the need to protect the fragile structures of Ggantija. By engaging the public, these initiatives contribute to the long-term preservation and appreciation of the site.

Collaborative partnerships between archaeologists, conservationists, and local communities are crucial for the sustained preservation of Ggantija. These partnerships foster knowledge exchange, community involvement, and the sharing of resources and expertise. Involving local communities in the preservation efforts enhances a sense of ownership and pride in the site, further contributing to its long-term protection.

In summary, the preservation of Ggantija's ancient structures relies on a range of techniques and strategies aimed at maintaining their stability, protecting them from environmental factors, and raising awareness among visitors. Regular monitoring, consolidation, protective coatings, drainage systems, vegetation management, conservation cleaning, educational initiatives, and collaborative partnerships are all integral components of the preservation process. Through these efforts, Ggantija's megalithic temples can be safeguarded for future generations to appreciate and study, ensuring the continued understanding and enjoyment of this remarkable archaeological site. The conservation of Ggantija, one of Malta's most significant archaeological sites, has been a collaborative effort that extends beyond national boundaries. International organizations, experts, and institutions have come together to contribute their knowledge, resources, and expertise to protect and preserve the ancient structures of Ggantija. This collaborative approach has been instrumental in enhancing conservation practices, advancing research, and ensuring the long-term safeguarding of Ggantija for future generations.

One notable international effort in the conservation of Ggantija is the collaboration between the Maltese authorities and UNESCO (United Nations Educational, Scientific and Cultural Organization). Ggantija has been inscribed as a UNESCO World Heritage site, recognizing its outstanding universal value and the need for its protection. This designation has brought international attention and support to the conservation efforts at Ggantija, providing access to funding, technical assistance, and expert advice.

Furthermore, international organizations such as ICOMOS (International Council on Monuments and Sites) and ICCROM (International Centre for the Study of the Preservation and Restoration of Cultural Property) have been actively involved in the conservation of Ggantija. These organizations provide expertise in heritage conservation, conduct research, and offer training programs to enhance the capacity of local professionals and stakeholders involved in the preservation of Ggantija.

Collaboration between academic institutions and archaeological teams from around the world has been integral to the conservation and research efforts at Ggantija. Scholars and experts from various disciplines contribute their expertise in archaeology, architecture, conservation science, and related fields to study and interpret the site. Through collaborative research projects, scientific analysis, and sharing of knowledge, a deeper understanding of Ggantija's significance and conservation needs has been achieved.

Partnerships between governmental agencies, local communities, and non-governmental organizations (NGOs) have also played a vital role in the collaborative conservation efforts at Ggantija. These partnerships ensure the involvement of local stakeholders, promote community engagement, and facilitate the sharing of responsibilities in the preservation and management of the site. Local communities are often the custodians of the cultural heritage and their active participation is essential in fostering a sense of ownership and stewardship.

International conferences, symposiums, and workshops focused on the conservation of Ggantija have served as platforms for knowledge exchange, networking, and capacity building. These events bring together experts, researchers, policymakers, and professionals from diverse backgrounds to share their experiences, discuss best practices, and address the challenges in the preservation of Ggantija. Such platforms contribute to the dissemination of information, the generation of new ideas, and the formation of collaborative networks.

Financial support from international donors, philanthropic foundations, and cultural heritage organizations has been crucial in funding the conservation initiatives at Ggantija. These contributions provide the necessary resources for research, conservation interventions, infrastructure development, and educational programs. The support of these international entities demonstrates a shared commitment to the preservation of cultural heritage and the recognition of the global importance of Ggantija.

In summary, the conservation of Ggantija has been a collaborative endeavor, drawing on the expertise, resources, and support of international organizations, academic institutions, governmental agencies, local communities, and various stakeholders. This collaborative approach ensures the sharing of knowledge, the implementation of best practices, and the sustainability of conservation efforts. By working together, these international efforts have contributed to the preservation and protection of Ggantija, safeguarding its ancient structures and the rich cultural heritage they represent.

Preserving Ggantija's ancient structures while providing public access and ensuring a sustainable visitor experience is a delicate balancing act. It requires careful consideration of conservation principles, site management strategies, and visitor engagement. Striking this balance allows for the enjoyment and appreciation of Ggantija's cultural heritage while minimizing potential risks to the site's integrity. Let us explore how sustainable preservation is achieved at Ggantija.

Site planning and design play a crucial role in ensuring sustainable preservation. The layout of visitor facilities, pathways, and interpretive signage is carefully designed to minimize the impact on the archaeological remains. Well-defined visitor routes and protective barriers help guide visitors and prevent them from accessing restricted areas, thus safeguarding the fragile structures of Ggantija.

Visitor capacity management is essential in maintaining a sustainable balance between accessibility and conservation. By setting limits on the number of visitors allowed on-site at any given time, overcrowding and potential damage to the archaeological remains are mitigated. This ensures that the site's integrity is preserved while providing visitors with an enjoyable and meaningful experience.

Educational programs and interpretive resources are integral to sustainable preservation. Through informative signage, guided tours, and interactive exhibits, visitors are provided with historical and cultural context, as well as an understanding of the significance of Ggantija. This enhances visitor appreciation, fosters respect for the site, and promotes responsible behavior.

Visitor engagement and participation in conservation efforts are encouraged at Ggantija. Opportunities for hands-on experiences, volunteer programs, and citizen science initiatives enable visitors to contribute to the preservation of the site. By involving the public in conservation activities, a sense of ownership and stewardship is fostered, enhancing the long-term sustainability of the site.

Regular monitoring and maintenance are vital in sustainable preservation. Ongoing assessments of the site's condition, including the monitoring of visitor impact, environmental factors, and structural stability, allow for timely interventions when necessary. Regular cleaning, vegetation management, and structural repairs ensure the preservation of the site's integrity and minimize potential risks.

Sustainable preservation also involves the consideration of environmental sustainability. Implementing environmentally friendly practices in energy usage, waste management, and water conservation reduces the ecological footprint of site operations. By embracing sustainable practices, Ggantija demonstrates a commitment to responsible stewardship and contributes to global efforts towards sustainability.

Collaboration and partnerships with local communities are instrumental in achieving sustainable preservation. Engaging with the local community fosters a sense of shared responsibility, encourages their active involvement, and ensures that the benefits of tourism and preservation are shared equitably. Local knowledge and expertise are valuable assets that contribute to sustainable management practices.

Lastly, ongoing research and innovation play a significant role in sustainable preservation. Continual scientific studies, technological advancements, and the application of best practices in conservation contribute to the development of new approaches and strategies. By remaining adaptive and open to new ideas, Ggantija can continuously improve its preservation efforts and adapt to evolving challenges.

In summary, sustainable preservation at Ggantija involves a careful balance between accessibility and conservation. Through site planning, visitor capacity management, educational programs, and visitor engagement, Ggantija ensures a meaningful and responsible visitor experience. Regular monitoring, maintenance, environmental sustainability, community collaboration, and ongoing research are integral components of sustainable preservation. By embracing these principles, Ggantija can be preserved for future generations to enjoy, while safeguarding its cultural heritage and ecological significance.

Chapter 8: Sacred Offerings and Rituals

The megalithic temples of Ggantija provide valuable insights into the religious and ritual practices of its ancient inhabitants. Through archaeological discoveries and careful analysis, researchers have gained a deeper understanding of the sacred offerings and rituals that took place within these magnificent structures. Let us delve into the fascinating world of ritual practices at Ggantija.

The presence of specialized areas within the temple complex suggests that Ggantija was a place of religious significance and communal gathering. Various chambers and enclosures were likely dedicated to specific rituals, each serving a unique purpose within the overall religious framework. The careful planning and construction of these spaces indicate the importance of rituals in the lives of the temple's builders and users. Archaeological excavations have uncovered evidence of animal bones, such as cattle, sheep, and goats, suggesting that animal sacrifices were part of the ritual practices at Ggantija. These offerings may have symbolized offerings to the divine, acts of gratitude, or requests for divine intervention. The selection of specific animals and the manner in which they were sacrificed likely held symbolic meaning within the religious belief system of the temple's inhabitants.

Ceramic vessels and stone utensils discovered at Ggantija indicate their use in ritual practices. These vessels may have been used for the preparation, storage, and consumption of ritual offerings, such as food, beverages, or sacred substances. Their elaborate decoration and craftsmanship suggest the significance attributed to these objects in the performance of rituals. The presence of figurines and statuettes within the temple complex suggests their role in religious rituals and worship. These representations of human and animal forms may have served as representations of deities or spirit beings, allowing worshippers to connect with the divine realm. The placement and arrangement of these figurines within the temple suggest that they played a central role in the ritual practices conducted at Ggantija.

Symbolic carvings and engravings on the megalithic stones themselves provide further evidence of ritual significance. These intricate patterns and designs may have held symbolic meanings or represented deities, spirits, or ancestral figures. The inclusion of these carvings in the temple's architecture suggests that they were integral to the religious experience and ritual practices of Ggantija.

The alignment of the temple's entranceways and chambers with celestial phenomena, such as the rising and setting of the sun, suggests that astronomical observations and celestial events played a role in the timing and organization of rituals at Ggantija. These alignments may have facilitated the coordination of important religious events, seasonal celebrations, or solstice and equinox rituals.

The rituals performed at Ggantija likely involved a range of activities, including prayers, chants, dances, and processions. The precise nature of these rituals remains a subject of speculation and interpretation, but their importance in the spiritual and social lives of the temple's inhabitants cannot be understated. These rituals would have fostered a sense of community, strengthened social bonds, and reinforced the religious beliefs of the community.

The offerings and rituals conducted at Ggantija were likely tied to the cycles of nature, agricultural fertility, and the well-being of the community. They may have been performed to ensure bountiful harvests, ward off evil spirits, seek divine protection, or express gratitude for blessings received. These rituals provided a means for the community to connect with the spiritual realm, seek divine guidance, and maintain a harmonious relationship with the natural and supernatural forces.

In summary, the megalithic temples of Ggantija offer valuable insights into the religious and ritual practices of its ancient inhabitants. The presence of animal sacrifices, ritual objects, figurines, carvings, and astronomical alignments suggests the significance of rituals in the lives of the temple's builders and users. The offerings and rituals conducted at Ggantija played a crucial role in community cohesion, spiritual beliefs, and the expression of devotion. By exploring these ritual practices, we gain a deeper understanding of the cultural and religious complexities of Ggantija's ancient civilization.

The megalithic temples of Ggantija hold significant clues to the symbolic meanings behind the offerings made within their sacred spaces. These offerings were not merely material gifts but carried deep cultural, religious, and spiritual significance for the ancient inhabitants of Ggantija. By unraveling the symbolic meanings of these offerings, we can gain insights into the beliefs and practices of this ancient civilization.

Animal sacrifices were a prominent form of offering at Ggantija, and their symbolic meanings can be interpreted in various ways. The selection of specific animals for sacrifice may have been influenced by their symbolic associations. For example, cattle, with their strength and fertility, may have represented abundance and prosperity. Sheep and goats, known for their agility and resourcefulness, may have symbolized agility in navigating life's challenges. The act of sacrificing these animals may have been seen as a gesture of giving back to the divine, acknowledging the interdependence between humans and the natural world. Ceramic vessels and stone utensils used in rituals at Ggantija carried symbolic significance as well. The craftsmanship and intricate designs of these objects suggest their role as vessels of communication between the earthly and spiritual realms. They may have symbolized the connection between the human and divine, acting as conduits for offerings, prayers, and spiritual energies. The use of specific materials, such as clay or stone, may have further emphasized their symbolic value, representing the primordial elements from which life emerged.

Figurines and statuettes found at Ggantija offer further insights into the symbolic meanings of offerings. These representations of human and animal forms may have been seen as embodiments of deities, spirits, or ancestral beings. They served as physical manifestations of the divine, allowing worshippers to establish a connection and seek guidance or protection. The careful placement and arrangement of these figurines within the temple complex suggest their role as intermediaries, bridging the gap between the human and divine realms.

Symbolic carvings and engravings on the megalithic stones themselves provide a rich source of symbolic meanings. Intricate patterns, geometric motifs, and depictions of animals or celestial bodies may have carried profound significance. These carvings may have represented cosmological concepts, the cycle of life and death, or specific mythological narratives. The placement of these carvings within the temple's architecture indicates their role in creating a sacred and spiritually charged environment.

The timing and alignment of rituals at Ggantija with celestial events also hold symbolic significance. Alignments with the rising or setting sun, solstices, equinoxes, or other astronomical phenomena may have symbolized the cyclical nature of life, the seasons, and the interconnectedness of the earthly and celestial realms. Such alignments may have marked important moments of transition, renewal, or the honoring of specific deities associated with celestial bodies.

It is essential to consider the cultural and religious context of the ancient inhabitants of Ggantija when interpreting the symbolic meanings of offerings. The specific beliefs, mythologies, and cosmologies of this civilization may have shaped the understanding and significance attached to these offerings. It is through a comprehensive analysis of archaeological evidence, comparative studies, and a deep appreciation for the cultural context that we can begin to unlock the intricate symbolic meanings embedded within the offerings at Ggantija.

In summary, the offerings made at Ggantija's megalithic temples carried profound symbolic meanings. Animal sacrifices, ritual objects, figurines, carvings, and celestial alignments all played a part in expressing beliefs, establishing connections with the divine, and honoring the cycles of life. These offerings served as vehicles of communication, embodying cultural values, and fostering a sense of spiritual connection with the cosmos. By unraveling the symbolic meanings of these offerings, we gain a glimpse into the rich tapestry of beliefs and practices of the ancient civilization that thrived at Ggantija. The megalithic temples of Ggantija offer fascinating insights into the ritualistic ceremonies that were central to the worship and belief systems of its ancient inhabitants. Through careful archaeological analysis and the study of artifacts and structures, we can begin to unravel the intricate practices and beliefs that shaped the religious landscape of Ggantija.

Ritual ceremonies at Ggantija were likely multifaceted, encompassing a range of activities and performances. These ceremonies served as a means for the community to connect with the divine, express reverence, and seek spiritual guidance and blessings. The temple complex itself, with its monumental architecture and sacred spaces, provided the setting for these rituals, creating a tangible link between the earthly and the divine realms.

The timing and organization of rituals at Ggantija were likely influenced by celestial events and natural cycles. The alignment of the temples with astronomical phenomena, such as the rising or setting sun, solstices, or equinoxes, suggests that these celestial events held significant religious and symbolic meaning. Rituals may have been timed to coincide with these celestial occurrences, marking moments of transition or emphasizing the connection between the human and divine realms.

The offerings made during ritual ceremonies played a central role in worship practices at Ggantija. Animal sacrifices, as mentioned previously, were a common form of offering. These sacrifices may have been accompanied by prayers, chants, and invocations, creating an atmosphere of devotion and solemnity. The act of sacrifice served as a means of communication with the divine, expressing gratitude, seeking blessings, or appeasing deities.

Ceramic vessels, stone utensils, and other ritual objects were used in the preparation, presentation, and consumption of offerings. These objects held symbolic significance and were carefully crafted and decorated, reflecting their importance in the ritual ceremonies. The precise manner in which these objects were used and handled would have been governed by established religious protocols and practices.

Music, dance, and processions were likely integral components of ritual ceremonies at Ggantija. The rhythmic beats of drums, the melodic tones of flutes, and the chanting or singing of hymns would have created an immersive and transformative experience for worshippers. Dance, with its expressive movements and gestures, may have been used to embody spiritual concepts, convey narratives, or invoke divine presence. Processions within the temple complex or in nearby sacred spaces would have allowed worshippers to physically engage with the sacred and reinforce their sense of collective identity.

The presence of figurines, statues, and carvings within the temple complex indicates their role in ritual ceremonies. These representations of deities, spirits, or ancestral beings would have served as focal points of worship and veneration. They may have been adorned with offerings, anointed with sacred substances, or engaged in symbolic gestures during rituals. The careful placement and arrangement of these sacred objects suggest their importance in creating a spiritually charged environment and facilitating the connection between worshippers and the divine.

Ritual ceremonies at Ggantija likely fostered a sense of community and social cohesion. They provided opportunities for individuals to come together, share in collective experiences, and reinforce communal bonds. The rituals would have been overseen by religious specialists, such as priests or shamans, who acted as intermediaries between the human and divine realms, guiding and officiating the ceremonies.

It is important to note that our understanding of the ritualistic ceremonies at Ggantija is based on interpretations derived from archaeological evidence and comparative studies. The specific details of these ceremonies may never be fully known, and they may have varied over time and across different communities. However, through the careful analysis of artifacts, structures, and cultural contexts, we can begin to glimpse the beliefs, practices, and spiritual experiences of the ancient worshippers at Ggantija.

In summary, the megalithic temples of Ggantija provide valuable insights into the ritualistic ceremonies that formed an integral part of the worship and belief systems of its ancient inhabitants. These ceremonies encompassed a range of activities, including offerings, prayers, music, dance, and processions. They were conducted within a sacred and symbolic environment, creating a connection between worshippers and the divine. The rituals served as a means of communication, expressing reverence, seeking blessings, and fostering a sense of community and collective identity. Through the study of these ritual practices, we can gain a deeper appreciation for the rich religious and cultural traditions of the ancient civilization that flourished at Ggantija. Ggantija, with its enigmatic megalithic temples, offers a glimpse into the material culture of the rituals that were practiced within its sacred spaces. The artifacts and objects discovered at the site provide valuable insights into the religious and ceremonial practices of the ancient inhabitants of Ggantija, allowing us to unravel the mysteries surrounding their ritualistic traditions. Among the most intriguing artifacts found at Ggantija are the ceramic vessels and stone utensils used in ritual ceremonies. These objects were meticulously crafted, exhibiting a high level of craftsmanship and artistic skill. Decorated with intricate patterns, geometric motifs, and symbolic designs, these vessels held a prominent role in the rituals of Ggantija. They were used for the preparation, presentation, and consumption of offerings, and their elaborate designs suggest their significance in facilitating the connection between the earthly and the divine.

The ceramic vessels found at Ggantija are diverse in shape and size, ranging from small bowls and cups to larger storage vessels. They were made using techniques such as coiling, molding, and firing, resulting in sturdy and well-crafted containers. The designs adorning these vessels include geometric patterns, animal motifs, and abstract symbols, reflecting the artistic sensibilities and religious symbolism of the ancient civilization. The careful attention to detail and the use of vibrant colors indicate the importance attached to these objects within the ritual context. Stone utensils, such as mortars and pestles, were also discovered at Ggantija. These tools played a vital role in the preparation of offerings, including grinding grains or herbs for ritualistic purposes. The stone utensils are often adorned with carvings or incised decorations, further highlighting their ritual significance. The intricate engravings on these objects may depict scenes from mythology, representations of deities, or symbols associated with fertility, abundance, and protection.

Figurines and statuettes are another significant category of ritual objects found at Ggantija. These small-scale representations of human and animal forms were likely used in the performance of rituals and as objects of veneration. Made from various materials such as clay, stone, or bone, these figurines exhibit remarkable craftsmanship and attention to detail. They often depict female figures, possibly representing goddesses or fertility deities, and animals such as birds or bulls, which may symbolize sacred or totemic creatures.

The figurines found at Ggantija are not merely artistic creations but hold deep religious and symbolic meanings. Their presence within the temple complex suggests their role as intermediaries between the human and divine realms, facilitating communication and invoking blessings. The careful positioning of these figurines within the sacred spaces of Ggantija indicates their importance in the rituals performed at the site.

Carvings and engravings on the megalithic stones themselves also contribute to our understanding of the material culture of Ggantija's rituals. Intricate patterns, abstract symbols, and zoomorphic representations adorn the stones, creating a visually stunning and spiritually charged environment. These carvings may have served as visual narratives, conveying mythological stories, cosmological concepts, or sacred symbols. The presence of celestial motifs, such as the depiction of the sun or stars, suggests a connection between the rituals and the celestial realm.

Apart from these specific ritual objects, Ggantija has yielded a wide range of artifacts that provide further insights into the material culture of the site. Personal ornaments, such as beads and pendants made from materials like shell, bone, or stone, suggest the use of adornments in rituals or as symbols of status and identity. Tools, such as stone axes or flint blades, indicate the practical aspects of everyday life and their potential significance in ritual contexts. The presence of animal remains, including bones or teeth, suggests their use in rituals, possibly as offerings or as symbolic representations of animal spirits.

Studying the material culture of Ggantija's rituals allows us to delve into the beliefs, practices, and symbolic systems of the ancient inhabitants. The meticulous craftsmanship, intricate designs, and careful placement of these objects within the temple complex indicate the profound reverence and spiritual significance attached to them. The rich variety of ritual artifacts and their diverse forms highlight the complexity and diversity of the religious practices at Ggantija.

However, it is important to approach the interpretation of these artifacts with caution, recognizing the limitations of our knowledge and the potential for multiple meanings and interpretations. The significance of these objects may vary depending on the specific context, cultural symbolism, or individual beliefs. Comparative studies, ethnographic research, and a deep understanding of the cultural and historical context are crucial in unraveling the material culture of Ggantija's rituals.

In summary, the artifacts and objects discovered at Ggantija provide invaluable insights into the material culture of the rituals practiced at the site. Ceramic vessels, stone utensils, figurines, carvings, and other artifacts reflect the artistic skill, religious symbolism, and ritualistic practices of the ancient inhabitants. Through the study of these objects, we can gain a deeper understanding of the beliefs, ceremonies, and cultural expressions of the ancient civilization that flourished at Ggantija.

The megalithic temples of Ggantija provide a fascinating glimpse into the cultural context of the Neolithic era and the sacred offerings that played a significant role in the religious practices of the ancient inhabitants. These offerings, carefully selected and presented within the temple complex, shed light on the beliefs, values, and spiritual traditions of the people who lived during this time.

The sacred offerings at Ggantija encompass a wide range of materials, including organic, mineral, and animal substances. These offerings were chosen with great care, reflecting the intimate connection between the human and divine realms and the desire to establish a harmonious relationship with the sacred forces of the natural world.

One of the most prominent forms of offering found at Ggantija is the deposition of animal remains. The presence of animal bones, particularly those of domesticated animals such as sheep, goats, and pigs, suggests that these animals played a significant role in the religious and subsistence practices of the ancient community. The deliberate selection and sacrifice of specific animals may have been guided by religious beliefs, symbolism, or the availability of resources. The offering of animal remains may have been seen as a means of communicating with the divine, seeking blessings, or expressing gratitude for the sustenance and prosperity provided by the natural world.

In addition to animal offerings, Ggantija has yielded a variety of other objects that were likely used as sacred offerings. Ceramic vessels, adorned with intricate designs and elaborate decorations, were commonly used to hold and present offerings. These vessels may have contained offerings of food, drink, or other substances that were considered valuable or symbolic. The careful craftsmanship and artistic embellishments on these vessels suggest the importance attached to the act of offering and the desire to present offerings in a visually appealing and respectful manner.

Mineral offerings, such as stones or minerals with special properties, also played a role in the religious practices at Ggantija. Certain stones may have been considered sacred or imbued with spiritual power, and their placement within the temple complex may have been intended to harness or channel these energies. The selection and arrangement of these mineral offerings would have been guided by specific beliefs or practices associated with the natural elements and their perceived connection to the divine.

The cultural significance of the offerings at Ggantija extends beyond the specific objects themselves. The act of offering was a deeply ingrained aspect of communal and individual religious practices, reflecting the belief in reciprocity and the importance of maintaining a harmonious relationship with the supernatural forces. The rituals surrounding the offering process likely involved prayers, invocations, or other symbolic gestures, emphasizing the spiritual significance of the act.

Understanding the cultural context of the Neolithic era is crucial in interpreting the meaning and purpose of the sacred offerings at Ggantija. The people who built and worshipped at Ggantija were intimately connected with the natural world, relying on the land for sustenance and survival. Their religious practices, including the act of offering, were deeply rooted in their relationship with the environment, the cycles of nature, and the belief in supernatural forces that governed their lives.

The study of the sacred offerings at Ggantija provides a window into the spiritual and cultural landscape of the ancient community. It offers insights into their worldview, religious beliefs, and the role of ritual practices in their daily lives. The careful selection, preparation, and presentation of offerings demonstrate the profound reverence and devotion of the ancient inhabitants towards the divine.

However, it is important to approach the interpretation of these offerings with caution, recognizing the limitations of our knowledge and the complexity of their cultural and symbolic meanings. The specific rituals, beliefs, and cultural practices associated with the offerings may have varied over time and among different communities. Comparative studies, archaeological evidence, and a nuanced understanding of the cultural context are essential in unraveling the cultural significance of the sacred offerings at Ggantija.

In summary, the sacred offerings discovered at Ggantija provide valuable insights into the cultural context of the Neolithic era and the religious practices of the ancient inhabitants. The animal remains, ceramic vessels, mineral offerings, and other objects found within the temple complex reflect the deep connection between the human and divine realms, the importance of maintaining harmony with the natural world, and the desire to establish a meaningful relationship with the supernatural forces. Through the study of these offerings, we gain a deeper appreciation for the spiritual beliefs, cultural practices, and symbolic expressions of the ancient civilization that thrived at Ggantija.

Chapter 9: Connections to Other Megalithic Sites

Ggantija, with its awe-inspiring temples and monumental structures, stands as a testament to the ingenuity and skill of ancient builders. As we explore the unique features and architectural marvels of Ggantija, it becomes evident that comparing it with other megalithic sites allows us to gain a broader perspective on the development of these ancient structures and the cultural significance they held for different civilizations.

One of the most notable comparisons can be made between Ggantija and Stonehenge, the iconic megalithic monument in England. While both sites date back to the Neolithic period, they exhibit distinct architectural characteristics. Ggantija is known for its massive stone structures, featuring immense megaliths that were meticulously crafted and stacked to create imposing temple complexes. In contrast, Stonehenge consists of circular arrangements of megaliths, with trilithons and lintels creating a unique architectural configuration. Both sites, however, share a common purpose in their alignment with celestial events, reflecting the ancient people's deep connection with the cosmos.

Another significant comparison can be made between Ggantija and Newgrange in Ireland. Newgrange is a passage tomb constructed with massive stone slabs and adorned with intricate carvings. Like Ggantija, Newgrange showcases advanced engineering techniques and a profound understanding of celestial alignments. Both sites have entrances designed to capture the rays of the rising sun during specific astronomical events, such as the winter solstice. This alignment not only highlights the astronomical knowledge of these ancient civilizations but also suggests a shared belief in the spiritual and symbolic significance of celestial phenomena.

When considering Ggantija's counterparts in Malta, the temples of Hagar Qim and Mnajdra come to mind. These temples, like Ggantija, were constructed with megalithic stones and demonstrate remarkable architectural precision. They too exhibit alignments with the sun, particularly during the solstices and equinoxes, emphasizing the ceremonial and astronomical functions of these sites. The temples of Hagar Qim and Mnajdra, along with Ggantija, contribute to our understanding of the cultural and religious practices of the ancient Maltese civilization, showcasing their sophisticated knowledge of celestial events and their integration into religious rituals.

Moving beyond the Maltese archipelago, other megalithic sites around the world offer intriguing points of comparison. For instance, the megalithic temples of Göbekli Tepe in present-day Turkey present an astonishing parallel. Dating back even further than Ggantija, Göbekli Tepe features massive stone pillars arranged in circular patterns, suggesting a communal gathering place with ritualistic and ceremonial significance. Both Ggantija and Göbekli Tepe challenge our understanding of early civilization and push back the timeline of complex monumental construction.

The comparisons between Ggantija and other megalithic sites highlight the shared characteristics, advanced engineering, and profound cultural significance of these ancient structures. While each site has its unique architectural style and cultural context, they collectively provide a glimpse into the capabilities and beliefs of our ancient ancestors. The megalithic monuments across different regions testify to the human fascination with celestial events, the pursuit of spiritual connection, and the collective efforts required to construct these monumental structures.

By studying and comparing these megalithic sites, we can unravel the mysteries surrounding their construction techniques, purpose, and cultural significance. The shared features and distinct differences observed among these sites contribute to a broader understanding of the achievements and complexities of early civilizations. They inspire awe and admiration for the ingenuity and vision of our ancestors, leaving us with a profound appreciation for the timeless legacy they have left behind in the form of these megalithic marvels.

In summary, the comparison of Ggantija with other megalithic sites offers valuable insights into the architectural styles, cultural practices, and spiritual beliefs of ancient civilizations. Each site, whether it be Stonehenge, Newgrange, Hagar Qim, Mnajdra, or Göbekli Tepe, contributes to our understanding of the rich tapestry of human history. These comparisons highlight the ingenuity, sophistication, and enduring legacy of these megalithic structures, underscoring the profound impact they had on the ancient communities that built them.

The megalithic temples of Ggantija offer a fascinating window into the cultural exchange and interactions between Neolithic communities. As we delve into the historical and archaeological evidence, it becomes clear that these ancient societies were not isolated entities but actively engaged in a dynamic network of communication, trade, and cultural diffusion.

One of the significant aspects of cultural exchange among Neolithic communities was the sharing of knowledge and techniques related to megalithic construction. The construction of monumental stone structures, such as the temples of Ggantija, required advanced engineering skills, specialized tools, and a collective effort from the community. The similarities in construction techniques, architectural styles, and megalithic elements across different regions suggest a transfer of knowledge and expertise between communities.

The exchange of ideas and architectural practices may have occurred through various means, including direct contact between neighboring communities, migration, and the diffusion of cultural traditions. The spread of megalithic construction techniques and the presence of similar architectural elements in different regions indicate the existence of communication networks and shared cultural values. These exchanges would have facilitated the transfer of technical knowledge, fostering innovation and the development of megalithic construction traditions across different landscapes.

Trade played a crucial role in facilitating cultural exchange during the Neolithic period. The movement of people and goods allowed for the sharing of ideas, technologies, and material resources. Neolithic communities engaged in long-distance trade, exchanging raw materials, finished goods, and possibly even religious and symbolic artifacts. This exchange of goods and ideas not only fostered economic development but also created opportunities for cultural interaction, influencing artistic styles, religious beliefs, and social practices.

The presence of shared motifs, symbols, and iconography in megalithic art across different regions further attests to the interconnectedness and cultural exchange between Neolithic communities. The intricate carvings and decorative elements found at Ggantija and other megalithic sites display common themes and artistic conventions. These similarities suggest a shared visual language and a common set of cultural symbols that transcended geographical boundaries.

The movement of people, whether through migration or temporary visits, also played a vital role in cultural exchange during the Neolithic period. People would have traveled between communities, bringing with them their traditions, beliefs, and practices. This movement of individuals contributed to the spread of ideas, cultural practices, and technologies, fostering a rich tapestry of cultural diversity within and between Neolithic societies.

It is important to note that cultural exchange was not limited to megalithic construction techniques and artistic expressions. The exchange of ideas encompassed various aspects of life, including subsistence strategies, agriculture, social organization, and religious beliefs. Neolithic communities would have shared agricultural practices, such as domestication of plants and animals, as well as techniques for food storage and preservation. The spread of new crops and agricultural knowledge would have influenced and shaped the subsistence practices of neighboring communities.

Religious and spiritual beliefs also experienced a degree of interconnectivity and mutual influence. Neolithic communities shared a deep reverence for the natural world and the supernatural forces they believed governed it. The similarities in ritual practices, the veneration of ancestral spirits, and the use of megalithic structures as sacred spaces reflect a shared understanding of the spiritual realm and the importance of maintaining a harmonious relationship with the divine.

In summary, the megalithic temples of Ggantija provide valuable insights into the cultural exchange and interactions between Neolithic communities. The similarities in megalithic construction techniques, artistic expressions, and symbolic representations across different regions indicate a vibrant network of cultural exchange, facilitated by trade, migration, and the sharing of knowledge. This exchange extended beyond mere material goods and included the transfer of ideas, technologies, and religious beliefs. The interconnectedness and cultural diffusion among Neolithic communities contributed to the development of unique architectural styles, artistic traditions, and social practices. By studying the cultural exchange during this period, we gain a deeper understanding of the interconnected nature of human societies and the rich tapestry of human history that unfolded during the Neolithic era.

The megalithic structures built by ancient civilizations across different regions share striking architectural similarities, pointing to common features and underlying principles in their construction. The examination of these shared characteristics provides valuable insights into the ingenuity and cultural connections of our ancestors.

One of the notable commonalities among megalithic structures is the use of massive stone blocks. These stones, often weighing several tons, were carefully selected, shaped, and positioned to create monumental structures. The precision with which these stones were fitted together without the use of mortar is a testament to the advanced engineering skills possessed by these ancient civilizations. This technique ensured the stability and longevity of the structures, defying the test of time.

Another recurring architectural feature is the use of trilithons, which are arrangements of two upright stones supporting a horizontal lintel. This architectural configuration can be observed in notable megalithic sites such as Stonehenge and Ggantija. The trilithon design not only provided structural stability but also created an impressive visual impact, emphasizing the monumental nature of these structures.

Circular arrangements of megaliths are another prevalent feature in megalithic architecture. Examples of this can be seen in sites like Stonehenge and the temples of Malta. These circular layouts often involved concentric rings or stone circles, suggesting a deliberate design choice with possible astronomical alignments. The circular form may have held symbolic and ritualistic significance, representing the cyclical nature of life, celestial movements, or communal gathering spaces.

Many megalithic structures exhibit precise astronomical alignments, which were likely intentional and served as a means of connecting with the celestial realm. These alignments were often linked to significant astronomical events such as solstices, equinoxes, or other celestial markers. The orientation of these structures toward specific celestial phenomena reflects the profound understanding of the cosmic rhythms possessed by these ancient cultures.

Notably, megalithic structures were often constructed in locations with natural features that amplified their significance. Sacred landscapes, such as hills, rivers, or other natural landmarks, were incorporated into the overall design and layout of these sites. This integration of the built environment with the natural surroundings suggests a deep reverence for the interconnectedness of the physical and spiritual realms.

Carvings and engravings on megalithic stones provide another common feature across various sites. Intricate and elaborate designs depicting geometric patterns, human figures, animals, or abstract symbols adorn the surfaces of these stones. These carvings likely held symbolic or religious significance, conveying cultural beliefs, mythologies, or spiritual narratives.

The use of megalithic structures as sacred spaces for communal gatherings, rituals, and ceremonies is another shared feature. These structures were not merely functional buildings but served as focal points for religious and social activities. The size and grandeur of these structures reflect the significance they held in the lives of the ancient communities, providing a sense of awe and sanctity.

While regional variations exist, these architectural similarities across megalithic structures suggest shared cultural practices, religious beliefs, and a collective human fascination with the divine, the celestial, and the cyclical nature of existence. The construction techniques, precise alignments, incorporation of natural features, and symbolic carvings reveal a sophisticated understanding of the physical and spiritual realms. The exploration of these architectural features and shared characteristics among megalithic structures offers glimpses into the interconnectedness of ancient civilizations. It highlights the universal human drive to create monumental structures that transcend time and bear witness to our ancestors' ingenuity and spiritual aspirations. By studying these architectural similarities, we gain a deeper appreciation for the shared human experiences that spanned across time and space, leaving a lasting legacy in the form of these remarkable megalithic structures.

The megalithic structures scattered across different regions of the world not only represent remarkable feats of engineering and architecture but also offer clues about the interconnectedness and trade networks that existed among Neolithic societies. The presence of similar megalithic construction techniques, architectural styles, and shared cultural symbols indicates a widespread exchange of ideas, materials, and technologies during this ancient era.

One of the key factors that facilitated the establishment of trade routes among Neolithic societies was the availability of valuable resources in different regions. Certain areas were rich in specific raw materials like stone, timber, or precious metals, while others possessed fertile lands suitable for agriculture. The need to acquire these resources for survival and the development of their communities likely motivated early humans to establish trade connections.

Stone, in particular, played a significant role in megalithic construction. Different types of stones were used depending on their availability and suitability for construction purposes. The transport of these massive stones over long distances suggests the existence of extensive trade networks, as communities sought out the best materials for their monumental projects. The movement of stones also implied the exchange of knowledge and techniques related to quarrying, shaping, and transporting these heavy loads.

The existence of shared architectural styles and construction methods across different regions is further evidence of trade and cultural interactions. The similarities in megalithic structures found in diverse areas such as Europe, Asia, Africa, and the Americas suggest a transfer of architectural knowledge and practices. These exchanges could have occurred through direct contact between neighboring communities or through more complex networks involving intermediaries who facilitated trade and cultural exchange.

Trade routes likely developed along natural pathways, such as rivers, coastlines, or mountain passes, which provided easier transportation and communication. These routes served as conduits for the movement of goods, ideas, and cultural practices. Along these trade routes, trading hubs and settlements may have emerged, fostering social interactions, intercultural exchanges, and the establishment of long-lasting relationships among communities.

The trade of raw materials, finished goods, and agricultural products was not the sole purpose of these networks. The exchange of cultural and religious artifacts likely played a significant role in the interconnectedness of Neolithic societies. Ritual objects, symbolic artifacts, and artistic creations may have been valued commodities, traded for their spiritual, social, or aesthetic significance. These exchanges would have influenced and shaped the religious beliefs, artistic styles, and cultural practices of different communities.

It is important to note that trade networks were not solely limited to physical exchanges of goods but also involved the transmission of ideas, beliefs, and knowledge. The movement of people, whether through migration, pilgrimage, or trade, would have facilitated the exchange of cultural practices, religious beliefs, and technological innovations. The interactions and cultural diffusion resulting from these exchanges would have contributed to the development of shared cultural traits and the enrichment of Neolithic societies.

The establishment of trade routes and networks among Neolithic societies not only fostered economic growth but also played a crucial role in the development of complex social structures. The exchange of goods and ideas led to the formation of interdependent relationships, alliances, and the spread of specialized knowledge and skills. These networks contributed to the growth and diversification of societies, laying the foundation for future advancements in agriculture, technology, and social organization.

In summary, the presence of megalithic structures across different regions indicates the existence of trade networks and cultural interactions among Neolithic societies. The movement of resources, knowledge, and symbolic artifacts suggests a vibrant exchange of ideas, technologies, and cultural practices. These trade routes not only facilitated economic transactions but also played a pivotal role in the development of complex societies, shaping the cultural, religious, and technological landscape of the Neolithic era. By tracing these connections, we gain valuable insights into the interconnectedness and shared human experiences that spanned across vast distances during this ancient period.

The megalithic temples of Ggantija in Malta stand as enigmatic structures that have captivated the curiosity of researchers and archaeologists for centuries. While Ggantija is unique in its architectural design and cultural context, intriguing links and connections can be drawn between Ggantija and other megalithic sites, shedding light on shared cultural, artistic, and possibly even spiritual influences.

One of the most remarkable connections between Ggantija and other megalithic sites is the presence of similar architectural features and construction techniques. Ggantija's massive stone blocks, expertly carved and meticulously arranged, exhibit striking similarities with structures found in other megalithic sites around the world. The use of large stone slabs, intricate corbelling, and the incorporation of massive trilithons are shared characteristics that hint at a common cultural heritage or an exchange of architectural knowledge.

Furthermore, the presence of distinct carvings and symbols on the stones of Ggantija holds parallels with those found in other megalithic sites. Intricate designs, such as spirals, concentric circles, and geometric patterns, can be observed in both Ggantija and sites like Stonehenge, Newgrange, and Carnac. These shared artistic motifs indicate a potential cross-cultural communication, symbolic language, or spiritual beliefs that were transmitted among these ancient societies.

Another fascinating connection lies in the alignment and orientation of megalithic structures with celestial phenomena. Ggantija, like Stonehenge and other sites, exhibits alignments with significant astronomical events such as solstices, equinoxes, and lunar cycles. This astronomical precision suggests a shared interest in celestial observations and a possible understanding of the cosmos among these ancient communities. The alignment of megalithic structures with celestial bodies may have served religious, calendar-keeping, or agricultural purposes, reflecting a common reverence for the celestial realm.

The presence of similar megalithic traditions across different regions also suggests the existence of ancient trade or cultural exchange networks. The transport of massive stone blocks over long distances indicates a level of technological sophistication and logistical organization that could only be achieved through complex networks of communication and cooperation. The sharing of architectural techniques, building practices, and the movement of skilled craftsmen may have facilitated the spread of megalithic traditions from one region to another.

Furthermore, the presence of similar mythologies and legends associated with megalithic sites provides additional evidence of interconnectedness. Stories and folklore surrounding these sites often involve giants, ancient gods, or supernatural beings, transcending geographical boundaries and echoing across different cultures. These shared narratives suggest a collective human fascination with these awe-inspiring structures and the belief in their divine or mystical origins.

While the exact nature and extent of the connections between Ggantija and other megalithic sites may remain elusive, the presence of shared architectural features, artistic motifs, astronomical alignments, and cultural narratives implies a network of cultural exchange, spiritual beliefs, and possibly trade among ancient societies. These connections transcend time and geography, painting a complex picture of a shared human heritage and a quest for understanding the mysteries of the cosmos.

As research and exploration continue, new discoveries and insights into the links between Ggantija and other megalithic sites may emerge. By unraveling these connections, we not only gain a deeper understanding of the cultural and artistic expressions of our ancestors but also glimpse the profound interconnectedness of human civilizations that thrived during the Neolithic period. The enigma of Ggantija and its connections to other megalithic sites will undoubtedly continue to inspire further exploration, research, and awe for generations to come.

Chapter 10: Ggantija's Legacy: Inspiring Wonder and Curiosity

Ggantija, with its awe-inspiring megalithic temples and rich cultural history, has left an indelible mark on the fields of archaeology and history. Its discovery and subsequent study have offered valuable insights into the lives, beliefs, and achievements of our prehistoric ancestors, reshaping our understanding of human civilization and its development.

First and foremost, Ggantija's sheer scale and architectural complexity have astounded archaeologists and historians alike. The massive stone blocks, carefully arranged to create towering temples, stand as a testament to the technological prowess and engineering abilities of the Neolithic people who constructed them. The precise fitting of these colossal stones without the use of mortar remains a marvel, challenging our modern perceptions of what was achievable in that era.

The excavation and analysis of Ggantija's archaeological remains have provided crucial information about the daily lives and social organization of its inhabitants. The discovery of burial sites, domestic structures, and artifacts has offered glimpses into Neolithic societies, their subsistence strategies, and their cultural practices. The study of Ggantija's pottery, tools, and other artifacts has enabled researchers to piece together the material culture and technological advancements of the time.

Moreover, the religious and ritualistic significance of Ggantija has opened a window into the spiritual beliefs and practices of the Neolithic people. The presence of sacred spaces, altars, and offerings suggests a complex system of beliefs and ceremonies centered around these monumental temples. The investigation of Ggantija's religious practices has shed light on the role of spirituality in the lives of ancient communities and their understanding of the divine.

Ggantija's significance extends beyond its immediate cultural and historical context. The site's exploration has sparked wider interest in megalithic structures around the world and their shared architectural and symbolic features. Comparative studies between Ggantija and other megalithic sites have allowed for cross-cultural analysis and the identification of common patterns, connections, and influences. Ggantija's role as a reference point has fueled further research into megalithic cultures, resulting in a deeper understanding of their social, religious, and technological achievements.

Furthermore, Ggantija's inclusion on the UNESCO World Heritage List has cemented its status as a globally recognized site of historical and cultural significance. Its recognition by the international community has not only brought attention to Ggantija itself but has also highlighted the importance of preserving and protecting other megalithic sites worldwide. The efforts to safeguard Ggantija have set an example for the conservation of ancient heritage, ensuring that future generations can continue to appreciate and learn from these remarkable structures.

The ongoing research and excavation at Ggantija continue to uncover new details and refine our understanding of this ancient complex. Advances in scientific techniques, such as radiocarbon dating and DNA analysis, have allowed for more accurate dating of the site and the exploration of genetic relationships among its inhabitants. The interdisciplinary nature of Ggantija's study, incorporating archaeology, anthropology, geology, and other disciplines, ensures a comprehensive understanding of the site and its significance in the broader context of human history.

In summary, Ggantija's enduring wonder lies not only in its impressive architecture but also in the profound impact it has had on our knowledge of the past. Through its excavation and study, Ggantija has illuminated the lives and achievements of our prehistoric ancestors, offering valuable insights into their culture, spirituality, and technological capabilities. Its influence extends beyond its immediate context, serving as a touchstone for the study of megalithic structures worldwide. As our exploration and understanding of Ggantija continue to evolve, its legacy as a monumental site of archaeological and historical importance remains intact, inspiring further research and appreciation for the marvels of our ancient past.

Ggantija, with its majestic temples and ancient mysteries, has played a pivotal role in shaping our understanding of the past. As one of the oldest and most remarkable megalithic sites in the world, Ggantija has captivated the imagination of researchers, archaeologists, and historians, inspiring a relentless quest for knowledge and discovery.

The significance of Ggantija lies not only in its architectural grandeur but also in its ability to unlock the secrets of our ancient ancestors. The temples, built over 5,000 years ago, offer a unique window into the Neolithic period, providing valuable insights into the lives, beliefs, and cultural practices of the people who built them.

The exploration and excavation of Ggantija have unearthed a treasure trove of artifacts and evidence, shedding light on various aspects of

Neolithic society. The discovery of pottery, tools, and personal items has revealed the material culture and technological advancements of the time. By examining these artifacts, archaeologists have pieced together a more comprehensive picture of daily life, from subsistence strategies to trade networks and social organization.

One of the most intriguing aspects of Ggantija is its religious and spiritual significance. The temples were undoubtedly sacred spaces where rituals, ceremonies, and communal gatherings took place. The study of Ggantija's religious practices has deepened our understanding of ancient beliefs, cosmology, and the importance of spirituality in early human societies. The presence of altars, symbols, and offerings suggests a complex system of worship and a connection to the divine.

Ggantija's colossal stone structures have posed numerous questions about the engineering feats and construction techniques employed by its builders. The transport and arrangement of massive stone blocks without the aid of modern machinery remains an enigma, challenging our notions of what was achievable in the Neolithic era. The meticulous craftsmanship and precision in creating the temples reveal a level of skill and knowledge that is truly awe-inspiring.

Furthermore, Ggantija's influence extends beyond its physical boundaries. Its existence has sparked debates, theories, and research on a global scale. Comparative studies with other megalithic sites have revealed commonalities in architectural design, artistic motifs, and cultural practices. These comparative analyses have broadened our understanding of ancient civilizations, cultural diffusion, and the shared human experience across different regions and time periods.

Ggantija's recognition as a UNESCO World Heritage site has ensured its preservation and protection for future generations. It stands as a testament to the importance of safeguarding our cultural heritage and learning from the past. The ongoing efforts to conserve and study Ggantija not only contribute to our understanding of the site itself but also serve as a model for responsible archaeology and heritage management.

The enduring allure of Ggantija lies in its ability to ignite curiosity and inspire further exploration. The questions it raises about the Neolithic period, ancient technologies, cultural practices, and human ingenuity continue to fuel research and inquiry. As new discoveries are made and new techniques are developed, our understanding of Ggantija and its significance in the broader narrative of human history will undoubtedly evolve.

In summary, Ggantija stands as a testament to human achievement, a gateway to our past, and a catalyst for knowledge and understanding. Its temples and artifacts provide valuable insights into the Neolithic period, offering a glimpse into the lives and beliefs of our ancient ancestors. Ggantija's influence reaches far beyond its physical boundaries, stimulating global discourse and inspiring further exploration. As we continue to unravel the mysteries of Ggantija, we deepen our appreciation for the ingenuity, creativity, and resilience of those who came before us.

Ggantija, with its remarkable temples and rich cultural heritage, has left a lasting legacy that extends far beyond its physical boundaries. Its influence can be seen in various aspects of human creativity, including art, architecture, and symbolism. The impact of Ggantija on these realms highlights the enduring significance and timeless inspiration that this ancient site continues to evoke.

One of the most apparent ways in which Ggantija has influenced subsequent artistic endeavors is through its architectural design. The monumental stone structures and intricate carvings of Ggantija have served as a source of inspiration for architects and builders throughout history. The sheer scale and grandeur of the temples have captivated the imagination, leading to the incorporation of similar elements in the construction of temples, palaces, and other monumental structures in different regions.

The symbolic motifs found at Ggantija have also influenced artistic expression. The intricate carvings and engravings on the temple walls have provided a rich visual vocabulary that has been interpreted and reimagined by artists across different periods. The recurring motifs of spirals, concentric circles, animals, and human figures have been incorporated into various forms of artistic representation, from paintings to sculptures, reflecting the enduring appeal and timeless allure of these ancient symbols.

Furthermore, Ggantija's spiritual and mythological significance has permeated artistic traditions. The ancient rituals and beliefs associated with the temples have inspired narratives, stories, and mythologies that have been passed down through generations. Artists and writers have drawn upon these legends and tales, incorporating them into literary works, paintings, and other forms of creative expression. The enduring allure of Ggantija's spiritual and cultural heritage continues to resonate with contemporary artists, keeping its legacy alive in the realm of artistic creation.

Ggantija's symbolism and cultural motifs have also found their way into decorative arts and crafts. The patterns and designs derived from the temple's carvings have been adapted and reinterpreted in textiles, pottery, jewelry, and other forms of traditional craftsmanship. These artistic expressions serve as a link between the ancient past and contemporary cultural traditions, preserving and celebrating the aesthetic and cultural heritage inspired by Ggantija.

Beyond the realm of art, Ggantija's influence can also be observed in architectural practices. The megalithic construction techniques and engineering marvels employed in the temples have inspired innovative approaches to building design and construction. The lessons learned from Ggantija's structural achievements have been incorporated into modern architectural practices, with architects drawing inspiration from the precision, durability, and monumental scale of the ancient temples.

Moreover, Ggantija's symbolic and cultural significance has resonated beyond the realms of art and architecture. The motifs and themes associated with the site have been adopted in various cultural contexts, becoming part of regional and national identities. Ggantija has become a symbol of pride, representing the rich historical and cultural heritage of Malta and serving as a testament to the creativity and ingenuity of its ancient inhabitants.

In summary, Ggantija's legacy in art, architecture, and symbolism is a testament to the enduring power of human creativity and the deep connections we forge with our ancient past. Its monumental temples, intricate carvings, and sacred symbolism have inspired artists, architects, and artisans across time, leaving an indelible mark on artistic expression and cultural traditions. Ggantija's cultural influence continues to be celebrated and cherished, ensuring that its legacy as a source of inspiration and cultural heritage remains vibrant and relevant in the modern world.

Ggantija, with its awe-inspiring temples and rich archaeological significance, stands as a gateway to Malta's prehistoric heritage. The site's historical and cultural importance has made it a popular destination for tourists seeking to immerse themselves in the ancient wonders of the island. Ggantija's allure lies not only in its monumental stone structures but also in the captivating stories it tells about the island's early inhabitants and their remarkable achievements.

For visitors, Ggantija offers a unique opportunity to step back in time and witness the remnants of an ancient civilization that flourished thousands of years ago. The temples, with their massive stone blocks and intricate carvings, are a testament to the ingenuity and craftsmanship of the Neolithic people who built them. Exploring the site allows visitors to appreciate the magnitude of their achievements and gain insight into their way of life.

The experience of visiting Ggantija is not just about admiring the physical structures but also about connecting with the cultural heritage of Malta. The site provides a glimpse into the beliefs, rituals, and social practices of the island's early inhabitants. The temples were undoubtedly sacred spaces where important ceremonies and rituals took place, serving as a focal point for communal gatherings and spiritual activities. Understanding the cultural significance of Ggantija enhances the visitor's appreciation of the site and its role in shaping Malta's identity.

Beyond the historical and cultural aspects, Ggantija's location amidst Malta's picturesque landscapes adds to its appeal as a tourist attraction. The temples are nestled in a serene and beautiful setting, surrounded by lush greenery and breathtaking views. Visitors can explore the site while immersing themselves in the natural beauty of the Maltese countryside, creating a truly immersive and memorable experience.

The accessibility of Ggantija is another factor that contributes to its popularity among tourists. The site is well-preserved and equipped with informative displays and signage, allowing visitors to navigate the temples and gain a deeper understanding of their significance. Guided tours and educational programs further enrich the visitor experience, providing context and expert insights into the archaeological findings and historical background of Ggantija.

Moreover, Ggantija serves as a starting point for exploring Malta's wider prehistoric heritage. The island is home to several other megalithic sites, each with its own unique characteristics and stories to tell. Visitors to Ggantija often combine their visit with trips to other nearby sites, such as Hagar Qim, Mnajdra, and Tarxien Temples, creating an immersive journey through Malta's ancient past.

The promotion and preservation of Ggantija as a touristic attraction have also contributed to the local economy and community development. The influx of visitors has stimulated the growth of tourism-related businesses, including hotels, restaurants, and souvenir shops, providing employment opportunities and supporting the local economy. Additionally, the revenue generated from tourism helps fund conservation efforts, ensuring the continued preservation of Ggantija for future generations to appreciate and learn from.

In summary, Ggantija serves as a gateway to Malta's prehistoric heritage, offering visitors a unique opportunity to delve into the island's ancient past. The site's historical significance, architectural marvels, and cultural insights make it a captivating destination for tourists seeking to explore Malta's rich archaeological heritage. Ggantija's accessibility, educational programs, and surrounding natural beauty further enhance the visitor experience. By promoting and preserving Ggantija, Malta showcases its commitment to honoring and sharing its prehistoric legacy with the world, inviting travelers to embark on a journey of discovery and appreciation for the island's ancient wonders.

Education and interpretation play a vital role in conveying the significance of Ggantija to future generations. As a site of immense historical and cultural importance, it is essential to impart knowledge and foster an understanding of Ggantija's role in shaping Malta's heritage. By engaging in effective educational practices and interpretation strategies, we can ensure that the legacy of Ggantija continues to inspire and resonate with future generations.

One of the key aspects of educating visitors and younger generations about Ggantija is through informative displays, exhibits, and interpretive signage. These tools provide valuable insights into the site's history, architecture, and cultural significance. By presenting well-researched information in a clear and accessible manner, visitors can develop a deeper understanding of the site and appreciate its significance within the broader context of human history.

Furthermore, educational programs and guided tours tailored to different age groups can greatly enhance the learning experience at Ggantija. These programs can be designed to cater to school groups, families, or individual visitors, providing them with the opportunity to engage in hands-on activities, interactive presentations, and guided explorations of the site. Such programs not only foster a sense of curiosity and discovery but also encourage critical thinking and a deeper connection with Ggantija's cultural heritage.

Digital technologies and virtual platforms also offer exciting avenues for education and interpretation. Virtual reality tours, augmented reality applications, and online resources can bring Ggantija to life, allowing individuals from all around the world to explore and learn about the site remotely. These technologies provide immersive and interactive experiences, enabling users to virtually walk through the temples, examine artifacts, and engage with historical narratives. By harnessing the power of digital tools, we can reach a broader audience and cultivate a global appreciation for Ggantija's significance.

Collaboration between academic institutions, archaeological experts, and local communities is crucial for the continued education and interpretation of Ggantija. By fostering partnerships and knowledge-sharing, we can ensure that the latest research findings and archaeological discoveries are incorporated into educational materials and interpretive programs. This collaborative approach promotes a deeper understanding of Ggantija's cultural significance and ensures that educational initiatives are based on accurate and up-to-date information. Beyond formal educational programs, community engagement plays a vital role in preserving and promoting Ggantija's significance. Local communities can contribute to the interpretation of the site by sharing their cultural traditions, oral histories, and personal connections to Ggantija. This inclusive approach helps create a sense of ownership and pride, instilling a deeper appreciation for Ggantija's cultural heritage among the local population and fostering a spirit of stewardship for the site.

In summary, education and interpretation are instrumental in communicating the significance of Ggantija to future generations. By employing informative displays, interactive programs, digital technologies, and collaborative efforts, we can ensure that the legacy of Ggantija is transmitted effectively to inspire and engage individuals of all ages. Through education, we foster an understanding and appreciation of Ggantija's cultural heritage, ensuring its enduring significance for generations to come. By nurturing a sense of curiosity, connection, and stewardship, we empower future generations to value and protect the invaluable heritage that Ggantija represents.

BOOK 4

LEGENDS OF THE ANCIENT STONES UNVEILING THE POWER OF BAALBEK'S MEGALITHIC TEMPLE

BY A.J. KINGSTON

Chapter 1: The Enigma of Baalbek: Introduction to the Megalithic Temple

Baalbek, with its majestic megalithic temple complex and enigmatic history, stands as a testament to the ingenuity and grandeur of ancient civilizations. Nestled in the fertile valleys of Lebanon, Baalbek's massive stone structures have captured the imagination of scholars, explorers, and historians for centuries. The site's rich archaeological heritage and lingering mysteries make it an irresistible enigma waiting to be unraveled.

The grandeur of Baalbek lies in its colossal stone blocks, some of the largest ever used in ancient construction. The Temple of Jupiter, with its six majestic columns, towers above the landscape, leaving visitors in awe of the architectural feat achieved by its builders. The sheer scale of the stones and the precision of their placement continue to astound modern observers, raising intriguing questions about the methods and tools employed by the ancient craftsmen.

Exploring the history of Baalbek reveals a complex tapestry of cultural influences and historical events. Originally a place of worship for the Phoenicians, Baalbek later became a prominent center of Hellenistic and Roman civilization. The site's evolution over time reflects the cultural shifts and political transformations that shaped the region. From its Phoenician roots to its Roman appropriation, Baalbek stands as a testament to the cultural fusion and continuity that characterized the ancient Mediterranean world.

However, it is the origins of Baalbek that remain shrouded in mystery. The precise techniques employed in the construction of the temples, the sources of the colossal stones, and the logistics of their transportation continue to puzzle researchers. Theories range from the involvement of ancient extraterrestrial civilizations to the use of advanced engineering techniques by an unknown civilization. These hypotheses, although speculative, demonstrate the enduring fascination and allure that Baalbek holds for those seeking to unravel its secrets.

The religious and mythological significance of Baalbek adds to its mystique. The site was dedicated to the worship of Baal, the Semitic god of storms and fertility, in ancient times. The intricate carvings and elaborate ornamentation adorning the temples testify to the religious fervor and the spiritual beliefs of the ancient worshipers. Baalbek's association with divinity and its sacred aura continue to captivate the imagination, raising questions about the rituals and ceremonies that took place within its sacred precincts.

The exploration and excavation of Baalbek have provided valuable insights into the site's history and cultural significance. Archaeological discoveries, including statues, inscriptions, and architectural fragments, have shed light on the religious practices, social organization, and daily life of the ancient inhabitants. These findings, combined with meticulous documentation and scholarly analysis, form the foundation for our understanding of Baalbek's past.

Preserving and protecting Baalbek is a vital task that requires a delicate balance between conservation and accessibility. Efforts to safeguard the site from natural elements, urban encroachment, and human impact are ongoing. The collaboration between local authorities, international organizations, and academic institutions ensures the responsible management and conservation of Baalbek for future generations.

The allure of Baalbek extends far beyond its historical and archaeological significance. The site's cultural and symbolic importance has inspired artists, writers, and poets throughout the ages. From ancient Roman poets to modern-day photographers and painters, Baalbek's captivating beauty and mysterious aura have left an indelible mark on the artistic imagination.

In summary, Baalbek's mystique persists, inviting exploration and speculation. Its massive stone structures, rich history, and enigmatic origins continue to captivate and intrigue. As we unravel the ancient enigma of Baalbek, we not only gain insights into the achievements of past civilizations but also contemplate the enduring mysteries that remind us of the limits of our knowledge. Baalbek's allure lies not only in its tangible remnants but also in the questions it poses, urging us to seek answers and unravel the ancient enigma that continues to fascinate us.

The Baalbek Temple Complex stands as a testament to the architectural genius and cultural richness of the ancient world. Located in present-day Lebanon, this awe-inspiring site has fascinated historians, archaeologists, and travelers alike for centuries. Its monumental structures, remarkable construction techniques, and intricate carvings speak volumes about the advanced civilization that once thrived here.

At the heart of the Baalbek Temple Complex is the Temple of Jupiter, a colossal structure that dominates the landscape with its towering columns and imposing presence. The sheer scale of the temple is a testament to the ambitious vision of its builders, who harnessed immense stone blocks to create a monument of unparalleled grandeur. Each column, weighing several tons, was meticulously carved and precisely positioned, showcasing the skill and craftsmanship of ancient architects and artisans.

Adjacent to the Temple of Jupiter is the Temple of Bacchus, dedicated to the Roman god of wine and fertility. This temple, characterized by its remarkably well-preserved columns and intricate reliefs, is a testament to the exceptional preservation of the site. The level of detail in the carvings and the harmonious proportions of the temple's design are a testament to the artistic and architectural achievements of the ancient world.

Beyond these monumental structures, the Baalbek Temple Complex boasts a rich array of smaller temples, including the Temple of Venus and the Temple of Mercury. These temples, although not as well-preserved as their larger counterparts, provide valuable insights into the diversity of religious practices and beliefs that once thrived within the complex.

The construction of the Baalbek Temple Complex is a marvel in itself. The immense stone blocks used in its construction, some weighing over 1,000 tons, have puzzled scholars for centuries. The origins of these massive stones and the methods employed to transport and position them remain subjects of debate and speculation. The sheer scale of the construction effort required meticulous planning, engineering prowess, and a deep understanding of stone-cutting techniques.

The historical and cultural significance of Baalbek extends far beyond its architectural splendor. The site has a rich history dating back to ancient times when it served as a center for worship and pilgrimage. Baalbek was associated with the Phoenician deity Baal, the Roman god Jupiter, and the Greek god Zeus, highlighting its importance as a religious sanctuary and cultural crossroads in the ancient world.

Over the centuries, Baalbek has witnessed the rise and fall of empires, serving as a testament to the enduring legacy of human civilization. From the Phoenicians and Romans to the Byzantines and Ottomans, Baalbek has been shaped by a multitude of cultures and civilizations, each leaving their mark on its storied history.

The exploration and excavation of Baalbek have unearthed a wealth of artifacts, inscriptions, and architectural fragments, shedding light on the rituals, beliefs, and daily life of its ancient inhabitants. These discoveries, coupled with scholarly research and analysis, have deepened our understanding of the site's cultural and historical significance.

Preserving and protecting the Baalbek Temple Complex is an ongoing endeavor that requires careful conservation and management. Collaborative efforts between local authorities, international organizations, and archaeologists are essential in safeguarding this ancient wonder for future generations. Conservation initiatives aim to protect the site from natural decay, environmental factors, and human activities while ensuring its accessibility to visitors who seek to immerse themselves in its rich history and cultural heritage.

In summary, the Baalbek Temple Complex stands as a remarkable testament to human ingenuity, architectural prowess, and cultural richness. Its monumental structures, intricate carvings, and historical significance continue to captivate and inspire. Baalbek remains an enduring symbol of the achievements of ancient civilizations and a window into the past, inviting us to contemplate the grandeur of the ancient world and the mysteries that lie within its hallowed halls.

Baalbek, the ancient megalithic temple complex in Lebanon, has long been a subject of intrigue and speculation. Its massive stone structures, enigmatic origins, and rich history have given rise to a myriad of mysteries that continue to captivate the imagination of scholars and explorers. From the sheer size of the stones to the purpose of the temples, Baalbek is a treasure trove of unanswered questions, inviting us to delve into the realm of speculation and uncover its secrets.

One of the most perplexing enigmas surrounding Baalbek is the transportation and placement of its colossal stones. The largest stone blocks used in the construction of the complex weigh over 1,000 tons, making them some of the heaviest ever quarried and moved by ancient civilizations. The sheer magnitude of this feat has led to numerous theories and speculations about the methods employed by the builders. Some propose the use of advanced, now-lost technologies or even the intervention of extraterrestrial beings. While these ideas may seem fantastical, they underscore the awe-inspiring nature of Baalbek's construction and the mystery that surrounds it.

The origins of Baalbek's megalithic temple builders also remain elusive. The site's history dates back thousands of years, and it has been associated with various cultures, including the Phoenicians, Greeks, and Romans. However, the precise identity of the original builders remains a subject of debate. Some suggest that an advanced civilization predating the known ancient cultures was responsible for Baalbek's construction. The presence of large stone blocks and intricate architectural details has fueled speculation that a highly sophisticated and technically advanced civilization existed in the region long before recorded history.

Another intriguing aspect of Baalbek is its relationship with celestial alignments. Some researchers have proposed that the temples were built with astronomical precision, aligning with celestial bodies and marking significant celestial events such as solstices and equinoxes.

These alignments, they argue, may have held religious or symbolic significance for the ancient builders. Whether these alignments are intentional or coincidental remains a subject of investigation, adding an extra layer of intrigue to Baalbek's enigmatic allure.

The purpose of Baalbek's temples has also sparked debate and speculation. While it is widely accepted that the complex served as a center of religious worship, the specific rituals and beliefs practiced within its walls are less clear. Some theories propose that the temples were dedicated to the worship of deities associated with fertility, abundance, and celestial forces. Others suggest that Baalbek was a site of pilgrimage and a hub of cultural exchange, drawing devotees and travelers from far and wide. The exact nature of the rituals and the significance of the temples within the broader cultural and religious context of the time remain elusive, leaving room for speculation and interpretation.

Uncovering the secrets of Baalbek requires a delicate balance between scientific inquiry and imaginative exploration. Archaeological excavations and research continue to provide valuable insights into the site's history and construction techniques. Yet, the enigmatic nature of Baalbek invites us to ponder the gaps in our knowledge and entertain alternative theories that push the boundaries of conventional understanding.

In summary, Baalbek's mysteries and speculations fuel our curiosity and ignite our imagination. The awe-inspiring scale of its stone structures, the unknown origins of its builders, and the purpose of its temples continue to elude definitive answers. As we continue to investigate and explore this ancient marvel, we are reminded of the vastness of human history and the enduring allure of the enigmatic. Baalbek stands as a testament to the ingenuity and ingenuity of the ancient world, challenging us to unravel its secrets and broaden our understanding of the past.

Chapter 2: Unraveling the Stone Enigma: Baalbek's Massive Construction

The Baalbek temple complex in Lebanon is renowned for its megalithic structures, particularly its gigantic stone blocks that have astounded scholars and visitors for centuries. The sheer size and weight of these stones raise intriguing questions about the ancient engineering techniques employed to quarry, transport, and position them. Understanding the origin and significance of Baalbek's gigantic stones is essential to unraveling the mysteries of this remarkable site.

The most famous stone at Baalbek is known as the "Stone of the Pregnant Woman." Estimated to weigh around 1,000 tons, this massive stone block remains partially buried, leaving only its exposed surface visible. Nearby, another enormous stone, referred to as the "Trilithon," consists of three individual blocks, each weighing approximately 800 tons. These stones, among others found at the site, challenge our understanding of ancient construction methods and the capabilities of the civilizations that erected them.

The quarrying process of Baalbek's gigantic stones is a subject of fascination and speculation. Scholars propose that the stones were quarried from nearby limestone quarries using a combination of stone-cutting tools, wooden sledges, and possibly even simple machines. The precision required to shape these enormous blocks suggests a level of expertise and craftsmanship far beyond what one might expect from the ancient world. Some theories even suggest the use of advanced techniques or technologies that remain lost to history.

The transportation of these colossal stones is another marvel. The distance from the quarry to the temple complex spans several kilometers, and the terrain includes hills and valleys. The method used to move such massive blocks across these challenging landscapes remains a subject of debate. Theories range from the use of ramps and sledges pulled by human labor to the utilization of levers, pulleys, or even anti-gravity devices, as proposed in more imaginative speculations. However, without concrete evidence, these theories remain speculative, and the precise techniques employed in moving the stones continue to elude us.

The positioning and placement of Baalbek's gigantic stones within the temple complex present yet another mystery. The precise alignment of the stones and their seamless integration into the overall design indicate a high level of architectural planning and engineering precision. Each stone had to be carefully positioned to ensure stability and structural integrity. The fact that these massive stones have remained in place for thousands of years further attests to the exceptional skill of the ancient builders.

The purpose behind the construction of these megalithic structures also sparks curiosity and debate. The enormous effort and resources invested in creating Baalbek's temple complex suggest a significant religious or cultural significance. Some theories propose that the temples were dedicated to deities associated with fertility, celestial forces, or divine rulership. Others suggest that Baalbek served as a center of pilgrimage, attracting worshipers from distant regions. The true purpose of Baalbek's megalithic structures may forever remain a subject of conjecture, as the ancient beliefs and practices associated with them have been lost to the passage of time.

In summary, the gigantic stones of Baalbek stand as a testament to the remarkable achievements of the ancient world. The massive size and intricate placement of these stones challenge our understanding of ancient construction methods and the capabilities of early civilizations. The quarrying, transportation, and positioning of these colossal blocks reveal a level of engineering skill and architectural finesse that continues to captivate and inspire. As we continue to study and explore Baalbek, we strive to unlock the secrets behind its megalithic marvels and gain deeper insights into the cultural and religious significance they held for the ancient builders.

The construction techniques employed in the creation of Baalbek, the ancient megalithic temple complex in Lebanon, have long been a subject of fascination and wonder. The massive size and intricate precision of the stone structures at Baalbek showcase the remarkable engineering skills of the ancient builders. Examining these construction techniques provides valuable insights into the ingenuity and technical prowess of the civilizations that once flourished in this region.

The first notable aspect of Baalbek's construction is the sourcing of the stones themselves. The limestone used in the construction of the temples was quarried from nearby quarries, which were strategically located to provide a ready supply of quality building material. The limestone used at Baalbek is known for its durability and suitability for large-scale construction projects. The quarrying process involved the extraction of large blocks using stone-cutting tools, likely with the assistance of wooden wedges and hammers. The precise shaping and smoothing of the stones were achieved through meticulous craftsmanship and manual labor.

Transporting these massive stone blocks from the quarries to the temple complex was a monumental undertaking. The exact methods employed for transportation remain a subject of speculation and debate among scholars. It is believed that a combination of wooden sledges, ramps, and human labor was used to move the stones across the rugged terrain. The sheer weight of the stones required a significant workforce and careful planning to ensure successful transportation. The exact logistics and techniques employed in this process remain elusive, leaving room for speculation and further investigation.

Positioning the massive stones into place was another remarkable feat of engineering at Baalbek. The temple complex includes structures with intricately fitted stones, such as the famous Trilithon, which consists of three colossal blocks weighing hundreds of tons each. The precision with which these stones were positioned and interlocked suggests a high level of architectural planning and craftsmanship. The builders utilized a combination of simple machines, levers, and pulleys to lift and position the stones accurately. The careful fitting and alignment ensured structural stability and longevity.

Another notable aspect of Baalbek's construction is the use of mortise and tenon joints, which allowed for secure interlocking of the stones. These joints involved carving holes (mortises) into the base of one stone and corresponding projections (tenons) on another stone to create a strong and stable connection. The precision required for such joints demonstrates the advanced skills of the builders in working with stone.

The integration of architectural elements, such as columns, walls, and stairs, into the overall design of Baalbek required intricate planning and execution. The columns, in particular, were carved from monolithic stone shafts and carefully positioned to support the weight of the structure above. The intricate detailing and decoration on these columns showcase the craftsmanship and artistic sensibilities of the builders.

In summary, the construction techniques employed at Baalbek showcase the remarkable engineering achievements of the ancient world. The sourcing, quarrying, transportation, and precise positioning of the massive stone blocks required exceptional skill and meticulous planning. The craftsmanship and architectural finesse exhibited in the fitting and interlocking of stones, as well as the integration of architectural elements, are a testament to the technical prowess and artistic sensibilities of the ancient builders. As we continue to study and explore Baalbek, we gain deeper appreciation for the engineering marvels of this ancient site and the legacy of the civilizations that left their mark on these magnificent structures.

Baalbek, the ancient temple complex in Lebanon, is renowned for its colossal stone blocks that have puzzled and amazed researchers and visitors for centuries. These enormous stones, some of the largest ever quarried and moved by human hands, stand as a testament to the engineering prowess and ambition of the ancient builders. Exploring the origin, transportation, and placement of these gigantic stones at Baalbek sheds light on the remarkable feats accomplished by the civilizations of antiquity.

One of the most impressive examples of Baalbek's gigantic stones is the "Stone of the Pregnant Woman." Estimated to weigh around 1,000 tons, this massive stone block lies in a nearby quarry, still attached to the bedrock. It is a monument to the sheer scale of the quarrying efforts undertaken by the ancient builders. How they managed to extract, shape, and transport such an enormous stone remains a subject of speculation and wonder.

Another notable feature is the "Trilithon," a structure composed of three colossal stone blocks estimated to weigh around 800 tons each. These stones were placed on top of each other to create awe-inspiring columns, forming part of the temple complex. The precision with which these stones were quarried, shaped, and positioned is a testament to the advanced engineering skills of the ancient craftsmen.

The quarrying process of these gigantic stones at Baalbek required ingenuity and meticulous planning. Stone-cutting tools such as chisels, mallets, and wedges were likely used to extract the stones from the quarry bedrock. The laborious task of shaping the stones would have involved skilled craftsmen chipping away at the rough surfaces, gradually transforming them into the desired dimensions. The precision achieved in the shaping of these massive blocks is remarkable, given the rudimentary tools available at the time.

Transporting these colossal stones from the quarry to the construction site posed an immense logistical challenge. The distance between the quarry and Baalbek spans several kilometers, and the rugged terrain posed obstacles that had to be overcome. The methods employed for the transportation of these stones remain a subject of speculation. It is believed that a combination of sledges, ramps, and the concerted efforts of a significant workforce was involved in their movement. The exact techniques and engineering solutions used to overcome the obstacles of rough terrain and steep inclines are still a matter of investigation.

Positioning these enormous stones into place required careful planning and execution. The interlocking of the stones through precise fitting and jointing techniques was essential for stability and structural integrity.

Mortise and tenon joints, in which holes (mortises) were carved into one stone and projections (tenons) were shaped on another to create a secure connection, were utilized in the construction of Baalbek. The fitting and alignment of these stones were executed with remarkable precision, allowing them to withstand the test of time.

The purpose behind the construction of these massive stone blocks at Baalbek remains a topic of speculation. Some theories suggest that they were meant to honor deities associated with celestial forces or to signify the grandeur of rulership. Others propose that their sheer size and weight were intended to convey a sense of power and divine authority. The exact beliefs and intentions of the ancient builders may forever remain a mystery, as the knowledge of their religious and cultural practices has been lost over the ages.

In summary, the gigantic stone blocks of Baalbek stand as a testament to the audacity and engineering genius of the ancient world. The extraction, shaping, transportation, and placement of these colossal stones required tremendous effort, skill, and planning. The precision achieved in their construction is a testament to the remarkable craftsmanship and technical expertise of the ancient builders. As we continue to marvel at the colossal stones of Baalbek, we gain a deeper appreciation for the ambition and achievements of the civilizations that created these awe-inspiring structures.

Chapter 3: A Journey Back in Time: Origins and History of Baalbek

The monumental construction of Baalbek, with its massive stone blocks and grand architectural design, has long been a subject of fascination and debate among scholars and researchers. The origins and purpose of this extraordinary site continue to elude us, leaving behind an enigmatic puzzle waiting to be deciphered. Examining the various theories and speculations surrounding Baalbek's construction sheds light on the complex narrative of this ancient site.

One theory posits that Baalbek's origins can be traced back to the Roman period, when the Romans built a temple complex atop earlier Phoenician and Hellenistic structures. The grandeur and sophistication of the Roman architecture at Baalbek are evident in the towering columns and intricately carved details that still grace the site. However, this theory does not fully account for the presence of the colossal stone blocks that predate the Roman era.

Another theory suggests that the construction of Baalbek can be attributed to a much earlier period, possibly the Phoenician or Hellenistic era. The Phoenicians, known for their seafaring and trading skills, may have been responsible for the initial development of the site. The Hellenistic influence is evident in the Corinthian columns that adorn the temple complex. However, this theory does not fully explain the remarkable scale and precision of the megalithic construction found at Baalbek.

A more intriguing and controversial theory proposes that Baalbek's megalithic construction predates the Phoenicians and Hellenistic periods by thousands of years, dating back to a much earlier and mysterious civilization. This theory suggests that the massive stone blocks, some weighing over 1,000 tons, were quarried, transported, and positioned by an ancient civilization with advanced engineering knowledge and capabilities that surpass those of later civilizations.

Supporters of this theory point to the extraordinary size and weight of the stone blocks, which surpass any known ancient construction methods. They argue that the precision in the fitting and interlocking of the stones, as well as the use of sophisticated jointing techniques, indicate a level of craftsmanship and engineering skill far beyond what was thought possible during the proposed time period.

The purpose of Baalbek's construction is also a subject of debate. Some theories propose that it was primarily a religious and ceremonial center, dedicated to deities associated with fertility, agriculture, or celestial forces. The positioning of Baalbek in alignment with astronomical phenomena, such as the summer solstice, has led to speculation about its role as an ancient observatory or site of celestial worship. Others suggest that Baalbek served as a political and cultural center, projecting power and authority through its impressive architecture.

The lack of written records from the ancient builders of Baalbek further complicates our understanding of its origins and purpose. Without direct testimony from those who shaped and raised these magnificent structures, we are left to decipher the clues embedded within the stones themselves and draw inferences from comparative studies of other ancient sites.

In summary, the origins and purpose of Baalbek's monumental construction remain shrouded in mystery and subject to ongoing research and speculation. The various theories proposed over the years provide glimpses into the complex narrative of this ancient site, but a definitive answer to the enigma of Baalbek has yet to be found. As archaeologists continue to unearth new evidence and explore alternative interpretations, the story of Baalbek continues to captivate the imagination and challenge our understanding of the ancient world.

Baalbek, with its rich historical tapestry, stands as a testament to the multilayered history of the region. Through the careful study of archaeological remains, inscriptions, and historical accounts, we can peel back the layers of time and uncover the fascinating chronicles that have shaped Baalbek into the remarkable site we see today.

The earliest known history of Baalbek dates back to the Phoenician period, around the 3rd millennium BCE. The Phoenicians, known for their seafaring prowess and commercial networks, established prosperous city-states along the Mediterranean coast. Baalbek, then known as "Baalat Gebal" or "Lady of the Mountain," was a significant religious center dedicated to the Phoenician deity Baal. The Phoenician influence is evident in the early temple ruins found at the site.

With the expansion of Alexander the Great's empire in the 4th century BCE, Baalbek came under Hellenistic rule. The city was renamed Heliopolis, meaning "City of the Sun," in honor of the Greek god Helios. During this period, the Greeks introduced their architectural and cultural traditions to the region. The magnificent temples of Baalbek, adorned with Corinthian columns and intricate friezes, exemplify the Hellenistic architectural style.

Following the decline of the Hellenistic Seleucid Empire, Baalbek came under Roman rule in the 1st century BCE. It was during this period that

Baalbek experienced its greatest expansion and witnessed the construction of the grandiose structures that still dominate the site. The Romans, impressed by the site's religious significance, dedicated the temple complex to their deities, particularly Jupiter, Bacchus, and Venus. The Roman architectural influence at Baalbek is undeniable. The massive stone blocks, some weighing hundreds of tons, were quarried from nearby mountains and meticulously arranged to create an awe-inspiring architectural ensemble. The Temple of Jupiter, with its towering columns and monumental entrance, serves as a testament to the grandeur and ambition of Roman engineering and craftsmanship.

In the 4th century CE, with the rise of Christianity, Baalbek underwent a transformation. The Roman temples were repurposed as churches, reflecting the shift in religious practices and beliefs. The presence of Byzantine mosaics and Christian symbols attests to this Christian era of Baalbek's history.

Over the centuries, Baalbek experienced successive waves of conquest and occupation. It fell under the control of the Islamic Caliphate, the Crusaders, the Mamluks, and the Ottomans, each leaving their mark on the site. Despite these periods of change and conflict, Baalbek's significance as a cultural and religious center endured, though it gradually declined in prominence.

The modern era brought renewed interest in Baalbek's historical and archaeological significance. Excavations and restoration efforts have revealed the layers of history embedded within the site, allowing us to unravel its complex past. Today, Baalbek stands as a UNESCO World Heritage Site, attracting visitors from around the world who seek to immerse themselves in the grandeur of its ancient ruins.

In summary, Baalbek's history is a testament to the cultural and architectural influences that have shaped the region over millennia. From the Phoenician origins to the Roman magnificence and subsequent periods of transformation, Baalbek's historical layers provide a glimpse into the rich tapestry of civilizations that have left their mark on this remarkable site. By unraveling its multilayered history, we gain a deeper appreciation for the enduring legacy of Baalbek and its significance in our understanding of the ancient world.

The history of Baalbek is a tapestry woven with the threads of cultural influences and exchanges. Situated at the crossroads of ancient trade routes, Baalbek served as a meeting point for diverse civilizations and a hub of cultural exchange. Through the study of archaeological evidence, historical accounts, and inscriptions, we can unravel the intricate web of cultural interactions that have shaped Baalbek's history.

The Phoenicians, renowned seafarers and traders, played a pivotal role in the early cultural development of Baalbek. They established a network of city-states along the Mediterranean coast, with Baalbek emerging as a significant religious center dedicated to the deity Baal. The Phoenicians' commercial connections brought them into contact with diverse cultures, influencing their religious beliefs, artistic expressions, and architectural styles.

With the expansion of the Hellenistic empire under Alexander the Great, Baalbek came under Greek influence. The Hellenistic period witnessed the infusion of Greek customs, language, and architectural traditions into the cultural fabric of the region. Greek deities and architectural motifs found their way into Baalbek's temples, blending with the existing Phoenician religious practices and artistic forms.

The Roman period marked a significant turning point in Baalbek's history, as the city became an integral part of the Roman Empire. The Romans, renowned for their assimilative approach to conquered cultures, adopted and incorporated local traditions into their own. Baalbek's transformation into a magnificent Roman city was marked by the construction of colossal temples, including the Temple of Jupiter and the Temple of Bacchus. These structures showcased the grandeur of Roman architecture while also incorporating elements from earlier cultures.

During the Byzantine era, Christianity took root in Baalbek, introducing a new religious and cultural dynamic. Byzantine mosaics, Christian symbols, and the repurposing of pagan temples as Christian churches reflect the influence of this period. Baalbek became a center for Christian worship and pilgrimage, attracting believers from near and far.

In the following centuries, Baalbek witnessed the rise and fall of various powers, including Arab dynasties, Crusaders, and Islamic empires. Each era brought its own cultural influences and transformations, leaving an indelible mark on the city. The diverse interactions and exchanges during these periods contributed to the rich cultural tapestry of Baalbek.

The Ottoman period marked a new phase in Baalbek's history, with the city becoming part of the expansive Ottoman Empire. Ottoman architectural styles and cultural practices left their imprint on the city, further enriching its heritage.

In the modern era, Baalbek's cultural influences continue to evolve. The site's status as a UNESCO World Heritage Site and its popularity among tourists from around the world highlight its enduring appeal and significance. The preservation and promotion of Baalbek's cultural heritage serve as a testament to the ongoing recognition and appreciation of its diverse historical influences.

In summary, Baalbek's history is a testament to the dynamic interactions and exchanges that have shaped its cultural landscape. The Phoenicians, Greeks, Romans, Byzantines, and subsequent civilizations all played a role in shaping Baalbek's identity, leaving behind a rich legacy of cultural influences. By exploring these interactions, we gain a deeper understanding of the diverse tapestry of cultures that have contributed to the unique character of Baalbek throughout history.

The process of rediscovering the past at Baalbek has been an arduous and rewarding journey. Through systematic archaeological excavations, researchers and scholars have unearthed a wealth of artifacts, structures, and insights that shed light on the fascinating history of this ancient site. From the early pioneering excavations to the modern scientific approaches, the discoveries at Baalbek have captivated the imaginations of historians, archaeologists, and the public alike.

The initial explorations of Baalbek began in the 19th century, when European travelers and scholars were first drawn to the grandeur of its monumental ruins. These early excavations, conducted with limited resources and methodologies, laid the foundation for subsequent research and sparked curiosity about the site's history and significance. Scholars like Ernst Herzfeld and Theodore Wiegand made significant contributions by documenting and mapping the architectural remains, providing crucial insights into the site's layout and structure.

In the mid-20th century, more comprehensive excavations took place under the direction of Lebanese and international teams. These excavations utilized advanced techniques and technologies to carefully uncover and analyze the remains of Baalbek. The systematic approach revealed not only the grand temples but also the intricate details of daily life, including domestic structures, workshops, and even a Roman theater.

The discoveries at Baalbek have provided valuable insights into various aspects of ancient life. The exquisite sculptures, intricate mosaics, and inscriptions found at the site have shed light on the religious practices, artistic expressions, and cultural beliefs of the Phoenician, Hellenistic, and Roman periods. The meticulous documentation and analysis of architectural features, such as the precision of stone construction and the engineering marvels of the colossal stones, have deepened our understanding of ancient engineering and craftsmanship.

One of the most significant finds at Baalbek is the Great Court, which encompasses the Temple of Jupiter and the Temple of Bacchus. The colossal stones used in the construction of these temples continue to perplex researchers. The sheer size and weight of these stones, some weighing over 1,000 tons, raise intriguing questions about the construction methods employed by ancient builders. The discoveries have prompted debates and theories about the means by which such immense stones were quarried, transported, and placed with such precision.

The ongoing excavations and research at Baalbek are yielding new insights into the site's history. Advanced techniques, such as ground-penetrating radar and 3D modeling, are being employed to uncover hidden structures and better understand the layout of the ancient city. Additionally, interdisciplinary studies involving archaeologists, historians, architects, and geologists are contributing to a more holistic understanding of Baalbek's past.

The discoveries at Baalbek have not only enhanced our knowledge of the site but also enriched our understanding of the broader historical context. By studying the artifacts and structures found at Baalbek in relation to other ancient sites in the region, researchers are able to draw connections and identify shared cultural and architectural elements. This comparative approach provides valuable insights into the interconnectedness of ancient civilizations and their cultural exchanges.

In summary, the archaeological discoveries at Baalbek have been instrumental in unraveling the mysteries of this ancient site. Through meticulous excavations, research, and interdisciplinary collaboration, researchers have unearthed valuable artifacts and gained insights into the cultural, religious, and architectural aspects of Baalbek's past. The ongoing exploration of the site promises to continue revealing new layers of history and further enriching our understanding of this remarkable ancient city.

Chapter 4: The Divine Architecture: Exploring the Temple Complex

Baalbek's majestic temple complex stands as a testament to the architectural splendor of ancient civilizations. Nestled in the fertile Bekaa Valley of present-day Lebanon, the grandeur and scale of Baalbek's temples leave visitors awe-inspired and curious about the minds and hands that crafted such magnificent structures. As one steps into this remarkable site, they are transported back in time, enveloped by the grandeur and mystique of an architectural masterpiece.

The Temple of Jupiter, the largest and most prominent structure in the complex, is a sight to behold. Its colossal columns and towering walls evoke a sense of reverence and admiration. The sheer size of the stones used in its construction is mind-boggling, leaving one to wonder about the engineering prowess of the ancient builders. These massive stones, some weighing over 1,000 tons, were transported from quarries miles away, a feat that continues to astound modern architects and engineers.

The temple ensemble of Baalbek unveils a world of intricate structures that have captivated scholars and visitors alike for centuries. Nestled amidst the picturesque landscape of the Bekaa Valley in Lebanon, Baalbek stands as a testament to the ingenuity and architectural brilliance of ancient civilizations.

At the heart of the ensemble lies the Temple of Jupiter, an awe-inspiring structure that dominates the site. Its massive stone walls, towering columns, and imposing podium create an atmosphere of grandeur and reverence. The sheer scale of the temple is awe-inspiring, with its outer dimensions reaching a staggering 88 meters by 48 meters. Each stone block used in its construction weighs several tons, a testament to the remarkable engineering and logistical efforts of the ancient builders.

The Temple of Jupiter is adorned with intricate carvings and decorative elements, reflecting the artistic prowess of its creators. Elaborate friezes depict mythological scenes and symbolic motifs, offering glimpses into the rich cultural and religious beliefs of the time. The elaborate Corinthian capitals atop the columns showcase the mastery of architectural design and craftsmanship.

Adjacent to the Temple of Jupiter is the Temple of Bacchus, dedicated to the Roman god of wine and revelry. This remarkably preserved structure showcases the grandeur of Roman architecture, with its monumental entrance, graceful columns, and intricately carved reliefs. The exquisite detailing on the temple's façade is a testament to the skill and artistry of the craftsmen who brought this architectural marvel to life.

Another notable structure within the ensemble is the Temple of Venus, which stands on a slightly lower terrace. Though not as well-preserved as its counterparts, the temple's ruins still reveal glimpses of its former magnificence. The remains of the temple's once-imposing columns and intricate architectural elements offer insight into the splendor that once graced this sacred space.

The temple ensemble of Baalbek is more than just a collection of impressive structures. It is a testament to the religious, cultural, and political significance of the region throughout the ages. These temples served as centers of worship, where devotees gathered to honor and seek divine blessings. They also served as symbols of power and authority, asserting the dominance of the ruling elite.

The architectural style of the Baalbek temples is a testament to the interplay between different civilizations and cultures that inhabited the region over time. The influence of Phoenician, Greek, and Roman architectural traditions can be seen in the columns, capitals, and decorative motifs that adorn the structures. This amalgamation of styles reflects the complex history and rich tapestry of cultural interactions that shaped the region.

Exploring the temple ensemble of Baalbek is like stepping back in time, immersing oneself in the grandeur and mystique of the ancient world. The sheer size and scale of the structures, coupled with their intricate detailing, evoke a sense of wonder and admiration. Each stone block, each carving, and each column holds within it a story, waiting to be deciphered and appreciated.

The preservation and restoration efforts at Baalbek have ensured that future generations can continue to marvel at the architectural marvels of the past. Ongoing archaeological excavations and research shed new light on the history and significance of the site, allowing us to piece together the puzzle of this ancient civilization.

In summary, the temple ensemble of Baalbek stands as a testament to the architectural brilliance and cultural legacy of ancient civilizations. Its intricate structures, massive stone blocks, and ornate detailing continue to inspire awe and wonder. The temples of Baalbek are not just monuments of the past; they are gateways to understanding the cultural, religious, and artistic achievements of our ancestors. As we explore these sacred spaces, we embark on a journey of discovery, unraveling the stories and mysteries of a bygone era.

The temples of Baalbek, with their imposing architecture and intricate design, stand as testament to the religious significance they held for ancient civilizations. These sacred structures were not merely architectural marvels, but were deeply intertwined with the religious beliefs and practices of the people who built and worshiped within them. At the heart of the temple complex is the Temple of Jupiter, dedicated to the chief Roman deity. It served as a focal point for religious ceremonies and was believed to house the presence of the divine. The temple's massive scale and grandeur were intended to inspire awe and reverence, creating a sacred space where worshippers could connect with the divine and seek spiritual guidance. The carefully planned layout of the temple, with its multiple chambers and sanctuaries, facilitated various religious rituals and ceremonies.

Adjacent to the Temple of Jupiter is the Temple of Bacchus, dedicated to the Roman god of wine and revelry. This temple played a vital role in the religious life of the ancient Romans, who believed in celebrating and honoring their deities through feasts and festivities. The temple's design, with its open courtyard and spacious interior, provided a suitable setting for the performance of religious rituals and processions.

The Temple of Venus, situated on a lower terrace, was dedicated to the Roman goddess of love and beauty. It served as a sacred space where worshippers could seek blessings and guidance in matters of love, fertility, and relationships. The temple's architecture, adorned with decorative elements and intricate carvings, reflected the importance of these themes in the religious and cultural beliefs of the time.

These temples were not just places of worship but also centers of religious education and spiritual guidance. Priests and priestesses played a crucial role in the religious rituals and practices conducted within these sacred spaces. They acted as intermediaries between the mortal realm and the divine, performing rituals, offering sacrifices, and interpreting signs and omens.

The religious significance of Baalbek's temples extended beyond the boundaries of the complex itself. They were part of a larger religious landscape, connected to other sacred sites and pilgrimage routes. Baalbek, with its grand temples, became a destination for pilgrims seeking divine blessings and spiritual experiences. The processions, ceremonies, and festivals held at Baalbek attracted worshippers from far and wide, fostering a sense of community and shared religious identity.

The intricate carvings, friezes, and sculptures that adorned the temples served not only as decorative elements but also conveyed religious narratives and symbolism. These artistic representations depicted scenes from mythology, legends, and religious rituals, offering worshippers visual cues and reminders of their beliefs. The symbolism embedded within the temple architecture and artwork created a multi-layered spiritual experience, inviting worshippers to connect with the divine on both a visual and symbolic level.

The religious significance of Baalbek's temples endured for centuries, even as the region experienced shifts in political power and religious beliefs. The temples were modified and adapted by different civilizations that ruled the area, reflecting the changing religious landscapes and cultural influences over time. Each successive civilization added its own layers of meaning and religious practices to the existing structures, further enriching the complex tapestry of spiritual significance associated with Baalbek.

Today, the temples of Baalbek continue to inspire awe and reverence among visitors from around the world. They stand as reminders of the enduring power of religious beliefs and the timeless human quest for connection with the divine. Exploring the architectural grandeur and spiritual significance of these ancient temples provides a glimpse into the religious worldviews and practices of the past, allowing us to appreciate the profound impact of religion on human history and culture.

Chapter 5: The Power of the Stones: Mythology and Spiritual Significance

The megalithic stones of Baalbek have long been shrouded in legends and mythical tales, adding an air of mystery and intrigue to this ancient site. These stories, passed down through generations, reflect the awe and wonder that the monumental stones have inspired in people throughout history. While some of these tales are purely imaginative, others are rooted in the beliefs and cultural narratives of the civilizations that once inhabited the region.

One of the most enduring legends surrounding Baalbek is the story of its construction by a race of giants. According to ancient folklore, the massive stones were said to have been moved and placed by supernatural beings or giants with incredible strength. These giants were believed to have been the builders of the temples, using their extraordinary powers to manipulate the enormous stones with ease. This legend, although fantastical in nature, reflects the astonishment and admiration that the colossal size of the stones evoked in the minds of ancient observers.

Another intriguing tale associated with Baalbek is the mythological connection to the god Baal. Baal was a prominent deity in the ancient Near East, worshipped as the god of storms, fertility, and agricultural abundance. According to myth, Baal was said to have performed extraordinary feats of strength and power, and it was believed that the megalithic stones of Baalbek were a testament to his divine presence and influence. The temples at Baalbek were thus considered sacred spaces where worshippers could commune with Baal and seek his blessings.

In addition to these mythical tales, Baalbek's stones have been linked to biblical narratives. Some believe that the massive stones were part of Solomon's Temple, mentioned in the Hebrew Bible. According to this interpretation, the stones were transported from a distant land to be used in the construction of the temple, showcasing the immense power and resources at the disposal of ancient kings. This connection to biblical stories adds another layer of significance to the already enigmatic stones of Baalbek.

Legends and folklore surrounding Baalbek also speak of hidden chambers and secret passageways within the megalithic structures. These tales fuel the imagination, evoking images of concealed treasures, mystical rituals,

274

and ancient mysteries waiting to be unraveled. While these stories may be steeped in myth and imagination, they contribute to the allure and fascination that Baalbek continues to hold for explorers, archaeologists, and visitors alike.

It is important to note that these legends and tales are not based on historical evidence, but rather on the imaginative interpretations and cultural beliefs of different civilizations throughout time. They reflect the human desire to explain the extraordinary and to imbue ancient sites with a sense of wonder and awe. Nonetheless, these legends play a crucial role in shaping the cultural significance of Baalbek, adding to its mystique and elevating it to the status of a legendary site of ancient marvels.

As we delve into the stories and legends surrounding Baalbek's megalithic stones, we are reminded of the power of human imagination and the enduring fascination with the extraordinary achievements of our ancestors. Whether rooted in mythology, religious beliefs, or cultural narratives, these tales contribute to the rich tapestry of folklore and legend that envelops Baalbek, making it not only an archaeological site of immense historical importance but also a place of mythical allure and enchantment.

The monumental stones of Baalbek hold profound symbolism and significance in the ancient beliefs and religious practices of the civilizations that once flourished in the region. These colossal stones, with their impressive size and imposing presence, were not merely structural components but were imbued with deeper meaning and sacred significance. They were seen as conduits for divine power, connecting the earthly realm with the spiritual world.

One of the key aspects of the symbolism surrounding the stones of Baalbek is their association with deities and divine forces. In the religious beliefs of the ancient Near East, stones were often regarded as embodiments of gods or divine beings. The megalithic stones of Baalbek were considered sacred, believed to be the dwelling places of gods or vessels through which spiritual energy flowed. The temples built with these stones were seen as gateways to the divine realm, where humans could interact with the gods and seek their favor.

The sheer size and weight of the stones also played a significant role in their symbolism. The effort required to quarry, transport, and manipulate such massive stones was considered a testament to the power and authority of the ruling elite or the gods themselves. The stones served as symbols of strength, stability, and permanence, reflecting the belief in the enduring presence and protection of the divine.

Furthermore, the positioning and arrangement of the stones within the temple complex carried symbolic meaning. The precise alignment with celestial bodies, such as the sun, moon, and stars, showcased a deep understanding of cosmology and the belief in the interconnectedness of the earthly and celestial realms. The orientation of the stones towards specific celestial events, such as solstices or equinoxes, reflected the belief in the cyclical nature of the universe and the importance of celestial phenomena in religious and agricultural practices.

The carvings and inscriptions on the stones of Baalbek also conveyed symbolic messages. Intricate reliefs depicting mythological scenes, divine figures, and religious rituals conveyed narratives of creation, divine power, and the interplay between gods and humans. These carvings served as visual representations of the beliefs, values, and cosmological concepts of the ancient cultures that inhabited the area.

In addition to their religious and symbolic significance, the stones of Baalbek held social and cultural importance. They served as gathering places for religious ceremonies, community celebrations, and communal activities. The temples were centers of social cohesion, where individuals from different walks of life came together to participate in rituals, seek spiritual guidance, and engage in communal worship. The stones were witnesses to the shared experiences, traditions, and communal bonds that characterized the ancient societies that revered them.

Today, the stones of Baalbek continue to captivate and inspire awe. Their immense size, architectural beauty, and rich symbolism evoke a sense of wonder and fascination. They stand as enduring reminders of the spiritual beliefs, cultural achievements, and technological prowess of the ancient civilizations that created them. The stones of Baalbek are not mere relics of the past; they carry within them the echoes of ancient voices, beliefs, and aspirations, inviting us to delve deeper into the mysteries of human history and the profound significance of the sacred stones that have shaped our collective heritage.

The stones of Baalbek, with their monumental size and awe-inspiring presence, are believed to possess spiritual resonance and hold potent energies and powers. Throughout history, people have been drawn to these sacred stones, perceiving them as conduits of divine energy and sources of spiritual power. It is in the mystical qualities attributed to the stones that their true significance lies.

One aspect of the spiritual resonance of Baalbek's stones is their connection to the Earth's energies. Some believe that the megaliths, deeply rooted in the ground, act as energetic anchors, harnessing the Earth's natural forces and channeling them in a profound way. It is said that the stones possess a unique vibration and resonate with the Earth's electromagnetic field, creating a sacred space where individuals can connect with higher realms of consciousness.

The alignment of the stones with celestial bodies, such as the sun, moon, and stars, further enhances their spiritual significance. The precise positioning of the stones to correspond with astronomical events, such as solstices or equinoxes, is seen as a deliberate act to tap into the cosmic energies and align with the rhythms of the universe. This celestial connection is believed to amplify the spiritual energy of the stones and facilitate a deeper communion between the earthly and celestial realms.

The stones of Baalbek are also associated with healing and transformation. Some claim that the stones emit healing energies that can bring balance and harmony to the body, mind, and spirit. It is believed that spending time in proximity to these stones can promote physical well-being, emotional healing, and spiritual growth. The powerful energy of the stones is said to cleanse and purify, allowing individuals to release negativity and open themselves to higher states of consciousness.

In addition to their healing properties, the stones of Baalbek are regarded as repositories of ancient wisdom and esoteric knowledge. They are believed to hold the secrets of the past, encoded within their crystalline structures. Those who attune themselves to the stones' vibrations and energies may access deep insights, ancient wisdom, and spiritual teachings that have been preserved throughout the ages. It is in this connection to the past and the accumulated wisdom of the ancients that the stones reveal their transformative power.

The spiritual resonance of Baalbek's stones is not limited to religious or cultural contexts but extends to individuals seeking personal growth, enlightenment, and a deeper understanding of the mysteries of existence. It is believed that by engaging with the stones through meditation, prayer, or contemplation, individuals can tap into their spiritual energies, expand their consciousness, and experience profound spiritual insights.

While the exact nature of the energies and powers associated with Baalbek's stones may remain elusive, their impact on the human psyche and spiritual experience is undeniable. Whether through their impressive size, celestial alignments, or profound energies, the stones of Baalbek continue to evoke a sense of wonder, reverence, and spiritual connection. They serve as reminders of our innate spiritual yearnings and our quest for deeper meaning and transcendent experiences in the presence of the sacred.

Baalbek's megalithic temple complex has long been associated with divine connections and has served as a site of rituals and ceremonies that were central to the religious practices of the ancient civilizations that revered it. These sacred rituals were seen as a means of establishing a direct connection with the divine, seeking blessings, and ensuring spiritual favor.

One of the key aspects of the rituals at Baalbek was the offering of sacrifices. Animals, such as bulls or goats, were ritually slaughtered and their blood was believed to carry symbolic significance, serving as a conduit between the human realm and the divine. The act of sacrifice was seen as a means of appeasing the gods, expressing gratitude, and seeking their protection and favor. These rituals were often performed by priests or designated individuals who held a sacred role within the community.

The processions and ceremonies conducted at Baalbek were elaborate and involved the participation of priests, attendants, and members of the community. These rituals often included chanting, singing, music, and dance, creating an immersive and sensory experience that heightened the spiritual atmosphere. The rhythmic movements and the repetitive nature of the chants were believed to induce a state of trance or altered consciousness, allowing participants to commune with the divine and experience a heightened sense of connection.

Baalbek's megalithic temples also served as sites for initiation rites and coming-of-age ceremonies. These rituals marked significant milestones in an individual's life, such as reaching adulthood, joining a religious order, or assuming a specific societal role. Through these ceremonies, individuals were initiated into the mysteries of the divine, receiving spiritual guidance, and embarking on a new phase of their lives.

The alignment of the temples with celestial bodies played a crucial role in the rituals and ceremonies conducted at Baalbek. The orientation of the temples towards the rising or setting sun, the solstices, or equinoxes held deep symbolic meaning. These celestial events marked important points in the agricultural and cosmic cycles, and the rituals performed at these times were believed to harness the energies of the sun, moon, and stars, enhancing their spiritual efficacy.

The rituals at Baalbek were not only focused on appeasing and communing with the gods but also on communal bonding and social cohesion. These ceremonies brought people together, reinforcing the sense of community and shared belief. The participation of individuals from different social strata emphasized the egalitarian nature of religious practice, where all members of society had the opportunity to engage in the rituals and experience spiritual transcendence.

While the specifics of the rituals and ceremonies at Baalbek may be lost to the depths of time, their importance and impact on the lives of the ancient worshipers cannot be underestimated. These rituals were not merely empty gestures but were deeply intertwined with the fabric of daily life, reflecting the spiritual aspirations, communal identity, and societal values of the civilizations that gathered at Baalbek's megalithic temples. They provided a sacred space where individuals could connect with the divine, seek solace, guidance, and celebrate the mysteries of existence.

Chapter 6: Celestial Connections: Baalbek's Alignment with the Stars

Baalbek, with its imposing megalithic structures, holds a celestial significance that has captivated the imaginations of scholars and seekers of ancient wisdom. The precise alignment of the temples with celestial bodies, such as the sun, moon, and stars, reveals an intricate understanding of the cosmos and a profound connection to the celestial realm.

One of the most striking celestial alignments at Baalbek is the orientation of the temples towards the rising or setting sun during significant astronomical events, such as solstices or equinoxes. These alignments were not accidental but intentional, indicating an astute awareness of celestial patterns and their correlation to the rhythms of the natural world. The alignment with the sun at these pivotal moments of the year held deep symbolic meaning, representing the cyclical nature of life, death, and rebirth, and reinforcing the connection between the earthly and celestial realms.

The moon also played a significant role in the celestial alignments at Baalbek. Some structures within the temple complex are aligned with the moon's cycles, marking its rising or setting during specific lunar phases. The moon's association with fertility, cycles, and the divine feminine would have held profound significance for the ancient worshipers at Baalbek, linking them to the rhythms of nature and the mysteries of life and creation.

The stars, too, were revered at Baalbek, and the temples were aligned with specific stellar positions. These celestial alignments not only served practical purposes, such as marking the passage of time or indicating agricultural cycles, but also carried deep spiritual and symbolic meaning. The stars were seen as celestial guides, representing the divine forces that governed the cosmos and influenced human destiny. By aligning the temples with specific stars or star clusters, the ancient builders of Baalbek sought to establish a direct connection with these cosmic forces, invoking their blessings and channeling their energies.

The celestial alignments of Baalbek's temples also have implications for its architectural design. The orientation of the structures, the positioning of the columns, and the layout of the complex were all carefully planned to harmonize with the celestial alignments. This meticulous attention to celestial details not only demonstrates the advanced astronomical knowledge of the ancient builders but also suggests that the temples were intended as celestial observatories, where celestial events could be observed and interpreted in relation to the spiritual beliefs and practices of the time.

The celestial significance of Baalbek goes beyond mere observation of celestial phenomena. It is believed that the alignments were intended to facilitate a deeper spiritual connection with the celestial realm. The celestial events served as focal points for rituals, ceremonies, and spiritual practices, providing an opportunity for individuals to attune themselves to the cosmic energies, commune with the divine, and seek guidance and blessings.

While the full extent of Baalbek's celestial significance may never be fully known, the celestial alignments of the temples offer glimpses into the profound spiritual and cosmological worldview of the ancient civilizations that revered this sacred site. Baalbek stands as a testament to the human quest to understand and connect with the vast mysteries of the cosmos, reflecting the timeless fascination with the celestial realm and its influence on human beliefs, rituals, and aspirations.

Baalbek, with its awe-inspiring megalithic temples, holds a profound connection to the cosmos through its intricate astronomical alignments. The precise positioning of the structures in relation to celestial bodies reveals a deep understanding of astronomical phenomena and a reverence for the cosmic forces that govern the universe.

One of the most remarkable astronomical alignments at Baalbek is the orientation of the temples towards the cardinal directions. The east-west alignment, with the main entrance facing the rising sun, signifies the symbolism of birth, new beginnings, and the promise of a new day. The careful alignment with the rising and setting sun during specific times of the year, such as solstices and equinoxes, further emphasizes the connection between the earthly realm and the celestial realm.

The alignment of the temples with specific stars or star clusters is another testament to Baalbek's profound astronomical knowledge. The Pleiades, a prominent star cluster in the constellation Taurus, holds significant celestial importance in the temple complex. Its alignment with certain structures suggests that the ancient builders considered it a celestial marker, a guide to the cosmic energies that influenced their lives and spiritual practices.

The moon, too, played a vital role in the astronomical alignments at Baalbek. Some structures are aligned with the moon's phases, marking its rising or setting during specific lunar cycles. The moon, with its waxing and waning, symbolized the ebb and flow of life, the cycles of fertility, and the connection between the heavens and the Earth. The alignment with lunar phases highlights the ancient worshipers' recognition of the moon's influence on their daily lives and the importance of lunar symbolism in their religious and spiritual practices.

Baalbek's astronomical alignments not only reflect an understanding of celestial movements but also suggest a reverence for the cyclic nature of time and the interconnectedness of cosmic forces. The alignments served as a means of attuning with the rhythms of the universe, allowing the worshipers to participate in the cosmic dance and harmonize their lives with the greater cosmic order.

The significance of these astronomical alignments extends beyond mere observation. They held profound religious and spiritual meaning for the ancient worshipers at Baalbek. The alignments were believed to facilitate a connection with the divine, allowing individuals to partake in the celestial energies and seek spiritual enlightenment. Rituals and ceremonies were often performed during specific celestial events, harnessing the power of these alignments to establish a direct communion with the cosmic forces and receive blessings from the celestial realm.

The meticulous attention to astronomical alignments at Baalbek not only speaks to the advanced astronomical knowledge of its builders but also underscores the temple complex's role as a sacred site dedicated to the harmonization of the human and the celestial. It stands as a testament to the human fascination with the cosmos and our perpetual quest to understand our place within the vastness of the universe.

Baalbek's astronomical alignments continue to inspire awe and curiosity, inviting us to contemplate the profound relationship between humanity and the cosmos. They remind us of the enduring human quest for spiritual connection and our innate desire to seek meaning and transcendence in the celestial realm. Baalbek's megalithic temples serve as a timeless testament to the ancient worshipers' reverence for the heavens and their profound insights into the cosmic dance that shapes our world.

The magnificent megalithic temples of Baalbek hold within their grandeur a deep sense of cosmic significance, intertwining the earthly and celestial realms in a tapestry of sacredness. At the heart of this cosmic dimension lies the profound understanding of the ancient builders of Baalbek, who recognized the intimate connection between the heavens and the earthly realm.

The celestial alignments of Baalbek's temples reveal an intricate knowledge of the celestial bodies and their movements. The orientation of the structures in relation to the sun, moon, and stars was carefully planned to create a harmonious union between the physical and spiritual worlds. These alignments were not merely practical considerations but held deep symbolic and ritualistic meanings.

The rising and setting of the sun played a central role in the celestial drama at Baalbek. The alignment of certain structures with the solstices and equinoxes marked significant moments in the solar calendar, such as the changing of seasons and the cycle of life. These alignments allowed the ancient worshipers to celebrate and honor the sun's life-giving power, acknowledging its role as a cosmic deity and a source of light, warmth, and fertility.

The moon, with its ethereal beauty and ever-changing phases, also took its place in the cosmic tapestry of Baalbek. The alignments of structures with lunar events, such as full moons or lunar eclipses, evoked a sense of wonder and mystery. The moon's influence on tides, cycles of growth, and human emotions was recognized and celebrated, integrating the lunar rhythms into the sacred rituals and beliefs of the ancient worshipers.

The stars, those distant celestial beacons, held a special place in Baalbek's cosmic realm. Certain structures were aligned with specific stars or constellations, emphasizing their significance in the spiritual and mythological narratives of the ancient world. The stars were seen as divine guides, mapping the heavens and guiding the course of human destiny. By aligning their temples with specific stars, the builders of Baalbek sought to establish a profound connection with the cosmic order and the eternal wisdom held within the stars' twinkling lights.

The celestial connections at Baalbek extended beyond the physical alignments. They were also woven into the rich tapestry of mythology and religious beliefs. Gods and goddesses associated with celestial bodies were venerated, and rituals were performed to honor and seek their blessings. The celestial realm was seen as a realm of divine beings and cosmic forces, and Baalbek's temples served as earthly gateways to commune with these celestial entities.

The cosmic dimension of Baalbek's temples transcends time and continues to inspire awe and fascination. The intricate astronomical alignments and the symbolic connections to celestial bodies speak to the eternal human quest for transcendence and a deeper understanding of our place in the cosmos. Baalbek's celestial connections invite us to contemplate the vastness of the universe, to ponder the mysteries of creation, and to recognize our interconnectedness with the cosmic web of life.

As we stand in the shadow of Baalbek's mighty stones, we are reminded of the profound wisdom of the ancient builders, who saw in the heavens a mirror of the divine and a pathway to spiritual enlightenment. The cosmic dimension of Baalbek's celestial connections beckons us to look beyond the earthly realm and embrace the infinite possibilities that lie in the realm of the stars. It reminds us that we are part of a cosmic symphony, intricately interwoven with the celestial rhythms that shape our world and ignite our souls with wonder.

Chapter 7: Mysteries and Legends: Tales Surrounding Baalbek

Baalbek, with its ancient megalithic temples, stands as a testament to the rich tapestry of myths and legends that have woven their way through its history. Within the walls of this majestic complex, tales of gods and heroes have echoed for millennia, passing down the stories of ancient civilizations and their deep reverence for the divine.

One of the most prominent figures in Baalbek's mythological landscape is Baal, the god after whom the city is named. Baal, often depicted as a mighty warrior wielding a thunderbolt, represented the power of storms and fertility. Legends tell of his battles with other gods and his role as a protector and provider of the people. The worship of Baal permeated the lives of the ancient inhabitants, who believed that his blessings brought abundance and prosperity to their land.

Another prominent deity associated with Baalbek is Astarte, the goddess of love, beauty, and fertility. Astarte was revered as a mother goddess and a patron of feminine energy. Her presence was believed to bring harmony and abundance to the land. Legends speak of her enchanting beauty and her role in the cycles of nature, where her influence could be seen in the blossoming of flowers and the birth of new life.

The epic tales of Baalbek also include heroic figures who embody bravery, strength, and wisdom. Adonis, a handsome young hunter, is among the most celebrated heroes. He was known for his exceptional beauty and his tragic fate, which symbolized the cycle of life, death, and rebirth. The story of Adonis captivated the ancient worshipers, who saw in his narrative the eternal struggle between love and loss, creation and destruction.

Myths surrounding Baalbek also include tales of divine interventions, supernatural creatures, and epic battles. The legends speak of powerful giants who once inhabited the land, constructing the monumental structures with their immense strength. These giants, known as the Kabiru, are believed to have possessed great wisdom and served as custodians of ancient knowledge.

Furthermore, Baalbek's myths intertwine with the wider ancient Near Eastern mythology, blending with stories of gods and heroes from surrounding cultures. The influence of Greek mythology, in particular, is evident in the syncretic traditions that emerged during the Hellenistic and Roman periods. Deities such as Zeus, Apollo, and Hercules became intertwined with the local pantheon, merging their narratives with the indigenous myths of Baalbek.

These myths and legends, passed down through generations, provided the people of Baalbek with a sense of identity, purpose, and connection to the divine. They served as a source of inspiration and guidance, offering explanations for natural phenomena, moral teachings, and a framework for understanding the complexities of the human experience.

Today, as we explore the remnants of Baalbek's grandeur, we are transported back in time to a world steeped in mythology and folklore. The ancient stories that once echoed through these sacred spaces continue to captivate and inspire, inviting us to delve into the realm of gods and heroes, and to contemplate the enduring power of myth in shaping our collective consciousness.

Baalbek's myths and legends serve as a reminder of the deep human longing to make sense of the world and our place within it. They connect us to a shared heritage and illuminate the universal themes of love, heroism, and the enduring struggle between good and evil. Through the echoes of these ancient tales, Baalbek beckons us to embrace the timeless power of storytelling and to recognize the profound influence that myths and legends have on shaping our cultural identities and understanding of the divine.

Baalbek, with its awe-inspiring megalithic temples, is shrouded in a veil of mythical narratives that have woven themselves into the very fabric of its existence. These stories, passed down through generations, have not only entertained and intrigued but have also shaped the perception and understanding of this ancient city. Through the tapestry of mythical narratives, we can catch glimpses of the profound beliefs and cultural values of those who walked these hallowed grounds.

One of the most enduring myths surrounding Baalbek is the tale of its origins. According to ancient legends, Baalbek was founded by giants who possessed great strength and knowledge. These giants, known as the Nephilim, were said to have been instrumental in the construction of the colossal stone blocks that make up the temples. Their monumental feat of engineering became a source of wonder and a testament to the immense power and wisdom they possessed.

In the realm of gods and goddesses, Baalbek finds itself entwined in the epic narratives of the ancient Near East. The god Baal, often associated with thunder and storms, is a central figure in many tales. Legends depict his struggles and triumphs, his battles with other deities, and his role as a divine protector and provider. The worship of Baal resonated deeply with the people of Baalbek, who believed that his benevolence brought fertility to the land and ensured prosperity and abundance.

Another prominent figure in Baalbek's mythical narratives is the goddess Astarte. Often depicted as a symbol of feminine beauty and fertility, Astarte held a significant place in the hearts and minds of the ancient inhabitants. Legends spoke of her enchanting allure and her power to bestow blessings upon those who sought her favor. Her presence was believed to bring harmony and balance to the natural world, and her worship was intertwined with the cycles of life and nature.

Myths surrounding Baalbek also encompass tales of heroic figures who embarked on daring quests and faced daunting challenges. These stories celebrate bravery, valor, and the triumph of good over evil. In some narratives, legendary heroes such as Hercules or Gilgamesh are said to have ventured to Baalbek, leaving their indelible mark on its history and forging connections between distant lands.

The mythical narratives of Baalbek also intersect with the realm of celestial beings. Legends speak of divine interventions, where gods and goddesses descended from the heavens to interact with mortals. These encounters were believed to have profound implications for both human and divine realms, shaping destinies and guiding the course of history.

As we delve into these mythical narratives, we begin to unravel the layers of meaning and symbolism that permeate the stones of Baalbek. These stories provide a window into the beliefs, values, and aspirations of ancient civilizations, offering insights into their understanding of the world and their place within it. They reflect the human quest to make sense of the mysteries of existence and to forge connections with the divine. In the echoes of these mythical tales, we find the enduring power of storytelling and the profound impact it has on shaping our collective imagination. Baalbek's mythical narratives continue to captivate and inspire, transporting us to a realm where gods, heroes, and ancient civilizations intertwine. They remind us of the timeless human desire to seek meaning and transcendence, and they invite us to reflect on the profound influence that myth and legend have on our understanding of the world around us. As we explore the majestic ruins of Baalbek, we are not merely witnessing the remnants of an ancient city but stepping into a realm where mythology and history intertwine. These mythical narratives, passed down through the ages, remind us of the enduring power of the human imagination and the enduring allure of the mystical and the divine. They invite us to embrace the enchantment of Baalbek's mythical past and to contemplate the profound insights it offers into the human experience. Within the mystical tapestry of Baalbek's legends and lore, a myriad of mythical creatures and beings find their place, adding an extra layer of enchantment to the ancient city's rich heritage. These extraordinary entities, often the subjects of awe and wonder, have captured the imaginations of generations and played integral roles in the stories and beliefs of the ancient inhabitants.

One of the most renowned mythical creatures associated with Baalbek is the mighty Griffin. Often depicted as a creature with the body of a lion and the head and wings of an eagle, the Griffin symbolizes power, wisdom, and protection. According to ancient tales, the Griffin was a guardian and custodian of sacred spaces, including the temples of Baalbek. Legends tell of its fierce loyalty, defending the city and its people against any threats that may arise. The image of the Griffin, often carved into architectural elements and artifacts, served as a symbol of divine protection and a reminder of the mythical realm's influence on mortal existence.

Another mythical being that finds its place within Baalbek's folklore is the Djinn. These supernatural entities, said to inhabit the unseen realms, held significant influence over human affairs. In the narratives of Baalbek, Djinn were often associated with both benevolence and mischief. They were believed to possess immense powers, capable of granting wishes or causing havoc depending on their whims. The presence of Djinn in Baalbek's mythical tales added an element of mystery and unpredictability to the city's cultural landscape.

The legends of Baalbek also speak of enchanting beings known as nymphs or nature spirits. These ethereal creatures, often associated with specific natural features such as springs, rivers, or forests, were believed to embody the essence and vitality of the surrounding landscape. In Baalbek, stories of nymphs whispered through generations, describing their graceful forms, melodious voices, and connection to the rhythms of nature. These mystical beings were revered as guardians of the land, bestowing blessings upon those who respected and cherished the natural world.

The mythical lore of Baalbek further intertwines with tales of shape-shifting creatures, such as the elusive werewolves and the enchanting sirens. Legends describe werewolves as humans capable of transforming into fearsome wolves under the influence of a full moon, while sirens, with their mesmerizing voices, lured unsuspecting sailors to their doom. These mythical beings served as cautionary symbols, representing the delicate balance between the human and the wild, and the dangers that lie in succumbing to primal instincts or succumbing to alluring temptations.

Additionally, Baalbek's mythical narratives feature celestial beings, including gods and goddesses who descend from the heavens to interact with mortals. These divine entities, with their otherworldly beauty and transcendent powers, shape the destinies of individuals and societies. Their influence is often portrayed through acts of benevolence or divine intervention, sparking both awe and reverence in the hearts of those who believe in their existence.

The legends and lore of Baalbek, with their mythical creatures and beings, serve as a testament to the human imagination and its profound capacity to create stories that reflect the complexities of the human experience. Through these tales, the ancient inhabitants of Baalbek sought to understand the mysteries of the world and to connect with the forces that shaped their lives.

As we explore the remnants of Baalbek's majestic temples, we are reminded of the enduring power of myth and the way it weaves together the realms of the tangible and the intangible. The mythical creatures and beings that inhabit Baalbek's folklore continue to captivate and inspire, inviting us to contemplate the enigmatic boundaries between reality and imagination. They remind us of the timeless allure of the mythical realm and its ability to enrich our understanding of the human condition. The ancient city of Baalbek, with its rich history and captivating legends, has wielded a profound influence on the cultures and belief systems that have emerged throughout the centuries. The power of myth in shaping human consciousness and inspiring collective imagination is unmistakable, and Baalbek's myths and legends have left an indelible mark on the tapestry of human culture.

One of the most significant ways in which Baalbek's legends have influenced culture is through their impact on religious and spiritual beliefs. Baalbek's myths, often intertwined with the worship of ancient deities, have shaped the religious practices and rituals of various civilizations. The stories of gods and goddesses associated with Baalbek, such as Ba'al and Astarte, have become integral parts of religious pantheons and have informed the cosmologies and moral frameworks of ancient societies. The spiritual significance attributed to Baalbek and its mythical narratives has imbued the site with a sense of sacredness, making it a destination for pilgrimage and worship throughout history.

Furthermore, the enduring nature of Baalbek's myths is evident in their incorporation into artistic expressions and literary works. Artists, poets, and writers have drawn inspiration from the city's legends, reimagining and reinterpreting them in various art forms. Baalbek's myths have been celebrated in epic poems, dramatic plays, and lyrical verses, breathing life into the characters and stories that have fascinated generations. These creative interpretations have served to preserve and transmit the cultural heritage of Baalbek, ensuring that its mythical tales continue to resonate and inspire.

Beyond artistic endeavors, Baalbek's legends have also influenced societal values and moral codes. The heroic feats, trials, and tribulations of mythical figures have provided archetypal narratives that offer guidance and moral lessons to individuals and communities. Themes of bravery, loyalty, sacrifice, and the struggle between good and evil, as depicted in Baalbek's legends, have informed ethical frameworks and shaped concepts of virtue in various societies. The stories of Baalbek have served as moral touchstones, prompting individuals to reflect on their own lives and choices, and inspiring them to aspire to noble ideals.

Moreover, the influence of Baalbek's myths extends beyond the realms of religion, art, and ethics. The narratives have played a role in shaping historical memory and cultural identity. The stories passed down through generations have provided a connection to the past and a sense of continuity with ancestral heritage. Baalbek's legends have served as cultural touchstones, reminding communities of their shared roots and fostering a sense of collective identity.

In the realm of scholarship, the study and interpretation of Baalbek's myths have contributed to the fields of archaeology, anthropology, and mythology. Researchers and scholars have delved into the depths of Baalbek's legends, seeking to unravel the historical truths embedded within the mythical narratives. Through the meticulous analysis of ancient texts, archaeological findings, and comparative studies, they have shed light on the cultural, social, and religious contexts that gave birth to Baalbek's legends. These scholarly endeavors have deepened our understanding of the ancient world and enriched our knowledge of human history.

The enduring influence of Baalbek's myths on culture and belief systems is a testament to the enduring power of storytelling and the human quest for meaning and transcendence. These ancient narratives continue to captivate, provoke contemplation, and inspire imagination, inviting us to ponder the mysteries of existence and our place within the grand tapestry of the cosmos.

As we explore the ancient city of Baalbek and immerse ourselves in its legends, we are reminded of the profound impact that myths can have on our lives and societies. The stories of Baalbek have transcended time, bridging the gap between the ancient and the modern, and inviting us to reflect on our shared humanity and the enduring power of the human imagination.

Chapter 8: The Lost Knowledge: Advanced Engineering Techniques

The monumental construction of Baalbek stands as a testament to the remarkable engineering prowess of ancient civilizations. The sheer scale and precision of the structures at Baalbek have baffled and captivated scholars and visitors alike, prompting the exploration of the secrets behind these ancient engineering marvels.

At the heart of Baalbek's engineering achievements lies the use of colossal stone blocks, some weighing up to 1,000 tons, known as the Trilithon stones. The transportation and positioning of these massive stones have remained a subject of fascination and speculation for centuries. The precision with which they were cut, shaped, and fitted together is a testament to the skill and ingenuity of the ancient builders.

One prevailing theory suggests that the stones were quarried from nearby locations, and their transportation involved a combination of manpower, sledges, and possibly even rudimentary ramps and lever systems. The sheer logistical challenge of moving such massive stones over considerable distances and then lifting them to their designated positions is a testament to the sophistication of ancient engineering techniques.

The precise fitting of the stones at Baalbek is another marvel of ancient craftsmanship. The joints between the blocks are so perfectly aligned that even the thinnest of blades cannot be inserted between them. The accuracy and stability achieved in the construction of Baalbek's walls and columns are a testament to the mastery of stonework and the meticulous planning and execution of the ancient builders.

One of the most remarkable features of Baalbek's construction is the use of interlocking stones known as Hellenistic masonry. The seamless integration of individual blocks into larger structures without the need for mortar or other binding agents is a testament to the precise shaping and interlocking techniques employed by the builders. This method ensured structural integrity while allowing for subtle adjustments and expansions as needed.

Furthermore, Baalbek's architectural design exhibits a sophisticated understanding of weight distribution and load-bearing principles. The massive stone columns of the Temple of Jupiter, for example, stand as towering symbols of the engineering achievements of the ancient builders. The ability to support such tremendous weight while maintaining structural stability required a deep understanding of the forces at play and the incorporation of appropriate design elements.

The advanced construction techniques employed at Baalbek are further evidenced by the intricate details and decorative elements found throughout the site. Elaborate carvings, reliefs, and ornamental features adorned the structures, showcasing the artistic mastery and technical skill of the builders. These decorative elements not only added aesthetic beauty but also served as a testament to the meticulous craftsmanship and attention to detail displayed in Baalbek's construction.

The engineering achievements of Baalbek continue to inspire awe and wonder, raising questions about the capabilities and knowledge of the ancient builders. The precision, scale, and complexity of the structures defy easy explanation and challenge our understanding of the technological capabilities of the time. They stand as enduring symbols of human ingenuity and the indomitable spirit of those who dared to dream big and push the boundaries of what was thought possible.

As we marvel at the engineering marvels of Baalbek, we are reminded of the remarkable achievements of our ancient ancestors. The construction techniques employed at Baalbek speak to a profound understanding of mathematics, physics, and architecture, and showcase the remarkable abilities of ancient civilizations to conceive, plan, and execute monumental building projects. The secrets of Baalbek's advanced construction continue to intrigue and inspire us, urging us to explore further and unlock the mysteries of our shared human heritage.

The construction of Baalbek stands as a testament to the mastery and expertise of its builders and architects. The remarkable precision and grandeur of the structures at Baalbek speak to the high level of skill and knowledge possessed by the ancient craftsmen who undertook this monumental endeavor.

The first aspect that showcases the expertise of Baalbek's builders is the selection and quarrying of the massive stone blocks. The use of such enormous stones, some weighing hundreds of tons, required a deep understanding of geology and the ability to identify suitable rock formations. The quarrying process itself would have required immense effort and ingenuity, involving the careful extraction and transportation of these colossal stones from distant quarries to the construction site.

The shaping and dressing of the stones is another aspect that highlights the expertise of the builders. The precision with which the stones were cut, chiseled, and shaped is a testament to their skill in working with stone. The surfaces are remarkably smooth and flat, with intricate carvings and decorative details that demonstrate a mastery of stonework and an eye for aesthetics.

The fitting and assembly of the stones at Baalbek reveal a meticulous attention to detail and a deep understanding of structural integrity. The massive stone blocks were carefully positioned and interlocked, creating a harmonious and stable composition. The joints between the stones are so precisely cut and fitted that they appear seamless, showcasing the precision and craftsmanship of the builders.

The architectural design of Baalbek further attests to the expertise of its architects. The grandeur and symmetry of the structures, the harmonious proportions, and the integration of decorative elements all point to a sophisticated understanding of architectural principles. The monumental columns, with their intricate capitals and decorative reliefs, exemplify the artistic and technical prowess of the builders.

The construction techniques employed at Baalbek also reveal an understanding of engineering principles. The massive weight of the stones and the structural challenges posed by such immense structures required innovative solutions. The builders incorporated arches, vaults, and other architectural features to distribute and balance the weight, ensuring the stability and longevity of the structures.

The expertise of Baalbek's builders is further evident in the longevity of the site. Despite centuries of wear and natural disasters, the core structures have endured, standing as a testament to the durability of their construction. The fact that Baalbek continues to awe and inspire visitors today is a testament to the skill and craftsmanship of its ancient builders.

The mastery and expertise displayed at Baalbek go beyond mere technical proficiency. They reflect a deep cultural and artistic sensibility, an appreciation for beauty, and a reverence for the divine. Baalbek was not just a feat of engineering; it was a labor of love and devotion, a testament to the human desire to create something awe-inspiring and enduring.

In summary, the construction of Baalbek stands as a remarkable testament to the expertise and mastery of its builders and architects. The selection and quarrying of colossal stones, the precision in shaping and fitting them, the architectural design, and the incorporation of engineering principles all speak to the remarkable skill and knowledge possessed by the ancient craftsmen who created this architectural marvel. Baalbek stands as a timeless reminder of human ingenuity and the enduring legacy of our ancestors' remarkable achievements.

The ancient city of Baalbek stands as a testament to the enduring impact of its technological prowess and engineering achievements. The advanced construction techniques employed at Baalbek have left an indelible mark on architectural history, influencing subsequent generations of builders and engineers. The engineering legacy of Baalbek can be seen in various aspects of its construction, showcasing the ingenuity and innovation of its ancient builders.

One of the most remarkable aspects of Baalbek's engineering legacy is the transportation and manipulation of colossal stone blocks. The ability to quarry, transport, and position stones weighing hundreds of tons required ingenious solutions and exceptional engineering skills. The builders at Baalbek developed sophisticated methods for moving and lifting these enormous blocks, utilizing advanced mechanisms such as ramps, cranes, and pulleys. These techniques laid the foundation for future engineering endeavors, inspiring later civilizations to push the boundaries of construction.

The precise fitting and interlocking of stones at Baalbek demonstrate an unparalleled level of craftsmanship and engineering precision. The builders created seamless joints between the stones, ensuring structural stability and longevity. The intricate artistry and attention to detail in the carving and shaping of the stones reveal a deep understanding of materials and their behavior. Such meticulous craftsmanship not only enhanced the structural integrity of the buildings but also added a touch of aesthetic beauty to the architectural marvels of Baalbek.

Another aspect of Baalbek's engineering legacy is its innovative use of architectural elements to distribute weight and ensure structural stability. The incorporation of arches, vaults, and massive columns played a crucial role in balancing the immense weight of the stone blocks and preventing structural collapse. These architectural features were not only functional but also contributed to the grandeur and magnificence of the structures. The engineering ingenuity displayed at Baalbek paved the way for the development of advanced architectural systems in later civilizations.

The enduring impact of Baalbek's technological prowess can be seen in the influence it has had on subsequent architectural achievements. The precision and scale of Baalbek's construction served as a source of inspiration for later generations of builders and engineers. The mastery of stone-cutting techniques, the knowledge of structural mechanics, and the ability to manipulate massive stones have been passed down through the ages, leaving an indelible mark on architectural traditions worldwide.

Furthermore, the technological advancements showcased at Baalbek challenged the limits of what was thought possible in ancient times. The ambitious scale of the structures, the sophisticated construction methods, and the mastery of engineering principles pushed the boundaries of architectural achievements. Baalbek's technological prowess paved the way for future advancements and stimulated further exploration and innovation in the field of construction.

The engineering legacy of Baalbek is not limited to its physical structures alone. It also encompasses the cultural and intellectual impact of its technological achievements. The awe-inspiring grandeur of Baalbek's architecture served as a symbol of power and divine connection, influencing religious and cultural practices. Its engineering feats inspired a sense of wonder and admiration, leaving a lasting impression on the collective imagination of generations.

In summary, the engineering legacy of Baalbek is a testament to the ingenuity, skill, and technological prowess of its ancient builders. The transportation and manipulation of colossal stones, the precision in fitting and interlocking them, and the innovative use of architectural elements all contribute to the enduring impact of Baalbek's engineering achievements. This remarkable legacy continues to inspire and captivate, reminding us of the extraordinary capabilities of ancient civilizations and the enduring power of human innovation.

Chapter 9: Reimagining the Past: Baalbek in its Former Glory

Reconstructing the ancient splendor of Baalbek's temple complex is a captivating endeavor that allows us to envision the grandeur and magnificence of this remarkable site. Through careful analysis of archaeological evidence, historical accounts, and architectural knowledge, scholars and experts have pieced together a visual representation of Baalbek's ancient temples, offering us a glimpse into the architectural marvels of the past.

At the heart of the complex stands the majestic Temple of Jupiter, dedicated to the Roman god of the sky and thunder. Its immense scale and commanding presence are awe-inspiring. The temple is characterized by its colossal columns, towering over the surrounding landscape. These columns, some of which still stand today, rise to a height of over 20 meters and are intricately carved with decorative motifs. The temple's façade showcases an impressive frieze adorned with intricate reliefs, depicting scenes from mythology and imperial propaganda.

Adjacent to the Temple of Jupiter is the Temple of Bacchus, a sanctuary dedicated to the Roman god of wine and revelry. This temple is renowned for its exceptionally well-preserved state, offering valuable insights into the architectural splendor of the Roman era. The Temple of Bacchus is notable for its elaborate Corinthian columns, finely sculpted friezes, and intricate detailing. The temple's proportions and harmonious design create a sense of balance and elegance, exemplifying the mastery of Roman architectural principles.

The temple complex also includes the Temple of Venus, a sanctuary dedicated to the Roman goddess of love and beauty. Although less well-preserved than its neighboring temples, the remnants of the Temple of Venus provide valuable clues about its original layout and architectural features. The temple is believed to have exhibited similar architectural elements to the other temples at Baalbek, including grand colonnades and intricate sculptural adornments.

Surrounding the central temples are numerous smaller structures and courtyards, forming a vast complex that once buzzed with activity and religious rituals. These ancillary structures, though often overshadowed by the grandeur of the main temples, contribute to the overall architectural harmony of Baalbek's temple complex.

Reconstructing the temple complex also involves imagining the surrounding landscape, which played an integral role in the spiritual and cultural significance of Baalbek. The temples were strategically positioned atop an elevated terrace, emphasizing their prominence and creating a visual spectacle for worshippers and visitors. The imposing backdrop of the Lebanon Mountains added to the dramatic setting, amplifying the awe-inspiring experience of approaching the temples.

Recreating the ancient splendor of Baalbek's temple complex requires a careful blend of historical research, architectural expertise, and artistic imagination. It is an ongoing endeavor, continually evolving as new discoveries and insights come to light. The visual reconstruction allows us to appreciate the architectural genius of the past, marvel at the skill and craftsmanship of ancient builders, and gain a deeper understanding of the cultural and religious significance of Baalbek.

Although time has taken its toll on Baalbek's structures, the visual reconstruction of the temple complex enables us to transcend the present and embark on a journey back in time. It allows us to immerse ourselves in the grandeur and opulence of the ancient world, fostering a greater appreciation for the architectural achievements of our ancestors. Through this reconstruction, Baalbek's ancient splendor is revitalized, inviting us to explore, learn, and connect with the rich cultural heritage of this extraordinary site.

Envisioning Baalbek in its original magnificence takes us on a journey back in time to a period of unrivaled grandeur and architectural prowess. It is a journey that allows us to witness the splendor of this ancient city, standing as a testament to the ingenuity and ambition of its builders.

As we step into the heart of Baalbek, we are greeted by the awe-inspiring Temple of Jupiter, its towering columns reaching towards the heavens. The colossal scale of the temple is overwhelming, with each column rising to a height that defies the imagination. These monolithic structures, crafted from massive blocks of stone, stand as a testament to the engineering marvels achieved by the ancient civilizations that once inhabited this sacred space.

Walking through the temple complex, we encounter the Temple of Bacchus, a sanctuary dedicated to the Roman god of wine and revelry. Its façade is adorned with intricate carvings and ornate details, each element a testament to the skill and craftsmanship of the artisans who worked tirelessly to bring this structure to life. The Temple of Bacchus is a symphony of architectural harmony, its proportions and design reflecting the principles of classical beauty and order.

Adjacent to the Temple of Bacchus, we find the Temple of Venus, a sanctuary dedicated to the Roman goddess of love and beauty. The temple, with its graceful colonnades and delicate embellishments, exudes an aura of elegance and refinement. It stands as a testament to the devotion and reverence that the ancient inhabitants of Baalbek had for their deities, their belief in the power and influence of the divine.

The temple complex is not limited to these grand structures alone. It encompasses a vast array of smaller temples, courtyards, and buildings that together create a tapestry of architectural wonders. Each structure serves a specific purpose, whether it be for worship, administration, or communal gatherings. As we explore the intricate layout of the complex, we are captivated by the interconnectedness of these structures, the harmonious blend of functionality and artistic expression.

Beyond the architectural marvels, the surrounding landscape plays a crucial role in enhancing the magnificence of Baalbek. Nestled in the fertile Bekaa Valley, the city is surrounded by majestic mountains that serve as a dramatic backdrop. This natural setting, combined with the grandeur of the temples, creates a mesmerizing tableau that captures the imagination and inspires awe in all who behold it.

To envision Baalbek in its original magnificence is to transport ourselves to a time when civilizations flourished and left an indelible mark on the world. It is a reminder of the human capacity for creativity, innovation, and the pursuit of architectural excellence. The glory of Baalbek's past is a testament to the enduring power of human achievement, a legacy that continues to captivate and inspire us to this day.

Although the passage of time has taken its toll on Baalbek, and the structures stand as fragments of their former glory, we can still envision the city's magnificence through the remnants that have withstood the test of time. Through archaeological discoveries, meticulous research, and artistic renderings, we can piece together the puzzle of Baalbek's past, allowing us to glimpse the splendor that once adorned this ancient city.

Envisioning Baalbek in its original magnificence is an act of reverence and admiration for the generations of builders, artists, and worshippers who contributed to its creation. It is an invitation to marvel at the achievements of our ancestors, to honor their legacy, and to gain a deeper appreciation for the beauty and complexity of the ancient world.

In the mind's eye, Baalbek stands tall, its temples resplendent, its glory eternal. As we embark on a journey through time, we find ourselves transported to the golden era of Baalbek, a time when the city thrived as a hub of culture, spirituality, and innovation. We step into a world where the grandeur of the temples and the vibrancy of daily life paint a vivid picture of a civilization at its zenith.

The air is filled with anticipation as we approach the magnificent Temple of Jupiter, the centerpiece of Baalbek's architectural ensemble. The sheer size and scale of the temple are awe-inspiring, with its colossal columns reaching towards the heavens, seemingly touching the celestial realms. As we venture further into the temple, we are greeted by a vibrant scene of devotion and reverence. Priests and worshippers engage in elaborate ceremonies, their voices mingling with the enchanting melodies of musicians and the aromatic scent of incense filling the air.

Moving through the bustling city streets, we encounter the Temple of Bacchus, a place of celebration and revelry. The temple's ornate façade, adorned with intricate carvings and exquisite details, reflects the joyous spirit of the ancient festivities held within its walls. The sound of laughter and music fills the air, while the aroma of food and wine tantalizes the senses. Baalbek comes alive with the joyous celebrations that mark the passage of time and the cycles of nature.

Beyond the temples, Baalbek is a thriving cosmopolitan center, bustling with artisans, merchants, and scholars from distant lands. The streets are alive with vibrant colors, as craftsmen ply their trades, creating exquisite works of art and craftsmanship. Markets are abuzz with the exchange of goods, as exotic spices, luxurious fabrics, and precious jewels find their way into the hands of eager buyers.

The city's cultural scene is equally vibrant, with theaters and amphitheaters showcasing captivating performances of drama, music, and dance. The ancient Greek and Roman influences blend harmoniously with the local traditions, creating a unique tapestry of artistic expression. Baalbek becomes a beacon of intellectual and artistic exchange, drawing scholars, poets, and philosophers who engage in spirited debates and share their knowledge with eager audiences.

Amidst the splendor of Baalbek's golden era, we witness the harmonious coexistence of different cultures and religions. The city is a melting pot of beliefs and traditions, with temples dedicated to various deities and sanctuaries where worshippers from different faiths find solace and inspiration. Baalbek becomes a symbol of tolerance and unity, a place where people from diverse backgrounds come together in mutual respect and understanding.

As we immerse ourselves in Baalbek's golden era, we gain a deeper appreciation for the achievements and aspirations of its inhabitants. Their architectural masterpieces, cultural contributions, and spiritual devotion leave an indelible mark on history, inspiring generations to come. Baalbek's golden era is a testament to the heights that human civilization can reach when creativity, ingenuity, and a thirst for knowledge come together in perfect harmony.

As our journey through time comes to a close, we carry with us the memories of Baalbek's golden era, forever etched in our minds and hearts. The grandeur, the passion, and the spirit of this ancient city remain as enduring legacies, reminding us of the immense potential of human endeavor. Baalbek's golden era continues to inspire us to reach for greatness, to embrace cultural diversity, and to cherish the remarkable achievements of our ancestors.

Chapter 10: The Legacy Lives On: Baalbek's Influence and Inspiration Today

The legacy of Baalbek, the mighty megalithic temple, reverberates through the corridors of time, leaving an indelible mark on human history. Its grandeur, cultural significance, and engineering prowess have captivated the imagination of scholars, artists, and explorers for centuries. As we trace the legacy of Baalbek, we uncover a tapestry of influence and inspiration that extends far beyond its ancient walls.

One cannot help but marvel at the immense scale and precision of Baalbek's construction. The colossal stone blocks, weighing several tons each, stand as a testament to the remarkable engineering achievements of the ancient world. The innovative building techniques employed by its creators have sparked fascination and admiration among architects and engineers across generations. The architectural legacy of Baalbek can be seen in subsequent monumental structures, inspiring awe and pushing the boundaries of human imagination.

Baalbek's cultural impact extends beyond its architectural splendor. The site has been a place of pilgrimage, attracting worshippers and seekers of spiritual enlightenment from various civilizations throughout history. Its sacredness is rooted in the religious practices and beliefs of the people who inhabited the region, fostering a sense of devotion and awe. Baalbek's temples served as centers of religious and cultural activities, shaping the belief systems and rituals of countless individuals.

The influence of Baalbek can be felt in the realms of art, literature, and mythology. The grandeur of its temples, the enigmatic legends surrounding its stones, and the spiritual significance attributed to the site have inspired artists, poets, and storytellers throughout the ages. Baalbek's prominence in ancient mythologies and legends has woven it into the collective consciousness of civilizations that emerged in its wake. It stands as a symbol of divine power and human aspiration, continuing to captivate the imagination of both scholars and dreamers alike.

Baalbek's endurance throughout the passage of time is a testament to its resilience and cultural significance. Despite periods of neglect, conquest, and transformation, the temple complex has managed to preserve its essence and intrigue. The site has been witness to the rise and fall of empires, the ebb and flow of cultures, and the evolution of human thought. Its survival is a testament to the enduring power of human creativity, ingenuity, and the reverence we hold for our ancient past.

As we explore the legacy of Baalbek, we are reminded of the importance of preserving and protecting our shared human heritage. The site's preservation efforts, both past and present, exemplify the commitment to safeguarding the treasures of our ancestors for future generations. It serves as a reminder that the past holds valuable lessons and insights that can shape our present and guide our future.

In summary, the legacy of Baalbek is a tapestry woven with threads of architectural marvel, cultural significance, and spiritual depth. Its enduring impact transcends time and borders, inspiring awe and admiration among all who encounter its magnificence. Baalbek's legacy invites us to ponder the mysteries of our shared human history and to appreciate the timeless beauty and ingenuity that reside within the ancient stones. Baalbek, the legendary megalithic temple complex, stands as a beacon of inspiration, igniting the creative fires of artists, architects, and designers across the ages. Its awe-inspiring grandeur, intricate craftsmanship, and mystical allure have left an indelible mark on the world of art, architecture, and design, shaping the course of human creativity. The artistic influence of Baalbek can be seen in various forms of expression, from the intricate carvings and reliefs adorning its colossal stones to the harmonious proportions and elaborate ornamentation that define its architectural elements. Artists throughout history have drawn inspiration from the intricate patterns, motifs, and symbolism found within Baalbek's temples, infusing their works with a sense of grandeur, spirituality, and ancient wisdom.

In the realm of architecture, Baalbek's monumental structures have served as a testament to human ingenuity and a source of architectural inspiration. The precise engineering techniques and ingenious construction methods employed in the creation of Baalbek's megalithic temples have influenced architectural styles and building practices around the world. From the intricate stone masonry to the mastery of structural stability, the lessons learned from Baalbek have been incorporated into architectural designs throughout history.

The allure of Baalbek's design and aesthetic has also extended its reach to the world of interior design and decorative arts. The intricate motifs and patterns found in the carvings and reliefs of Baalbek have inspired the creation of intricate tapestries, ornamental sculptures, and decorative elements. The rich symbolism and cultural significance associated with Baalbek have been incorporated into furniture designs, textile patterns, and even modern-day installations, creating a connection between the ancient past and the contemporary artistic expressions.

The impact of Baalbek's cultural influence extends beyond the realm of art and architecture. Its mythical tales, legends, and spiritual symbolism have found their way into literature, poetry, and music. Writers and poets have sought to capture the essence of Baalbek's mystical aura in their works, invoking its ancient mysteries and invoking a sense of wonder and awe. Composers and musicians have drawn inspiration from its powerful presence, creating melodies and symphonies that echo the grandeur and sacredness of Baalbek's temples.

Baalbek's cultural influence has transcended time and geographical boundaries, shaping the way we perceive and appreciate the world around us. Its influence can be seen in the architectural wonders of ancient civilizations, the intricately crafted artworks of various cultures, and the spiritual and mythological beliefs that have permeated human consciousness. Baalbek's legacy serves as a reminder of the enduring power of artistic expression and the profound impact that ancient sites can have on the human imagination.

As we continue to explore and appreciate the artistic and cultural significance of Baalbek, we are reminded of the intrinsic connection between human creativity and our shared cultural heritage. The influence of Baalbek on art, architecture, and design is a testament to the timeless beauty and universal appeal of its artistic expressions. It invites us to delve into the depths of our creative potential, drawing inspiration from the past while pushing the boundaries of artistic innovation. In summary, Baalbek's cultural influence on art, architecture, and design is profound and far-reaching. Its majestic presence, intricate craftsmanship, and spiritual symbolism continue to inspire and captivate generations of artists and designers. The legacy of Baalbek serves as a reminder of the power of human creativity and the eternal beauty that can be found in the harmonious union of art, architecture, and cultural heritage. While the ancient origins of Baalbek may seem distant in the annals of history, its spiritual significance continues to resonate in the hearts and minds of people today. Despite the passage of time and the transformation of belief systems, Baalbek's sacredness endures, transcending boundaries and captivating the imagination of spiritual seekers. For many, Baalbek represents a living connection to the divine, a place where the earthly and the celestial converge. The imposing megalithic structures and the enigmatic energy that permeates the site evoke a sense of awe and reverence. Visitors from around the world are drawn to Baalbek in search of a deeper understanding of their own spiritual journey and a glimpse into the mysteries of the universe.

Baalbek's temples, once dedicated to ancient deities, have evolved to become spaces of introspection, contemplation, and communion with the sacred. Spiritual practitioners and seekers of various traditions find solace and inspiration within the sacred confines of Baalbek. Meditative practices, ritual ceremonies, and prayerful moments become pathways to connect with the divine energies that have imbued the site for centuries.

The pilgrimage to Baalbek is more than a physical journey; it is a quest for spiritual enlightenment and personal transformation. As pilgrims traverse the ancient paths and stand in the presence of the monumental stones, they are enveloped by a sense of profound connection to something greater than themselves. The vibrations of millennia-old rituals and devotions reverberate through the ages, creating a tangible link between past and present.

In the modern era, Baalbek's spiritual significance has also found expression in interfaith dialogue and ecumenical gatherings. The site has become a meeting ground for people of diverse faiths and beliefs, fostering mutual understanding and shared reverence for the sacred. Baalbek serves as a symbol of unity, reminding us that beneath the surface of religious differences, there is a common thread that unites humanity in its quest for transcendence.

The preservation and conservation efforts at Baalbek are not solely focused on the physical structures but also on safeguarding its spiritual essence. Recognizing the importance of maintaining the site's sanctity, measures are taken to ensure that it remains a space of spiritual solace and inspiration for future generations. By protecting the integrity of the site and promoting responsible tourism, the sacredness of Baalbek is preserved and its spiritual legacy is honored.

As we contemplate Baalbek's spiritual continuity, we are reminded of the enduring power of sacred spaces. They serve as bridges between the earthly and the divine, nurturing our spiritual growth and offering glimpses into the profound mysteries of existence. Baalbek stands as a testament to the human quest for transcendence, a beacon of spiritual enlightenment that transcends time and connects us to the essence of our shared humanity.

In a world often filled with distractions and disconnection, Baalbek's spiritual significance reminds us of the importance of seeking moments of reverence and reflection. It calls us to listen to the whispers of the divine, to find solace in the sacred, and to recognize the inherent interconnectedness of all beings. Baalbek's enduring spiritual legacy invites us to embark on our own inner pilgrimage, to explore the depths of our souls, and to honor the sacredness that resides within and around us. In summary, Baalbek's role as a sacred site in modern times is a testament to its enduring spiritual significance. It serves as a sanctuary for seekers of truth and meaning, a place where the divine and the human converge. As we continue to explore the mysteries of Baalbek, may we be inspired to cultivate our own spiritual connection, fostering unity, and embracing the profound beauty of the sacred in our lives.

Baalbek, with its awe-inspiring megalithic temples and rich historical legacy, has become a significant destination for cultural heritage and tourism. Situated in the heart of the fertile Bekaa Valley in Lebanon, Baalbek attracts visitors from around the world who seek to immerse themselves in the wonders of ancient civilizations and explore the enduring legacy of human ingenuity.

Tourism plays a crucial role in the preservation and promotion of Baalbek's cultural heritage. The influx of visitors provides vital resources for the ongoing conservation and restoration efforts, ensuring that the magnificent temples and their intricate details are protected for future generations. Through tourism, Baalbek can continue to shine as a beacon of cultural pride and historical significance.

For tourists, a visit to Baalbek is a transformative experience. As they step foot into this ancient site, they are transported back in time, walking in the footsteps of past civilizations. The colossal stone blocks, intricate carvings, and grand architecture serve as tangible links to the greatness of the past. Visitors are able to witness firsthand the architectural prowess of the ancient builders and gain a deeper appreciation for the rich cultural heritage that has shaped our world.

Baalbek's significance as a UNESCO World Heritage site further enhances its appeal to tourists. The designation acknowledges the outstanding universal value of the site and raises global awareness about its historical and cultural importance. This recognition attracts a diverse range of travelers, including history enthusiasts, archaeology aficionados, and curious explorers, all eager to uncover the secrets of Baalbek's past.

Education also plays a vital role in the appreciation and understanding of Baalbek. Museums and interpretive centers near the site provide informative displays and exhibits that delve into the history, architecture, and significance of Baalbek. Educational programs and guided tours offer visitors the opportunity to engage with knowledgeable experts who share their insights and expertise, enriching the overall experience.

Furthermore, Baalbek's cultural heritage serves as a platform for cross-cultural exchange and dialogue. It acts as a meeting point for people from diverse backgrounds, fostering an appreciation for different traditions and promoting intercultural understanding. Baalbek's international appeal brings together individuals who share a common passion for history, archaeology, and the preservation of cultural treasures.

The economic benefits of tourism in the region cannot be overlooked. The influx of visitors contributes to the local economy, generating employment opportunities and supporting small businesses, such as hotels, restaurants, and souvenir shops. This economic growth not only benefits the local community but also helps to sustain the ongoing preservation efforts at Baalbek.

However, it is essential to strike a balance between tourism and the preservation of Baalbek's integrity. Sustainable tourism practices and responsible visitor behavior are vital to ensure the long-term preservation of the site. Measures must be taken to minimize the impact of tourism on the fragile archaeological remains and to promote respectful engagement with the cultural heritage.

In summary, Baalbek's role in cultural heritage and tourism is multifaceted. It offers visitors an immersive journey into the past, igniting a sense of wonder and awe. As a UNESCO World Heritage site, it attracts global attention and serves as an educational resource for learning about ancient civilizations. Moreover, tourism at Baalbek brings economic benefits to the local community while fostering cross-cultural exchange. By striking a balance between preservation and responsible tourism practices, Baalbek can continue to shine as a beacon of cultural heritage, inviting visitors to unravel the mysteries of its magnificent temples and connect with the richness of human history. Baalbek, with its awe-inspiring temples and rich historical significance, has a lasting and profound impact on all who visit its hallowed grounds. From seasoned scholars to curious travelers, Baalbek's eternal appeal captivates the imagination and leaves an indelible impression.

For scholars and researchers, Baalbek offers a unique opportunity to delve into the depths of ancient civilizations. Its monumental architecture, intricate carvings, and archaeological remains provide a treasure trove of information, inviting scholarly investigation and interpretation. The site's complex history and its significance in the context of various civilizations make it a subject of fascination for historians, archaeologists, and anthropologists.

Visitors, too, are spellbound by the sheer grandeur and mystique of Baalbek. As they step foot into this ancient sanctuary, they are immediately transported to a bygone era, where the echoes of ancient rituals and the footsteps of long-forgotten worshippers resonate. The colossal stones, meticulously crafted columns, and intricately designed reliefs evoke a sense of awe and wonder, reminding us of the remarkable achievements of our ancestors.

Baalbek's appeal extends beyond its architectural marvels. It is a place of spiritual significance and a testament to the human quest for divine connection. The aura of sacredness that envelops the temples touches the souls of visitors, invoking a sense of reverence and humility. Many find solace and inspiration within the sacred space, reflecting on the mysteries of existence and contemplating the enduring legacy of ancient wisdom. The allure of Baalbek is not limited to its physical presence. It possesses an intangible quality that transcends time and space, stirring the imagination and sparking contemplation. It invites us to ponder the purpose and meaning of our own existence, as we marvel at the ingenuity and creativity of those who came before us.

The impact of Baalbek is not restricted to the duration of a visit. It lingers in the minds and hearts of those who have been touched by its grandeur. The memories and emotions evoked by the experience become a part of the individual's personal narrative, shaping their perspective on history, culture, and the interconnectedness of humanity.

Baalbek's lasting impression extends beyond the individual level. It serves as a catalyst for cultural exchange and dialogue, fostering a deeper understanding and appreciation of diverse traditions and beliefs. Scholars and visitors alike engage in meaningful conversations, sharing insights and interpretations that contribute to the collective knowledge and appreciation of our shared human heritage.

Moreover, Baalbek's influence extends to the realm of artistic expression. It has inspired countless works of literature, poetry, music, and visual arts. Its timeless beauty and profound symbolism find resonance in the creative endeavors of artists who seek to capture its essence and transmit its message to future generations.

In summary, Baalbek's eternal appeal lies in its ability to transcend time and connect people across generations and cultures. Its majestic temples and rich history leave an indelible mark on the hearts and minds of visitors and scholars alike. The site's spiritual significance, architectural splendor, and cultural resonance continue to inspire, educate, and captivate. Baalbek stands as a testament to the enduring legacy of human ingenuity and the power of ancient sites to evoke wonder, contemplation, and a deep appreciation for our shared human story.

Conclusion

In this remarkable book bundle, "Megalithic Temples," readers embark on an extraordinary journey through the captivating realms of Stonehenge, Gobekli Tepe, Ggantija Temples, and Baalbek. Across four volumes, the mysteries, secrets, and timeless wonders of these megalithic structures are unveiled, revealing a rich tapestry of history, spirituality, and human ingenuity.

In "Mysteries of the Megaliths: Unraveling the Secrets of Stonehenge," readers are immersed in the enigmatic world of one of the world's most iconic ancient sites. From its awe-inspiring stone circles to its celestial alignments, the secrets of Stonehenge are explored, inviting readers to contemplate the spiritual significance and profound mysteries that have intrigued generations.

"Timeless Guardians: Exploring the Enigmatic Gobekli Tepe" takes us back even further in time, to the origins of civilization. Unearthed in modern times, Gobekli Tepe has rewritten our understanding of ancient cultures and their technological prowess. Delving into its intricate carvings, architectural marvels, and spiritual significance, this volume unveils a lost world of immense beauty and complexity.

"The Forgotten Giants: Journey to the Ggantija Temples of Malta" invites readers to the Mediterranean island of Malta, where the Ggantija Temples stand as silent witnesses to an ancient civilization. Amidst the fascinating megalithic structures, readers will discover the mysteries of their construction, the rituals and beliefs of their creators, and the enduring legacy of a forgotten people.

Lastly, "Legends of the Ancient Stones: Unveiling the Power of Baalbek's Megalithic Temple" introduces readers to the majestic Baalbek, a site shrouded in myth and awe. Through meticulous research and vivid storytelling, this volume reveals the grandeur of Baalbek's monumental stones, the engineering marvels that created them, and the legends that have woven themselves into the fabric of this ancient site.

Collectively, these four volumes offer an unparalleled exploration of megalithic temples, weaving together the threads of history, spirituality, and human achievement. From the mystical realms of Stonehenge to the enigmatic secrets of Gobekli Tepe, from the forgotten giants of Ggantija to the power and symbolism of Baalbek, this book bundle takes readers on a transformative journey, deepening their understanding of ancient civilizations and inspiring a profound appreciation for the enduring legacy of these megalithic marvels.

Whether you are a history enthusiast, an archaeology aficionado, or a curious explorer, "Megalithic Temples" is a treasure trove of knowledge and wonder. Open its pages, and embark on a captivating expedition through time and space, where the echoes of ancient rituals and the power of human imagination still reverberate.

About A. J. Kingston

A. J. Kingston is a writer, historian, and lover of all things historical. Born and raised in a small town in the United States, A. J. developed a deep appreciation for the past from an early age. She studied history at the university, earning her degree with honors, and went on to write a series of acclaimed books about different periods and topics in history.

A. J.'s writing is characterized by its clarity, evocative language, and meticulous research. She has a particular talent for bringing the lives of ordinary people in the past to life, drawing on diaries, letters, and other documents to create rich and nuanced portraits of people from all walks of life. Her work has been praised for its deep empathy, its attention to detail, and its ability to make history come alive for readers.

In addition to her writing, A. J. is a sought-after speaker and commentator on historical topics. She has given talks and presentations at universities, museums, and other venues, sharing her passion for history with audiences around the world. Her ability to connect with people and make history relevant to their lives has earned her a devoted following and a reputation as one of the most engaging and insightful historical writers of her generation.

A. J.'s writing has been recognized with numerous awards and honors. She lives in California with her family, and continues to write and speak on historical topics.

Milton Keynes UK
Ingram Content Group UK Ltd.
UKHW020817171123
432750UK00018B/965